Smart Girls

Smart Girls

Success, School, and the Myth of Post-Feminism

**SHAUNA POMERANTZ AND
REBECCA RABY**

With a Foreword by Anita Harris

UNIVERSITY OF CALIFORNIA PRESS

University of California Press, one of the most distinguished university presses in the United States, enriches
lives around the world by advancing scholarship in the
humanities, social sciences, and natural sciences. Its
activities are supported by the UC Press Foundation and
by philanthropic contributions from individuals and
institutions. For more information, visit www.ucpress.edu.

University of California Press
Oakland, California

© 2017 by The Regents of the University of California

Library of Congress Cataloging-in-Publication Data

Names: Pomerantz, Shauna, author. | Raby, Rebecca,
    1968– author. | Harris, Anita, 1968–
Title: Smart girls : success, school, and the myth of
    post-feminism / Shauna Pomerantz and Rebecca Raby
    with a foreword by Anita Harris.
Description: Oakland, California : University of
    California Press, [2017] | Includes bibliographical
    references and index.
Identifiers: LCCN 2016030544 (print) | LCCN 2016033472
    (ebook) | ISBN 9780520284142 (cloth : alk. paper) |
    ISBN 9780520284159 (pbk. : alk. paper) |
    ISBN 9780520959798 (Epub)
Subjects: LCSH: Girls—Education. | Girls—Conduct
    of life. | Sex differences in education. | Academic
    achievement.
Classification: LCC LC1481 .P66 2017 (print) | LCC LC1481
    (ebook) | DDC 371.822—dc23
LC record available at https://lccn.loc.gov/2016030544

Manufactured in the United States of America

25 24 23 22 21 20 19 18 17
10 9 8 7 6 5 4 3 2 1

To all the young people who so generously
shared their stories with us

Contents

Foreword

BY ANITA HARRIS

What challenging times for girls to be smart. In 2008, Amy Poehler established her Smart Girls online community to encourage young women to "change the world by being yourself" and cultivate girl activism, STEM (science, technology, engineering, and mathematics) competencies (especially digital), and "smartist" identities. In 2013, Legendary Entertainment acquired Smart Girls for an undisclosed amount, an unparalleled opportunity for the company to generate marketing revenue by, in its own words, accessing "geek" consumers.[1] Listen to the lyrics of Weezer's 2010 track entitled "Smart Girls" ("Where did all these smart girls come from? / Someone tell me how to get me some. / Never get enough, of those smart girls, / Sleeping in the buff"), or parse a 2016 interview in *Billboard* with Zayn Malik, formerly of the phenomenally successful boy band One Direction, in which he declared that he likes "girls that are a bit chunky in certain areas—the nice areas. I like a fuller woman," but that girls should also be capable of "an intellectual conversation as well, where someone can construct a sentence beyond what hair and make-up they're wearing, and talk about something political or about the world."[2]

The "smart girl" has become a brand and a market. She is also a sexual stereotype, with intelligence newly revived in contemporary culture—both mainstream and alternative—as a necessary asset for heterosexual desirability. At the same time, she is constructed as the winner in a world of self-made opportunity where smarts and determination will get you anywhere, and we are invited to take for granted that high-achieving girls and their exceptional accomplishments are the rightful resolution, and the final chapter, of the book of feminism. But beyond the marketing, stereotypes, and hyperbole, the smart girl is an increasingly complex lived identity. In this book, we are invited into the lives of fifty-seven Canadian girls, as well as seventeen boys, who self-identify as smart, and we learn about the complexity of this experience. How do smart girls themselves perceive success, what are their strategies and resources for maintaining so-called perfection, and what impact does this have on their wellbeing and aspirations? How does academic success sit within youth and school cultures of popularity and norms of heterosexual desirability? How is enduring sexism dealt with in an environment in which young people are told that feminism is no longer needed? What forms of social and racial stratification lie beneath the image of successful girls as a homogenous cohort?

It has been acknowledged for some time that girls are no longer subjected simply to exclusion, belittlement, and marginalization in schools or in our culture. In fact, in many ways, girls have become the new educational success stories. An easy reading of this situation is that feminism has done its work, the "girls are alright," and it is probably time to now concentrate on boys. Shauna Pomerantz and Rebecca Raby describe this as the "smart girl story," and it is a compelling one. It certainly allows us to celebrate how far girls—and feminism—have come, but like any broad-brush claim, it favors the big declaration (props to the girls taking over the world!) over the close and fine-grained experience (how real girls live the complex experience of success in a post-feminist world). It also threatens to extinguish other important dimensions of the experience of high achievement. In particular, it leaves little room for acknowledgement of stress, suffering, and struggle; it glosses over enduring forms of sexism that continue to shape girls' everyday lives; and it provides no glimpse of the future prospects of smart girls as they leave education and enter the workforce. A more complex analysis, and a harder read, is that educational success is neither an answer in itself nor something that is seamlessly achieved, and it certainly does not constitute the end of the story.

Smart Girls is therefore a very timely and welcome corrective to this dominant narrative about high-achieving girls and the ease with which they sustain their identities as clever and successful academically as well as appropriately feminine in the terms that are relevant to contemporary culture. This book gets behind and beyond the stereotype of trouble-free success in both of these domains to explore the everyday experiences of young women's struggles as they grapple with these demands and expectations against the backdrop of post-feminism. Of course, notions of "girls on top," especially in terms of educational attainment, have circulated for some time. But this book interrogates this stereotype in the current context—where the smart girl has been supersized to the "supergirl"—and through the lens of in-depth empirical research with smart girls themselves, a perspective often absent from our public and academic debates. It gets straight to the heart of girls' lived experiences to understand how micro and macro social hierarchies, especially as they play out at the intersections of class, race, sexuality, and religion shape the constitution and contours of their gendered success.

Michelle Fine suggests that a foreword should be like a bathroom wall that invites you to scribble about your "favorite, thick messy struggles in the book."[3] In the spirit of this analogy, I will list my favorite struggles that *Smart Girls* engages with.

STRUGGLE # 1: INTERROGATING SUCCESS

The book breaks open what we mean by success and how it is achieved. Success here is not limited to academic achievement; we are reminded that girls can never afford to stop trying to succeed in perfecting femininity, too, especially by managing demands to be attractive, popular, and caring. It insists on a much more critical analysis of success than that which currently dominates debates about girls' achievements, not least by looking at the costs and effects this kind of success has on girls' self-esteem, health and well-being, relationships, and hopes for the future. And it brings back into focus the less visible apparatuses that foster and support the success so typically attributed to personal capacity alone: the social institutions and cultural and economic resources that scaffold and cut across individual achievement and structure advantage and opportunity. It also draws attention to the *work* of succeeding: the relentless efforts to do well, to perfect every activity, to be "well-rounded," and most of all, to not let the labor of success show inappropriately, especially in terms of diminishing one's fun or friendly personality. Girls' success emerges here as an ongoing process rather than an outcome; a never-ending production rather than a product; a verb rather than a noun.

And importantly, one critical dimension of this constant personal endeavor is where it leaves collective action and critical reflection. As girls turn in on themselves to do the work of success, and as a post-feminist world teaches them that they are now on their own, they are perhaps less able to join up their struggles and develop solidarities with one another. How are girls themselves living this and finding ways through it? Old ways of conceptualizing activism, and complicity, may not capture how girls struggle with a world that tells them that they have now arrived, and furnishes some real evidence of success, and yet at the same time raises the stakes subtly, and higher, with every achievement they make. While girls' agency and personal efforts for resistance and critical reflection shine through in this book, the challenge of sustained connection and shared structural analysis is the shadowy backdrop to this glow.

STRUGGLE # 2: SUSTAINING OUTCOMES

Smart Girls invites us to think about what happens when high achieving girls and young women leave environments of academic excellence and high standards at high school or university, armed with brilliant minds, instilled with you-can-do-anything attitudes by our post-feminist, individualist culture, and theoretically on track for top careers. The answers can be sobering. A study of three generations of Harvard MBA graduates has found that men and women define success in the same ways, and women are actually more likely to seek career growth, but their ability to realize these achievements is starkly differentiated, with men more likely to hold senior management positions with significant responsibilities and women less likely to be satisfied with their careers.[4] While educational opportunities for women have expanded rapidly, work cultures have been slow to change. Consider Professor Nalini Joshi, one of Australia's top mathematicians and one of the first women to be elected to the Academy of Science, who has said that when she attends Academy functions "wearing a black suit, with a name badge, I am often mistaken for one of the serving staff. And I am not alone."[5] In Australia, while more than 50 percent of doctorates in the natural and physical sciences are awarded to women, only 14 percent of science professors are women.

It is also well established that a gendered pay gap persists, and as a *Washington Post* article points out, according to the US Bureau of Labor Statistics, while women hold over 50 percent of professional jobs in the United States, they constitute only 14.6 percent of executive officers, 8 percent of top earners, and 4.6 percent of Fortune 500 CEOs.[6] A study of millennial women in top multinational organizations finds that the primary reason young women in their twenties and thirties leave high-flying jobs is because they are underpaid and underutilized and lack opportunities for career development.[7] It should also be noted that young women are still not able to access crucial informal professional networks where key decision makers are found. *Smart Girls* asks us how well we are equipping girls to deal with these realities and whether educational success plus self-belief are enough to combat them.

STRUGGLE # 3: LOCATING THE BOYS

The third struggle that this book brings to light is that of grappling with girls' experiences and viewpoints in relation to boys. One of the ongoing issues for research and thinking about opportunities and challenges for girls has always been deter-

mining what place boys have in the discussion. Shauna Pomerantz and Rebecca Raby show that it is no longer enough to just
counter those age-old catch cries of "what about the boys?" with
an evidence base demonstrating the enduring disadvantages
that girls face by comparison. We must also consider how young
masculinity is produced and experienced through discourses of
girls' success and how gender relations operate among young
people in the context of this story. What happens to heterosexuality and the structuring of personal relationships between boys
and girls in a popular culture context that no longer simply den-
igrates female intelligence (with sayings such as "Boys don't
make passes at girls who wear glasses") but now also commodi-
fies, "sexifies," and brazenly sells smarts and encourages young
men to demand that girls proffer them their looks *and* brains for
evaluation and consumption in the heterosexual marketplace?
How do smart (and not-so-smart) boys position themselves in
relation to smart girls as competitors, allies, friends, and dates?
How have boys' efforts for success changed in concert with the
rise of the smart girl?

The importance of boys as stakeholders in the lives of young
women—as social actors for whom this nuanced gender order is
meaningful and also problematic as a source of power and sometimes misery—needs to be grappled with in careful ways. This
book amply demonstrates that the zero-sum framing of girls
versus boys in unequal battles for attention, resources, and support in schools and beyond can be limiting. It is particularly
innovative and important in offering insights from boys themselves, who are almost always missing as real agents in discussions and research about girls' success. *Smart Girls* is able to bring
smart boys into the conversation and critically hear their perspectives in truly meaningful, helpful ways.

Through the narratives of Ella, Wren, Brooke, and other young women, accompanied by the stories of the smart boys who also participated in this study, we glean a far deeper understanding of what it means to be a smart girl today. We learn that it comes with costs, deals, and struggles—and requires class and family resources—that the stereotypes cannot capture. And we grasp how bright and brave young women are finding a way through these stereotypes to produce a messier, but more authentic, picture of a modern girl who is clever and conflicted, who is the product of feminism *and* post-feminism, and who needs us to suspend our assumptions and listen to her.

Acknowledgments

Coauthorship is an adventure—and not one to be undertaken lightly! Writing a book with someone else means you will be pushed in new directions, experience moments of frustration, grapple with regular critique, and reckon with your own limitations. At the same time, coauthorship enables you to share successes, learn how to give constructive feedback, play to each other's strengths, and become a better writer and thinker. In writing this book, we most certainly experienced this adventure to the hilt—each of us always knowing we could lean on the other and often taking turns holding the reins. *Smart Girls* is the product of deep, committed, collegial collaboration—and it is stronger for it.

Besides our fruitful partnership, there were, of course, numerous other collaborations that enabled this book to come to fruition. We would like to thank the University of California Press, our editor, Naomi Schneider, and her editorial assistant, Will Vincent, for believing in our project and helping bring it to a broader audience. Thanks as well to Genevieve Thurston for her awesome editing and to Dore Brown for managing the production of this book. We would also like to thank the reviewers of our book proposal and manuscript, who offered us insightful and thoughtful critiques. Special thanks go to Leslie C. Bell, Dawn H. Currie, and Anita Harris for their generosity of spirit and time and their wholehearted mentorship. Early on, when this book was just in its proposal stage, Bronwyn Davies offered us some sage advice—and we are very grateful for her words of wisdom. Thanks also to Jon Eben Field for helping us through a qualitative software crisis and for reading and offering feedback as the manuscript evolved over two years. Thank you to Larissa Bablak for coauthoring an article that informed chapter 5 as well as to Mary-Beth Raddon for reading and offering feedback on chapter 5.

We wish to extend our deepest thanks to Anita Harris for providing us with the foreword to this book. We are honored to have Anita engage with our project in such a profound way. Her work has been inspirational to us, and we wish to acknowledge her dedication to, and prominence within, the field of girlhood studies and youth studies, as well as her powerful critiques of neoliberalism and post-feminism. Her ideas permeate this book.

We gratefully acknowledge the support of the Social Sciences and Humanities Research Council of Canada for funding our study from 2010 to 2013. We also greatly appreciate the funding from Brock University that enabled our pilot study, as well as the funding from Brock University's Council for Research in the Social Sciences for indexing support. Thank you to the Department of Child and Youth Studies at Brock University for encouraging and contributing to cutting-edge research on young people. We are also very grateful for the wonderful research assistants who helped us along the way: Larissa Bablak, Kristina Gottli, Mary Spring, Andrea Stefanik, Ishrat Sultana, Ana Vintan, and Alexandra Watson.

Shauna's acknowledgments: I would like to thank Hart and Nancy Pomerantz for their constant encouragement, support, and kindness. Thanks also to the entire Pomerantz-Goldsilver-Morgenstern-Field clan for always asking about and taking an interest in my work. Thanks to the friends who supported me through this process over tea or wine: Carolyn Begg, Lisa Betts, Bob Christopher, Fanny Dolansky, John Grant, Erin Knight, Sandra Starmans, Clelia Scala, Katreena Scott, Stephanie Tomori, Harry Tournemille, Sandra Tournemille, and Liz Vlossak. Special thanks to Miriam Field and Shane Field for making me laugh, helping me keep a good perspective, and dragging me away from my desk on sunny days. My deepest thanks go to Jon Eben Field, who makes all of my work possible. Thank you for your editing, ideas, cooking, kindness, music, and love.

Rebecca's acknowledgments: I am lucky to have an incredible mentor at Brock University, Jane Helleiner. I am grateful to Jane for the interest she has shown in my development as a scholar and the wise guidance that she has provided me. I would also like to thank Helen McFadden, Jill Patterson, Mary-Beth Raddon, Kathryn Payne, Andrea Doucet, Nancy Cook, and David Butz for asking questions and sharing various insights about this book project along the way. Holly Patterson, thank you for your support and for the many other forms of invisible labor that have been so important in helping me hold up my end of this book project. You and Levi both rock my world.

Finally, we would both like to acknowledge the many interesting, smart, creative, and involved young people who populate and animate these pages. This book could not have been written without you, and we thank you for your time, patience, and stories.

CHAPTER ONE

Are Girls Taking Over the World?

> By virtually every measure, girls are thriving in
> school; it is boys who are the second sex.
>
> Christina Hoff Sommers, "The War
> against Boys"

Wren was all set to take on the world after graduation.[1] About to
complete her senior year as an honor roll student, she was
beyond excited about the prospect of starting university in the
fall—the first in her family to do so. Involved in her school
council, captain of the scrap-booking club, and an A+ pupil (her
school average was a cool 92 percent), Wren had already been
accepted to two of the four schools she had applied to and felt
confident that the other two would come through. Like all the
girls in her working-class[2] group of friends, Wren's future looked
bright. She was optimistic, passionate, and caring; she knew that
she wanted to change the world for the better. "The majority of
my girlfriends are as driven as me," she told us. "They all know
what they want to do, where they want to go, and are very motivated about pursuing those goals." When Wren noted that the
vice president and secretary of the school council were both

girls, as were the editor of the school paper and the president of the film club, she reflected for a moment and then said, "Girls are just generally more organized with their thoughts about what they want to do ...[3] Yeah, I think a lot of my female friends are generally more motivated to succeed."

"I've always been a pretty academic student," Wren said, sitting across from Shauna during her interview, wearing her class-of-2015 dark blue hoodie, sporting a loosely tied ponytail, and displaying the bronze manicure she had just gotten in preparation for the semiformal fundraiser that Friday night.[4] Her goal was to study international development and then, if all went well, embark on a short-term career as a humanitarian aid worker before possibly becoming a teacher. And Wren's determination was certainly paying off. She was considered a good bet for receiving the citizenship award at her graduation ceremony and felt passionate about the legacy she was leaving behind as she embarked on the next leg of her academic journey. Indeed, she was the most recognizable person in her school: "I would say I'm popular because everyone knows me." She wasn't popular for being a party girl or gossipy, as is often the case; rather, she was popular for being kind, hardworking, and thoroughly dedicated to her school. "I care about my school quite a lot," she emphasized. "Some of the things I do are invisible to the students, so I don't always get praised for it, but my goal is to make it the best time of everyone's life." Though she was involved in the anti-bullying club, art club, choir, leadership camp, and ME to WE (an organization that empowers youth to change the world through volunteerism and social involvement) and had recently instituted the flourishing scrap-booking club, she still found time to make good on this goal. Before graduation, she had a few more projects up her sleeve: trips, fundraising, spirit activities, and then … prom. "I've worked up to the power," she said of her status. "It's a good feeling. It's nice to have it pay off."

Though not a "girly girl," Wren admitted that she would enjoy the ritual of dressing up for graduation day when it came in June—but that outfit would not be anywhere near as fancy as the one she had for prom. She had saved up money from babysitting and other odd jobs to buy her moderately priced, yet stylish, graduation dress. Friends would come over to do their hair and makeup and compare their dresses. But ultimately, they would talk about how unreal it all felt. "It's kinda scary to think about it," Wren admitted, "but it's also quite meaningful. It's not the end of your school life, but it symbolizes the end of your child life. It just symbolizes moving on." When Wren walked across the stage that summer in cap and gown, she would do so with sheer exhilaration and pride. "It feels like I've earned this," she stated matter-of-factly. "I work really hard, about a 9.7 out of 10." The other 0.3 was lost to a recently acquired Netflix addiction. "Part of stress relief," she joked. "Otherwise, it'd be a 10 out of 10." Wren's laughter reminded her that taking time away from school work was *not* the end of the world, even though sometimes it felt like the whole world might come crashing down on her head if she did not keep her eye on the prize at all times.

SMART GIRLS: THE FACE OF THE FUTURE?

Are girls taking over the world?[5] It would appear so based on Wren's story and many others just like it. In fact, throughout the Western world, we have been bombarded with accounts of girls' skyrocketing academic success. The twenty-first century smart girl is defined by her ability to glide through high school collecting

As, racking up awards, and paving her own way to a bright future. Single-minded "alpha girls,"[6] over-scheduled "perfect girls,"[7] even-tempered "gamma girls,"[8] and do-it-all "supergirls"[9] can be found in books,[10] magazine articles,[11] and newspaper headlines, giving the impression that there is an endless parade of young women who epitomize ubiquitous, seemingly effortless success. Such descriptions offer an enduring image of bright, disciplined, hardworking girls who excel in school and are poised to not just take on the world but take it over. Examples include: "The New Girl Power: Why We're Living in a Young Woman's World"; "Why Are Girls Higher Achievers?"; "Compelling statistics show boys rank behind girls by nearly every measure of scholastic achievement"; "At Colleges, Women Are Leaving Men in the Dust."[12] This narrative has also frequently played out in popular culture. From Hermione Granger of the *Harry Potter* series to Gabriella from the *High School Musical* franchise and from Dora of *Dora the Explorer* to Alex Dunphy of *Modern Family*, girls have indeed become the face of academic stardom. Beyoncé even chants it in her pop hit, *Run the World (Girls)*: "I'm reppin' for the girls who takin' over the world, / Help me raise a glass to the college grads!"[13]

This girl, we are repeatedly told, is the face of the future. But after reading numerous descriptions of girls' unstoppable, inevitable success, we began to wonder about the story that was not being told. While not all girls are academically successful, the ones who are face differing contexts that radically shape their experiences. Why are accounts of girls' high achievement in school reduced to a standardized story that makes it appear as though being smart is stress-free and unsurprising? Where are the stories of struggle, tension, and negotiation? Where are the stories of sexism in classrooms and social worlds that still create stumbling blocks for girls?[14] Where are the stories about what happens to girls after high school and college, when they face gender inequality in the workplace? And where are the stories of girls who are silenced by a homogeneous narrative that leaves so many significant contexts, including passion, frustration, and concession, to the wayside?

Joining in a conversation with other feminists working in the areas of gender, schooling, and academic success,[15] we wanted to investigate the smart girl experience precisely because it has become a highly visible story in Western culture with real power to shape how we think about, treat, and allocate resources to girls. The typical story of girls' academic success narrowly shapes adult perceptions of girls, restricting what is considered to be normal ("Aren't girls supposed to do well in school?"), possible ("But girls today can do anything, so achieving your goals should be a snap!"), and realistic ("Juggling straight As, student council, and soccer is what it takes to succeed in today's world!"). These limitations become all the more poignant when we consider the diversity and inequality that this smart girl stereotype erases. After all, who *is* the successful girl featured in books, magazines, and newspapers? Most likely, she is white, middle- or upper-middle-class, Western, and from a progressive household, where higher education is not just valued but ingrained in the family's culture. "Race,"[16] socioeconomic class, sexuality, religion, nationhood, age, and other crucial contexts are woefully underrepresented or completely ignored, suggesting that a girl's success is based solely on her gender[17] ("Girls are just smarter than boys"), but without an understanding that gender is never a stand-alone category that operates in exclusion of all the other contexts that feed into who a girl is and how she comes to see herself.

In order to offer a different kind of story—one that digs deeper into the complex and intersectional identity of smart girlhood—we talked with girls who saw themselves as academically successful (or as potentially academically successful) and asked them what it was like to be smart within the context of their schools.[18] What we found was that, although most were doing very well academically, all of them had stories to tell about how they managed and negotiated[19] high achievement, what it had cost them socially or emotionally, and what concerns they had about the future that related to being independent and making a good living. For the most part, we learned that being a smart girl was not an easy identity to occupy in school—it took work, worry, and the kind of structural and familial support that not all girls can access. These hidden contexts suggest that the smart girl stereotype with which we are now so familiar in the West does a grave disservice to girls'—and boys'—struggles by obscuring how adults understand young people's experiences of school and social life and their concerns for the future.

While Wren's life may have the elements of that all-too-familiar tale—a girl with straight As who is involved in extra curricular activities, bound for college, and deeply committed to her future success—her story, along with the other stories in this book, offers a much broader understanding of what girls' experiences of academic success look like. For example, Wren admitted that maintaining her GPA was deeply stressful. "I do stay up very late every night, till 2 or 3 am," she told Shauna. "All my friends are in the same boat. We all have a lot of responsibility."

One of the self-imposed responsibilities on Wren's plate was worrying about the future. She described a main stressor in her life and the lives of her friends: how to merge work with having a family. "I think girls have the immanent, 'Am I going be a mom? Am I going to travel, be a mom, go to university? Am

I going to do *this?* Am I going to do all *that?*'" Wren mused. "Boys *never* think, 'Am I going to be a dad?'" She and her friends spent a lot of energy thinking and talking about the intricacies of timing: "How old is too old, and what age is right, and how much are you supposed to have done and fit all this stuff in and then still be a mom? Or are you even going to *be* a mom?!"

Wren's disclosure of stress and her concerns about combining work and family serve as a sharp reminder that many girls are not simply gliding through school, no matter what their report cards say. Rather, they must—to greater and lesser extents— engage in strategic negotiations to balance their academic success with other complex identity contexts. The goal of this book is thus to move beyond stereotypes and delve into the lives of smart girls by offering multilayered portrayals that help to contextualize simplistic headlines, magazine covers, and popular psychological accounts. Each chapter tackles a particular element of this negotiation, such as the stress of managing a supergirl persona, overt and covert strategies that go into simultaneously being an academically successful student *and* a successful girl, how girls deal with sexism in relation to academic success (including ambivalent feminist moments), and the intersectional challenges of negotiating academic success alongside entwined class-based and racialized backgrounds.

By contextualizing the lives of smart girls, we hope to offer a window into girls' academic success that moves away from the idea that they are "taking over the world"[20]—a common story that has led to both excitement and panic—and swings back to a narrative from a previous era, which views girls as worthy of support, resources, and political interventions. In short, we hope to put girls back on the agenda.[21]

GIRLS AGAINST BOYS:
THE NEW DOMINANT SEX?

The smart girl stereotype can only be understood in conjunction with another homogenizing story that has also captured attention in the West for over twenty years: the failing boy. Garnering considerable press in the United Kingdom, Australia, Canada, and the United States,[22] the failing boy has become one of the most gripping—and debated—narratives in Western education. While girls such as Wren are held up as exemplars of academic success, boys are routinely framed as struggling and lost.[23] In fact, girls' success has been repeatedly blamed for boys' failure, as if only one gender can or should do well at a time. One is contingent on the other: as girls are seen to ascend like stars, they are routinely held responsible for the perception that boys are plummeting like stones.[24]

It is widely reported that girls are now outperforming boys in high school tests, SATs, college acceptances, and undergraduate grades,[25] which would seem to set girls up for better lives by giving them, among other things, higher self-esteem, greater happiness, and improved financial security.[26] But many have asked: What about the boys?[27] The purported displacement of boys by girls has elicited outcries that the playing field is now tilted in girls' favor, as evidenced by these headlines: "Why Boys Are Failing in an Educational System Stacked against Them"; "Why Our Schools Are Failing Boys"; "The Boys at the Back"; and "How to Make School Better for Boys: Start by Acknowledging That Boys Are Languishing While Girls Are Succeeding."[28] A well-referenced *Business Week* cover story describes girls as building "a kind of scholastic Roman Empire alongside boys' languishing Greece."[29] The metaphor of transitioning empires is fitting given the refrain of attack: framed as hardworking, multi-tasking, and self-inventing, girls are represented as ready and able to take down the existing gender regime. Girls' success is thus viewed as a hostile coup—a dangerous and tumultuous changing of the guard that must be kept under watch. While individual girls like Wren are congratulated for their hard work and high achievement, there is a deeply rooted anxiety in the West surrounding the notion that girls, as a social group, are now poised to vanquish boys as the "natural" heirs to the throne.[30]

. . .

However, it was not so long ago that girls were the underdogs in education. In the 1970s, 1980s, and early 1990s, liberal second-wave feminists set their sights on schooling as a form of gender-based oppression.[31] They demanded that schools become more hospitable, less toxic environments for girls that would not shortchange their futures by channeling them into dead-end and feminized courses.[32] Emphasizing women's ability to rise up in a meritocracy, liberal feminist strategies entailed balancing gender representations in textbooks, encouraging girls to participate in mathematics and sciences, and engaging girls as self-reliant and independent learners who could achieve if they applied themselves.[33]

In the mid-1990s, as a result of liberal feminist lobbying to bring gender balance to schools, as well as the newly instituted neoliberal imperative to reward American schools that garnered higher standardized test scores,[34] statistics emerged that suggested a new gender gap: girls were doing better than boys on standardized tests and overall averages, outshining boys on literacy scores, and encroaching on traditionally male terrains, such as mathematics and sciences. Feminist interventions to reform the gender imbalance in education had seemingly worked, but according to some critics, maybe a little too well.[35] Rather than being a cause for celebration, these highly publicized findings instigated panic. Condemned as the "feminization" of schooling, feminist interventions were blamed for the perceived failure of boys.[36]

In her book *The End of Men,* Hanna Rosin offers these well-circulated figures: in the United States, women now earn 60 percent of master's degrees, close to half of law and medicine degrees, and 42 percent of MBAs. Women now also earn close to 60 percent of all bachelor's degrees, meaning that, for the first time in history, women receive more education than men.[37] The *Washington Post* also notes that, in 2012, "nationally, girls had a higher [high school] graduation rate, at 84 percent, while boys had a rate of 77 percent."[38] And in the first of a six-part series on failing boys in the *Globe and Mail,* one of Canada's national newspapers, it was reported that boys "earn lower grades overall in elementary school and high school. They trail in reading and writing, and 30 per cent of them land in the bottom quarter of standardized tests, compared with 19 per cent of girls. Boys are also more likely to be picked out for behavioural problems, more likely to repeat a grade and to drop out of school altogether."[39]

These disparities have been explained through a combination of neuroscience and the feminization of schooling thesis, which suggests that schools have become unfairly tilted in girls' favor. According to some developmental psychologists, boys' and girls' brains are hardwired differently.[40] For example, boys are said to be better at spatial problems, physical activity, and problem-based thinking, while girls are said to be better at language, communication, and relational play.[41] It has been repeatedly argued that the curriculum has been modified to appeal to girls in order to address liberal feminist complaints so that it now revolves around skills at which girls presumably excel, while the talents of boys are believed to be increasingly disparaged.[42] The feminization of schooling thesis is bolstered by critiques about the disproportionately high numbers of female teachers at the elementary school level, which, critics complain, gives girls unfair advantages:[43] the "female perspective" is favored, female teachers do not understand boys' "natural" kinesthetic abilities, and boys are punished for being rowdy, needing to move around, and doing the things that boys do.[44]

As these arguments have gathered speed,[45] an imagined future of smart girls growing up to be excessively powerful women has instigated fear, not only over boys' educations but over the crisis of masculinity this gender reversal would seemingly cause. There is talk of the "end of men,"[46] "the rise of women,"[47] "the new sexism,"[48] and "the war against boys."[49] Girls, once the underdogs in education, are now being criticized for having too much power.[50] But are girls really taking over the world? Do statistics on educational success tell the whole story? Or is there more to this simplistic narrative that has dominated educational debates for the past twenty years? Amidst the feverish pitting of "successful girls" against "failing boys," the day-to-day struggles of smart girls have been ignored, as have the political, social, and economic contexts that enable the stereotype of the smart girl to flourish.

WHAT SEXISM? POST-FEMINISM AND GIRL POWER

The positioning of girls as the new dominant sex in the classroom is part of a broader social trend known as post-feminism.[51] Post-feminism suggests that girls in the West are beyond the need for feminism because they now live in a world where sexism no longer exists. After all, if girls are outdoing boys in school, how can they possibly be experiencing gender inequality? Following this logic, American psychologist Dan Kindlon writes about the emergence of "alpha girls"—girls who have attained the highest level of success of any generation of girls in American history. These girls are smart, confident, and self-reliant.[52] They neither ask for any special treatment nor complain. These girls feel that the world is their oyster and are comfortable with their newfound power.

Kindlon argues that what makes this all-encompassing success possible is the fact that today's North American girls are 100 percent unhampered by their gender, enabling a feeling of limitless possibility: "They think of themselves as a post-feminist generation. They are the living, breathing embodiments of the inner revolution that women in the last generations so ardently desired and fought for."[53] According to Kindlon, the alpha girl has been liberated by the success of feminism; she no longer needs to rely on a so-called victim mentality to help her get a leg up. He concludes that the "alpha is a leader in a generation of girls on the rise. She is deployed in large numbers at the borders of adulthood—ready to make her mark on our world."[54] In such a world, there is no room for gender inequality; it has been expunged, and, along with it, the need for feminist politics.[55]

Kindlon's argument rests on the post-feminist assumption that feminism has won and that girls are now reaping all the benefits of living in a golden era where gender no longer matters. With the playing field presumably leveled, complaints of sexism now sound antiquated, whiny, and wounded. Instead, post-feminism relies on a narrative of individualism, which suggests that girls are in charge of their own fate: success is up to them, and as such, failure can no longer be attributed to larger structural issues that once held girls back. With gender inequality considered a thing of the past, girls are now seen to have unlimited access to success. But the flip side to this belief is that girls can no longer cry foul when they experience gender inequality: sexism is thus framed as a personal, rather than social, defect. But what cost does this have?[56]

The girls in this book grew up in a culture defined by and infused with girl power.[57] As the popular incarnation of post-feminism, girl power has helped to reinforce the myth of gender equality at the everyday level. From sexual agency to lavish consumerism to assertive individualism, girl power has aided in the belief that girls today can do, be, and have anything they want without fear of sexism or other inequalities in school or beyond to slow them down.[58]

Originating as a rallying cry for young women trying to make space for themselves in the male-dominated punk scene of the early 1990s,[59] girl power was initially invested with collective political action and critiques of the sexism, racism, and homophobia that governed both mainstream and underground music industries.[60] As a call to arms, girl power was all about the DIY punk code of anticonsumerism and anticorporatism—*grrrl* power! But by the mid-1990s, it had become a catchphrase for the mega pop band the Spice Girls.[61] According to the official Spice Girls book, girl power is about believing in yourself, having control over your own life, staying true to your friends, and demanding equality in your relationships.[62] Friendship, fun, female empowerment, and loyalty pervaded girl power, which conveyed the unequivocal message that girls could do anything they wanted as long as they stood by each other—and looked good doing it.

This post-feminist ethos has shaped not only the way girls understand themselves but also the political climate in which adults interpret and judge the actions of girls. Girls are now seen to embody individualized freedom, which often includes the "choice" to consume, hook up, ace school, find a job, and upset the traditional gender order in education and beyond.[63] In fact, when the term "girl power" was introduced into the *Oxford English Dictionary* in 2001, it included the idea of self-invention as part of its definition: "A self reliant attitude among girls and young women manifested in ambition, assertiveness, and individualism."[64] It is this kind of girl power—celebrating the newfound autonomy of girls and young women through consumer, sexual, and educational freedom—that has become central to girls' understanding of themselves and adults' understanding of girls.

.   .   .

Returning to Wren's story, it is hard to argue that she is a victim of gender inequality. The president of her school, a straight-A student, happy, and well adjusted, Wren is the spitting image of Kindlon's alpha girl, and she also reflects the media construction of what "real" girl power looks like: she seems to have the world at her fingertips, to have it all. But when Shauna asked Wren if she had experienced sexism, she only paused momentarily before launching into a string of stories. She recounted her annoyance when, on an exchange trip to Italy, she was stared at and harassed for being a "larger girl," which she felt was an example of gender discrimination. She also explained that she was not yet on the dating scene and wondered if it was because the boys at her school were intimidated by her academic and administrative success: "Girls are supposed to swoon over men with power, but if a guy can't swoon over a girl with power, then that's inequality!" And with prom on the horizon, she also lamented the still-pervasive custom of boys asking girls out.

After listing these disappointments, Wren thoughtfully concluded that such gender disparities "just weren't fair" and were definitely examples of sexism.

As a product of post-feminism and its popular incarnation of girl power, the smart girl stereotype obscures sexism by representing girls as doing, being, and having it all while failing to acknowledge the kind of struggle or stress that might be associated with gender inequality. But there is more to the story than either post-feminism or the smart girl stereotype demonstrates. Although post-feminism erases the possibility of sexism by insisting that girls are living in a gender-neutral world, sexism still abounds in all areas of social life and at all levels of power. To look at just a few examples in the workplace, women hold less than 17 percent of corporate board seats in[65] and make up only 5.2 percent of CEOs of Fortune 500 companies.[66] Women hold only 19 percent of the seats in the U.S. Congress.[67] Female lawyers earn 83 percent of what their male counterparts earn and make up only 20.2 percent of all partners in U.S. legal firms.[68] In powerful and lucrative STEM fields—science, technology, engineering, and mathematics—the gender disparities are even more glaring. Only one in seven engineers is female; women hold only 27 percent of computer science jobs; and even though women are touted as earning more bachelor's degrees than men, they receive less than 20 percent of computer science degrees.[69] Overall, women still earn only seventy-eight cents to every dollar that men earn.[70] In fact, across all university degrees, women earn less than men, with the gap widening as the level of education increases.[71]

When gender intersects with "race," the pay gap becomes even more pronounced. For example, in the United States, Hispanic and Latina women earn 54 percent and African American women earn 64 percent of what white men earn.[72] Hispanic,

Latina, and African American women are also less likely to graduate high school than white women or men, and they face discrimination in the workplace, further heightening the pay gap. When educational backgrounds are equal, women of color are still paid less than their white counterparts.[73]

What these figures make startlingly clear is that, while some girls excel in school, this success does not translate into a transformation of power at the highest levels, and economic inequality stubbornly endures.[74] It is still very much a man's world. So why does the stereotype of the flourishing smart girl set to take over the world persist?[75]

DESPERATELY SEEKING IDEAL
NEOLIBERAL SUBJECTS

Post-feminism and its popular incarnation, girl power, are situated within the broader social, political, and economic trend known as neoliberalism. Neoliberalism was a powerful undercurrent in 1980s politics during the Reagan years in the United States, the Thatcher years in the United Kingdom, and the Mulroney years in Canada, and it continues its ascendancy in the twenty-first century. It entails the valorization of competition, an entrepreneurial spirit, the steady extraction of the state from economic and social matters, and the belief that we are able to make ourselves into what we want.[76] Neoliberalism incudes the seductive notion that we are in charge of our own fate no matter what circumstances we have been dealt.[77] But the flip side to this seemingly empowering ethos is that we must fend for ourselves and not expect any sort of social or economic support from our governments.[78] Under neoliberalism, we are cut off from state involvement and expected to not just survive but thrive.[79]

In this era of personal accountability and shrinking social safety nets,[80] neoliberalism demands citizens who are flexible in education, work, and social life—citizens who are willing to pull their weight and work hard without complaint. Post-feminism is a part of this neoliberal ethos because it applies all of these characteristics to girls and young women, who are now told they are living a life without the constraints of gender and other kinds of inequality, leaving them free to explore any opportunities, ascend to any heights, and make any choices.[81] But again, the drawback to this ethos is that girls and young women can no longer expect any political or social support in relation to gender injustice, making claims of sexism difficult and the need for feminist politics a hard sell.[82]

It is this kind of logic that has contributed to the construction of what Australian youth studies scholar Anita Harris terms "future girls"—girls who are ideal global citizens.[83] Future girls, Harris suggests, are girls and young women capable of weathering the changes afoot in our new economic and social order without complaint. They soldier on, working as hard as possible, without whinging or whining. Their future-oriented approach not only serves them well but also serves the needs of global capitalism, which requires particular kinds of students and workers if it is to continue its political and economic dominance. And it is the academically successful girl who is the best example of this kind of ideal neoliberal subject, able to remake herself with ease by relying on a wide skill set, shine as a decision-maker in the face of multiple choices and options, and excel in a variety of capacities through perseverance and a plucky can-do attitude.[84] But what becomes abundantly clear in the construction of smart girls as ideal neoliberal subjects who work hard and get the job done is that many impossible demands and responsibilities are placed on their shoulders.[85] This kind of pressure has created contradictory conditions for girls, who are told they can succeed at anything they choose, although only a few actually do. And for those who do not succeed? They are left to wonder what they did wrong at a time in Western history when girls are supposed to be able to accomplish anything they set their minds to.[86]

This is the backdrop against which our study is set: the widespread belief that we are living in a post-feminist era, where girls are seen as having achieved not just gender equality but gender superiority, even though sexism remains pervasive; and the broader political, economic, and social trend of neoliberalism, within which girls are constructed as ideal global citizens because they are seen as compliant and adaptable and, therefore, as assets to global capitalism. Yet when faced with everyday experiences of gender inequality alongside narratives of empowering and competitive individualism, many girls in our study struggled to make sense of their academic identities as girls who are supposed to have it all. These are the stories that help to counterbalance the stark juxtaposition of successful girls and failing boys.

THE SMART GIRLS STUDY

The stories in this book were collected during a research project conducted in Southern Ontario, Canada, between 2008 and 2013.[87] Including the subjects in our pilot study, we interviewed fifty-seven self-described smart girls between the ages of twelve and eighteen in order to learn how they negotiated being smart in school.[88] After much discussion about what we meant by "smart," we decided to focus on academic achievement determined by criteria like grades, but left some room for disruption of this narrow measure. Our recruitment materials asked for participants who were "doing very well in school (or could if you tried)." We also asked, "Do you tend to receive As in your courses?" and, "Do you think of yourself as smart?" During our interviews, we asked participants how they defined the word "smart." Many girls emphasized grades or being book smart, but some also discussed the relevance of being street-smart, by which they often meant being socially savvy. Both of these definitions align with neoliberal objectives, as we discuss in the next chapter.

Though we privileged academic success in our recruitment materials, some girls who did not receive particularly high grades or who only received high grades in certain subjects still volunteered. In our discussions with these girls, the nuances of academic success were evident: the relevance of school subjects and their varying academic statuses, the financial resources that can facilitate high grades, how some students are disinterested in the structures of schooling, and the complexity of the category "smart girl," which certain girls occupied more comfortably than others. The less obviously academic girls in our study continued to complicate and challenge the smart girl stereotype for us and helped us rethink and redefine our own constrained notions of what it means to be "smart."[89] For these reasons, those girls who did not fit the traditional smart girl mold were extremely important to our study. Yet as we dug deeper into the stories of the girls we interviewed, even those that initially seemed to uphold the smart girl stereotype (i.e., white, middle-class overachievers), we found that *all* of the girls frequently scuttled the commonsense links between gender and success that permeate everyday perceptions.

We asked the girls what it was like to be smart, how they perceived their academic identities, and how being academically successful overlapped with being (or not being) a successful girl. This examination included how being smart affected girls' experiences of popularity, femininity, and sexism. It also included an exploration of how academic success was entwined with other identity contexts, such as class and "race." About half of the girls chose to be interviewed together with a smart friend, which likely enabled them to feel more comfortable in the presence of an adult researcher, and most were interviewed a second time about six months later.[90] Frequently, participants chose to be interviewed in nonacademic settings, such as local coffee shops, their homes, public libraries, and food courts in malls.[91] They chose their own, sometimes quite creative, pseudonyms.

We also interviewed a subset of seventeen boys between the ages of twelve and eighteen who, like the girls, self-identified as smart. They were similarly given the option of an individual interview or an interview with a smart friend and were able to choose the interview location. We were committed to including boys in this book, which is focused on girls, for a number of reasons. First, in order to deeply contextualize girls' experiences, we felt it was necessary to hear from boys and engage with their understandings of academic success. We did not want to presume to know what boys thought, nor did we want to leave them out of a project that, in many ways, is contingent on boys' experiences of academic success, too. Moreover, in order to offer rich and meaningful stories, we felt we needed multiple perspectives on particular issues relating to gender, such as classroom and social world dynamics. For example, while girls are often cast in the role of teacher's pet, boys are granted access to the more affable role of class clown. When we asked boys about these gendered categories, many had different viewpoints than the girls did, and this contributed fresh perspectives on the meaning of academic success within a school setting. The stories we collected from boys are thus relayed in relation to the stories from girls, and they offer an important—and mostly unheard—position that deepens our understanding of gender, schooling, and academic success. While this is a book about girls, our discussion of boys' academic success and their understandings of gender in the context of school highlights the importance of hearing from boys on this topic.

Our participants came from a total of fifteen schools across Southern Ontario, including high schools, middle schools, and upper-level elementary schools. The schools were nondenominational public schools, Catholic public schools, and private schools.[92] The majority of our participants came from the small city of Secord, a blue-collar, deindustrializing border town hit by the kind of economic restructuring brought about by manufacturing closures that have similarly disadvantaged other North American cities over the past thirty years.[93] While our interviewees came from a wide range of economic backgrounds, most had at least somewhat financially stable families, which reinforces the association between economic security and academic success.[94] Of the fifty-seven girls we interviewed, forty-five were white, ten were East, South, or Southeast Asian, one was Arabic, and one was black. Of the seventeen boys, fifteen were white, one was South Asian, and one was Southeast Asian (see appendix).[95]

READING SMART GIRLS

This book is organized around topics that help contextualize the lives of smart girls and negate the simplistic story that is overrepresented in media and popular psychological accounts. In chapter 2, we begin this contextualization by exploring the media construction of the supergirl—the girl who is not only academically successful but also skilled at sports, extracurricular activities, and social life. No other example seems to offer better proof that girls today have it all. Yet the stories relayed to us by girls who might be deemed supergirls suggest that this kind of intensive success comes at a price. The stress and anxiety associated with maintaining perfection is daunting and potentially damaging to girls, who push themselves beyond reasonable limits to stay on top. Such consequences are further compounded by the invisible privilege of class-based and family advantages, which very few girls can access. While the supergirl makes über achievement look highly attainable and readily available, the economic and social support needed to sustain this identity means that it is hardly generalizable to all girls.

In chapter 3, we explore tensions in smart girls' lives by focusing on how girls and boys negotiate gender and peer culture. We focus on the collisions and overlaps between the most culturally valued forms of femininity and masculinity as they intersect with academic success. While girls are deemed to be the new dominant sex in education and beyond, we offer stories in this chapter that illustrate the strategies the girls in our study used to negotiate their smart identities within their school's social world.[96] We explore the challenges of a smart girl identity in relation to popularity, sexual desirability, fitting in, and standing out. In some instances, girls played down their academic success for fear of becoming loners with no friends. In other instances, girls dumbed down because they believed it would make them more popular and attractive to boys. There were also girls who played up their academic success to garner accolades, awards, and respect, although sometimes at the expense of popularity and sexual desirability.

In this chapter, we also explore the strategic negotiations of girls in contrast to those of boys, who used different tactics to manage their academic success. In some instances, boys were able to navigate the complexity of being smart in school more easily than girls, particularly if they offset this potentially damaging social position with other skills, such as sports or humor. The boys did not feel they had to hide being smart, but they did hide doing work in order to get high grades; they did not want to be seen as caring too much, because it suggested that they were unathletic, antisocial bookworms. Both girls and boys worried about how they were perceived in relation to their academic success, but girls were more careful about being seen as too smart, while boys were more careful about being seen as too studious.[97]

Chapter 4 offers another context for girls' academic success by focusing specifically on sexism in the classroom and on how girls imagine their futures. While many of the girls in our study drew on a post-feminist outlook that emphasized individualized success or failure and denied the existence of sexism, they sometimes recognized, and then lamented, the sexist contexts that shaped their lives. In this chapter, we explore the tension between girls' common assumptions of gender equality and the sexism they (or we) identified. While most of our participants maintained that the genders were equal, contradictions and epiphanies arose in our interviews. For example, a participant might deny sexism one moment and then provide a concrete example of it the next without noticing that she had done so; or a participant might first deny the existence of inequality but realize later in the interview that it was present in her life and then provide an example of how it angered her or affected her in some specific way. When girls did not see sexism in their lives, it sometimes created tensions, which they interpreted as personal problems that they needed to solve alone.

In this chapter, we also juxtapose the stories girls told about their perceptions of gender dynamics in school to those of boys, who offered a very different perspective. While girls often felt that boys were favored by teachers—allowed to joke around, play the class clown, and derail lessons on a dime—many boys expressed feelings of gender discrimination around assumptions that they were automatic troublemakers. In these cases, some boys felt that teachers favored girls, who were seen as quiet, studious, and well behaved, and that, as a result, girls did not receive the same level of surveillance as boys did. These contradictory layers interject points of complexity and contradiction into the typical stories of academically successful girls and academically challenged boys. They also highlight how pervasive gender assumptions can be difficult for both girls and boys to negotiate.

In chapter 5, we focus on other contextualizing features of smart girls' lives: intersections of class and "race." These interwoven complexities are crucial to countering the typical story of smart girls as homogeneous winners in education. In our interviews, class emerged as a powerful force in the lives of smart girls. On the one hand, it was a source of judgment between students and thus a tool that some girls used to bolster their privilege and exclude others. Many of the participants in our study made comments evaluating schools based on the class make-up of the neighborhoods the student populations came from, noting the importance of wearing expensive brand-name clothing and making broad generalizations about wealthy and poor families. There were also moments when girls recognized the parental support they received, noted the value of a private school education, or lamented the challenges they faced because their families were less well-off than others. But on the other hand, class was also something that was hidden and simplified. Many girls failed to recognize their own privilege, for instance, or said that everyone at school gets along, although it was clear that it helped a girl's social status to wear popular styles. Class inequality was also viewed as an individual issue that arose from the personal skills of the wealthy and the personal deficits of the poor rather than from structural dimensions, such as high unemployment. Many feminist researchers have pointed out that working-class girls face specific challenges in school that go largely unseen.[98] Broader issues, such as structural factors and the middle-class assumptions of the school, were unacknowledged by even the most politically astute girls that we interviewed. Similarly, "race" emerged as a central feature in definitions of academic success, particularly in relation to the stereotype of the "smart Asian." The girls in our study with Asian backgrounds lamented that they were often pigeonholed as being automatically good at school but laughed off these racist stereotypes as "just joking around," yet such assumptions reproduce a narrow idea that being "too smart" is not only antisocial but also the mark of a cultural outsider.

In the concluding chapter, we focus on two themes that offer glimpses into places in smart girls' lives where possibilities for social transformation might be fostered. First, we explore ways that some of the girls in our study were contesting popular femininity through microresistances. These small yet potentially influential challenges to popular femininity help shift the landscape of girlhood by subtly expanding who and what a (smart) girl can be. Second, we focus on the importance of school culture in fostering girls' comfort with academic success. If the culture of the school was open to less traditional forms of gender and sexuality, it seemed that smart girls had a much better chance of thriving rather than hiding. Negotiations and complications were minimized where it was cool—or at least not socially disastrous—for girls to openly engage their academic identities with pride and visible satisfaction. While there was certainly no perfect refuge for smart girls—who all had to contend in some way or another with the complexities and constraints that being smart entailed—some schools clearly presented this kind of support more than others. Both of these themes offer a glimpse into ways that girls, boys, teachers, administrators, parents, and media commentators might support smart girls, making space for them to pursue academic success without apprehension.

Lastly, the final chapter makes a renewed call for greater care in making broad statements—in media outlets and academic research—about girls and boys in school. Greater attention must be given to intersections of identity, such as gender, "race," class, sexuality, age, and nationhood, including privileges and disadvantages that cut across these categories. We offer one such example in the next chapter. While the celebrated supergirl of the twenty-first century may seem to be an identity that is attainable for girls who try hard enough, we explore the class-based and family supports that it takes to succeed at absolutely *everything* and offer a critique of the possibility of actually being a supergirl without succumbing to the stress and sleeplessness of striving so high.

CHAPTER TWO

Driven to Perfection

For girls, it's be yourself, and be perfect, too.

Sarah Rimer, "For Girls, It's Be Yourself"

During her first interview, Ella was in the last grade of Agatha Benchley Elementary, a downtown school she had switched to a few years before, where she was enrolled in a gifted education program. She was very happy with this move, even though she told us that "people think of it as more like a ghetto school."[1] She explained that the students at Agatha Benchley came from mixed economic backgrounds, unlike other schools that were considered "preppy" or "stuck up," and she said that it was a supportive, friendly environment where being smart was valued. This support was important to Ella, who was deeply committed to her schoolwork and, like a number of the girls we interviewed, described herself as a perfectionist. As she explained: "So everything has to be, like, perfect on the dot!" She added that, when she does not make the right decisions, or when she gets something wrong on a test, she gets upset, worries profusely, and then tries to work and study even harder. That said, Ella was not exclusively focused on school to the neglect of everything else.

She wanted to be perfect at *everything*—and she seemed able to pull it off.

.   .   .

While the smart girl stereotype has continuously been perpetuated in media accounts throughout the last decade or so—and seen as proof positive that girls can do, be, and have anything they want—a more elite narrative has emerged: that of the supergirl.[2] Not only is the supergirl academically successful and future focused, but she is also able to excel across multiple aspects of school, including extracurricular activities, clubs, sports teams, community service, and peer relationships. The supergirl is seemingly able to successfully navigate the demands of being smart *and* popular, sporty *and* academic, and involved in school-sanctioned activities *and* comfortable in her school's social world.[3] In short, the supergirl can do it all, do it well, and do it with confidence. And it is this new archetype that has raised the bar even higher for what is considered to be "normal" for girls, shaping and shifting expectations among teachers, parents, school administrators, and reporters, who have become deeply invested in describing the habits of the supergirl to a curious audience. As *New York Times* reporter Sara Rimer writes, these "amazing girls" are "high achieving, ambitious and confident." In fact, they seem to triumph in just about everything they do.

Like Kindlon's alpha girl—who "doesn't feel limited by her sex; she is a *person* first and then a woman"[4]—the supergirl also functions as the best evidence possible that girls today are living in a gender-neutral world. The supergirl is viewed as being able to push herself to great success without being thwarted by individual or structural limitations, which are not believed to exist anymore. The supergirl is certainly not hindered by gender inequality; instead, she is a girl who seems to be able to do anything, be anything, strive for anything, and win anything. But does such a girl actually exist? Or is she yet another stereotype that reinforces the idea of girls' individual success at the expense of a more nuanced and structural contextualization? While the supergirl offers a seductive portrait of girlhood, it is a product of our current post-feminist and neoliberal times and, as such, demands further examination.

As Lakshmi Chaudhry of *The Nation* reports, "Everything a boy can do, this gal can do and more … and maybe even better."[5] And in the *BusinessWeek* article that describes girls as building "a kind of scholastic Roman Empire alongside boys' languishing Greece," supergirls are labeled as "alpha femmes" who have taken over everything in school, from student activities to honor roll accolades.[6] But the success attributed to the supergirl is far from the end of the story—there is a more complicated and sometimes more troubling side that is often overlooked. As Chaudhry goes on to explain, success is not making these girls happy: they are stressed out and anxious as they feel constant pressure to excel, starting in grade school and continuing through to university. Chaudhry also suggests that gender inequality continues to lurk behind this drive for perfection, arguing that, because women are devalued, they feel the need to "earn respect, love or acceptance by being a hot babe, good mom, school valedictorian, concert pianist, MVP or, preferably, all of the above."

Rimer's account of "perfect" girls also reveals the high price of perfectionism. In her interviews with girls who fit the supergirl profile, she notes that, "being an amazing girl often doesn't feel like enough these days when you're competing with all the other amazing girls around the country who are applying to the same elite colleges that you have been encouraged to aspire to practically all your life."[7] In *Supergirls Speak Out,*[8] American journalist Liz Funk concurs with Rimer's view, based on her interviews with girls aged fifteen to twenty-seven. She suggests that, while supergirls may boast incredible résumés and seem to have the world at their feet, they are so beset by perfectionism and competition that they are on a path to self-destruction. Funk believes that this underlying drive and self-dissatisfaction emerges from growing up in a sexist society that does not allow girls to simply accept themselves—or be accepted by others—for who they are: "Most supergirls' self-distraction is to lure their thoughts away from broader issues of being raised with a latent understanding that it's not good to be a girl."[9]

Really, if there are indeed such things as supergirls, the definition must also include being anxious about the future, focused on individualized competition, and driven to perfectionism in an attempt to surmount ongoing gender inequality. The supergirl drive for success and perfection comes at a cost, not just to themselves but also to other girls (and possibly boys). In the face of a need for recognition, girls strive to do more and more, continually raising the bar for each other to impossible heights that are often out of reach, especially for girls who do not have a breadth of resources and supports.

In this chapter, we explore the experiences of the girls in our study who appeared to fit the supergirl persona. We illustrate how the construction of the supergirl resonates with this particular juncture in Western history and how certain schools and families are key to facilitating supergirls' success. The girls we introduce here endeavored to excel across the board and largely succeeded in their efforts due to powerful support systems.[10] They also faced the more personal challenges of striving for illusive perfection. As for other smart girls whose experiences we explore in subsequent chapters, the lofty harmony of super-girl achievements was elusive—if not impossible.

FITTING IN AND STANDING OUT

Returning to Ella, she was one of the rare girls in our study who seemed to fit the celebrated supergirl persona. She was smart, sporty, popular,[11] and completely in control. White, lower-middle-class, and one of the younger girls that we interviewed, she was a worldly, self-possessed, and confident twelve-year-old during her first interview and a thriving thirteen-year-old doing well in her new high school when we interviewed her the second time. The first interview with Ella was on the day before she flew to France for a three-month exchange—an opportunity that had been organized by her mom. Shauna sat down to talk to Ella in the sparsely furnished bedroom she shared with her sister. She had a stylish, artsy look about her, even though she wore loose-fitting sweatpants and a casual, off-the-shoulder sweatshirt. She was relaxed and keen to talk.

Ella did very well in school and was one of the few participants in our study who had skipped a grade. As the youngest of six children, she did not stand out in her family, however, because her "whole family was gifted." Her mom, who made a living from renovating and flipping houses, was particularly supportive of Ella, advocating for her at school, ensuring that she was academically stimulated, and encouraging her to stay on top of her various activities—interventions Ella generally appreciated, although sometimes resented. Her dad, a salesperson, had a more laid back role in Ella's life. Though Ella described herself to friends as "poor," her family was clearly culturally rich, valuing education, travel, and the arts. Her mom, in particular, made sure that Ella was involved in enriching experiences that would grant her cultural capital—the knowledge, skills, and ways of being that are valued within dominant institutions, such as school, and often ensure success.[12]

Sitting in the sun-soaked room, which her mom had painted, Ella explained to Shauna that she was very much into the arts, particularly music. She was taking piano and guitar lessons, plus she had played the lead in the school musical that year. Ella talked about how creativity was just as important to her as being smart: "It's not about thinking what your limits are, it's about thinking outside the box and just being imaginative." Ella was also an athlete, involved in both school and community sports leagues. In fact, Ella made a mark for herself by being the only girl on a local hockey team for a number of years. At first, this gender difference was a challenge, as other teammates assumed that she would not be a strong player, but gradually they came to realize that she was a natural on skates and could hold her own in the rink. As if schoolwork, music, and sports were not enough, Ella was also involved in an advocacy group for children's rights. When Shauna commented on how busy she was, Ella joked that it was a miracle she found time to be interviewed for our study.

Over the course of our interviews, we learned that some girls with the same kind of ambition and perfectionist yearnings as Ella were unpopular in school. She told us that some of these girls were called "brown-nosers" or "teacher's pets." Seen as trying too hard and being overly focused on grades, they were accused of having unsocial and boring lives. But Ella escaped this fate. She was a popular girl, friendly and well known by a lot of her peers. She had a small group of solid friends she had met through the gifted education program. But she also talked about the importance of being friendly to everyone and fitting in easily with people who were different from her. By her own account, Ella was also attractive to boys. She had started dating a few months earlier, and when she and a boy named Eddie broke up, a number of other boys began to crowd around with interest. She relayed this story with a suppressed smile on her lips—she was proud of her status but knew it was better not to boast.

By the time of the second interview, Ella had settled into ninth grade at Blue Ridge High, a large high school in a middle- to upper-middle-class neighborhood. Blue Ridge had extensive academic programming, including French immersion.[13] After taking a short break from her French immersion program for her trip to France, Ella was now happily reenrolled. She was already making new friends and getting used to her new classes, which she described as a "little bit harder, obviously, because I'm in high school." Despite the new academic challenges, Ella was still pushing herself, taking grade ten vocals and music theory. She was also still popular and reported that she could still skillfully manage her social life alongside her drive for perfection in her schoolwork—though it was becoming more complicated to do this as she aged.

. . .

To all extents, Ella fits the profile of a supergirl—a girl who is able to embrace the myriad elements of her life with relative ease. She had good friendships and popularity, was very successful in her coursework, and played the starring role in her school's musical. Ella was one of about ten girls in our study who enjoyed this kind of all-around success. These girls did not see their academic prowess as a liability because for them, smartness was coupled with other skills and resources, including supportive school environments and families that allowed them to both fit in and stand out.

But while the media narrative of the supergirl suggests that this kind of multileveled success occurs individually, in the following section we explore the broader contexts that have produced the idea of the supergirl, an idea that is then affixed to particular girls, like Ella. As part of the ideal neoliberal subject, the supergirl is a specific symbol of our current era of risk and individualism. While deemed a lone shining star, the supergirl is actually entwined in a constellation of school contexts, family resources, and peer climates that are certainly not available to all girls. We also consider how, while girls like Ella may seem to have it all, they are also negotiating the challenges and dizzying contradictions of gender inequality and perfectionism.

DIY SUCCESS: THE "SELF-MADE" GIRL

The girls in our study were determined to be successful, and they often alluded to an internal drive that made them exclusively responsible for their own success.[14] Candace, a white, upper-middle-class sixteen-year-old with professional parents who was dedicated to both sports and music, offered an example of this kind of personal ambition when she suggested that she had total control over how she did in school: "The only person that can make me do better in school is *me*." For Candace, as for many of the girls in this book, doing well in school meant trying hard, getting the job done, and relying on no one but herself. Similarly, Janey and her sister, Margot, white girls from a middle-class family, prioritized individual hard work and self-motivation. Margot explained, "Well, like, our parents never, like, pushed us in school, like, 'You have to get As.' It just kind of happened. We did it on our own." And Janey added, "We both have, like, goals.

We set our own goals, and we know what we have to do to get them, so it's more, like, self-motivation."

The personal responsibility that most of the girls in our study took on is an example of the neoliberal imperative of individualism. The girls were intent on making the "right choices" and translating those choices into future success in careers in medicine, teaching, forensics, writing, finance, arts, law, and architecture—goals they saw as accessible and contingent on their own intelligence, will, and wise choices.[15] While some of the girls appreciated the significant support and guidance they received from their parents, structural factors such as class-based privilege rarely seemed to enter their understandings of success. Most of them considered high achievement to be something they had earned through personal skills, hard work, and ambition rather than any kind of external privilege. And most did not at first think about complications of gender inequality or other forms of oppression. As we explore more deeply in chapter 4, the girls in our study were influenced by a post-feminist perception of gender equality. But as other feminist researchers have noted, we need to explore these complex political, economic, and social contexts to understand the supergirl as a narrow and specific notion of girlhood that resonates with neoliberal citizenship.[16] The widespread focus on personal success that we found in our study, and that was symbolized in particular by girls who might be seen as supergirls, must be grounded in the current historical moment, which is heavily marked by the confluence of post-feminism and neoliberalism. This confluence depends on individualized competition and success, self-regulation, and personal ambition—all of which should be demonstrated without a trace of complaint.

SUPERGIRL RISING: THE "RIGHT" CHOICES, RISK, AND THE NEOLIBERAL CONTEXT

Widespread local and global changes relating to the rise and intensification of neoliberalism have been integral to the discussion of supergirls for over a decade. This political, economic, and social strategy of deregulated trade, private enterprise, and the steady extraction of the state from the provision of social services prioritizes personal traits such as competition, self-reliance, and individual responsibility. These values, in turn, foster the notion that individuals are entirely responsible for their own success and failure, regardless of privilege or disadvantage.[17] Despite a strong current of individualism that has always run through American culture, it is through the rise of neoliberal policies and ideals that the valorization of individualism has really intensified.

Many people have certainly benefited from neoliberalism, which has brought about the globalization of markets, an expanded availability of cheap consumer products, and flexibility for businesses. But for many others, neoliberal policies have contributed to the erosion of the middle class and the increasing gap between the very wealthy and the very poor, largely through decreased taxation and government services, increased privatization, and attacks on unions and workers' rights.[18] Shifts toward a globalized economy, cheap transportation, and free trade have also depleted manufacturing in many local communities, including the small, deindustrializing city of Secord, where many of the participants in our study lived.[19]

These material and ideological shifts have been linked to a decline in predictable career trajectories and the rise of insecurity and precarity facing young people.[20] Ironically, the very ideologies and forces generating this instability also foster the belief that we must negotiate it all on our own: we are expected to make the "right" choices in order to achieve success all by ourselves. The risks we face along the way must be dealt with individually, and the consequences are, in turn, linked to individual responsibility. In other words, there is a belief that we have become perpetually flexible, free, and autonomous to make decisions, but only within a broader social environment that is unequal and increasingly insecure.[21] The autonomy and options of the risk society may sound exciting, conjuring up images of a cowgirl or cowboy on the frontier, but the risk society involves negotiating all on one's own a world of rising inequality across the globe, unstable employment, and a flimsy safety net. Feelings of insecurity now permeate all social classes,[22] although of course what feels risky for some may be devastating for others, depending on one's support network and financial means.[23]

CAN GIRLS DO IT ALL?

As we explored in chapter 1, Anita Harris introduces the idea that neoliberal and post-feminist views have come together to *specifically* position girls as "the ideal flexible subject[s] of [this] new economy,"[24] confidently embracing high career expectations, faith in hard work and credentials, and the importance of good, individual choices.[25] The neoliberal philosophy of individual responsibility resonates with liberal feminist girl power ideals through an emphasis on girls' ability to be who they want to be, challenge traditional limitations, and embrace autonomy and choice. As Harris argues, the new economy "evokes, although thoroughly liberalizes, feminist principles."[26] Neoliberalism has fostered a new economy that coincides with feminist achievements in securing increased opportunities for women through legal protections and economic shifts. For example, the expansion of the feminized service and social services industries and the contraction of manufacturing have led to new employment possibilities for young women.

The success of some girls has also been attributed to gender flexibility, which makes girls in particular so well positioned within this neoliberal climate since they are seen as capable of straddling traditional femininity and masculinity simultaneously. We are no longer surprised that girls are aspiring to work in ambitious professions or that they are confident in school. For example, Kindlon suggests that alpha girls are so accomplished and at ease with themselves because they have been able to embrace masculine competitiveness and rationality, in part through having close relationships with their fathers.[27] Others suggest that girls are seen to have both the "soft skills,"[28] that are embraced by the current business world and rationality and drive, which have generally been considered to be more masculine traits.[29] But while this social shift has led to concern over the so-called end of men,[30] as we have argued, such successes have not translated into a broad shift in power between men and women. Similarly, the story of girls' skyrocketing success does not take into account other important caveats, such as the toll of striving for perfection, the sexism women continue to face, the challenge of balancing contradictory features of traditional gender roles, and a world that suggests girls have it made but remains exacting and punishing in its judgments of successful women.[31]

The twenty-first century supergirl represents the culmination of the ideal, flexible neoliberal girl subject. But while supergirls are exciting figures of assumed feminist success and neoliberal drive, they are also part of a social context that suggests girls can never be good enough—heavy competition means that smart girls must always do more, and do it better, in order to stay on top. And it is only a small percentage of girls who can fulfill the promises of empowerment, choice, and responsibility that are now viewed as inherent to girlhood.[32] Most girls share the same beliefs and aspirations as those who seem to be super-girls but face structural conditions that prevent them from succeeding as expected—and these girls may blame themselves for what they perceive as their failure to achieve what is expected of them and what they expect of themselves.

GRADES, GOODNESS, AND GRACE

Within this powerfully competitive political, economic, and social climate, school grades are paramount: they represent personal success in the present, and are important when it comes time to apply for university and, later on, for a job. Almost all of the girls in our study placed great importance on grades and saw them as key indicators of their smartness and their ability to succeed.[33] Anything less than an A could lead to worry, not just about the future but about one's inherent smartness, too. But the girls also had other ways of measuring smartness that fostered a narrow, elusive, and conservative definition of supergirl success. Through our interviews, we learned that smartness was also about being "good," being involved, and being social—all ways the bar was raised from smart girls' success to supergirl levels.

In an era of "multiple intelligences,"[34] we expected more talk about different kinds of smartness, like athletic intelligence and musical talent. Instead, what repeatedly came up were terms like "street smarts" and "social smarts." At first, these expanded understandings of what it means to be smart seemed to disrupt a narrow, established focus on traditional academics and suggested diverse possibilities for smart girl success, but really, these comments were about making "good" decisions (i.e., being self-disciplined and nice), both of which are about conforming to established schooling and considered integral to individualized personal success. In other words, these broader definitions of being "smart" resonate with a narrow good girl, can-do, supergirl identity.

When our participants talked about street smarts, they were not generally referring to the skills and strategies that young people might develop when living with precarity.[35] With few exceptions,[36] the girls saw being street smart as knowing themselves and making good choices, like avoiding drugs and alcohol or studying rather than going to a party. Ultimately, making good choices was about behaving responsibly and being a good girl.

. . .

Julia and Abbey were sisters who, like Ella, fit the supergirl persona. They came from a white, upper-middle-class family and grew up in a large home. For both interviews, they were well dressed in a preppy style that denoted their social status and material wealth. Julia was involved in piano, percussion band, jazz band, synchronized skating, and swimming. She also worked six hours a week at a part time job. Abbey was three years younger and involved in piano, swimming, basketball, and dance. In order to get a better sense of how the sisters defined academic success, Shauna asked them how smart kids behaved at school. Abbey's immediate response was, "They make smart decisions," including choosing the right friends and staying out of trouble. Julia agreed: "Yes, making decisions about drinking and driving. Obviously [smart kids] are going to say no. For drugs, they would say no." Other girls in our study similarly equated being smart with being responsible.[37] For these girls, being good, much like getting high grades, was about self-discipline and focus on future success, both hallmarks of neoliberalism. But these kinds of comments also made it clear that being good is far from a neutral assessment: it involves meeting powerful middle-class assumptions about following a narrow path to success, a path that fits well within established institutions.[38] For the supergirl, self-invention and future success in a culture of uncertainty and individualism is about doing everything right, and here we see how this includes compliance. It also includes being involved in school culture, from extracurricular activities to a thriving social life.

JUST DO IT: EXTRACURRICULARS

Ella engaged in a long list of extracurricular activities that would make anyone's head spin. At the end of eighth grade, she was taking guitar and piano lessons, had the lead in her school musical, and was involved in sports (both at her school and in her community) and clubs. Ella's deep focus on schoolwork also compelled her to take an advanced math class for extra credit. This level of commitment was not unusual in our interviews. Many of the girls we talked with were similarly juggling a dizzying array of activities—they kept so many balls in the air that we often wondered how they did it.

Extracurriculars provide a wealth of opportunities; they can improve academic achievement, cultivate sociality and responsibility, and contribute to positive development.[39] For many of the girls in our study, like Ella, heavy involvement in extracurricular activities was just part of the package—their smart girl "portfolio." Good friends Brooke, Laney, and Jamila met with us at a local café. White and middle-class, Brooke came from the most financially secure family of the three. Due to her popularity, extracurriculars, and high grades, she also most resembled a supergirl. Laney came pretty close, however. Over lunch, she explained that being smart is not just about good grades or being able to do math questions but also about deep school and community participation outside of the classroom through extracurriculars, including sports, and part time jobs. Jamila was Middle Eastern and came from a working-class family. She was also very involved, participating in school music productions and working part-time, but less at the center of things than a supergirl would generally be. Between the three friends, they participated in schoolwork, part-time jobs, regular choir, chamber choir, jazz, band, improv, dance, cross-country, the school musical, and student council.

The supergirls in our study were not only very involved but also seemed to thrive on an intense level of extracurricular participation. Their many commitments brought them friendships, feelings of belonging and importance, and pride in their skills. Their commitments also tended to be conventional, further cementing inclusion within normative expectations and established institutions. To become successful, young people increasingly feel they need to gain the skills and social connections that will serve them both in the present and in the future, and the supergirls in our study were keenly aware of this imperative. They were involved in activities for fitness, fun, and friends, but they were also thinking ahead: How could they stay as competitive as possible for their future success? These girls were working hard—both on their schoolwork and in the complex web of other commitments that kept them busy before, during, and after school—and they were ever hopeful that all the effort would pay off in university acceptances and successful careers.[40]

GIRLS JUST WANT TO HAVE FUN: BEING SOCIAL

Another component of the supergirl identity is being nice and friendly. Brooke, who was very active on her student council while also juggling sports, music, and a part-time job, said that part of being smart is getting a "sweet report card," but another part is having good communication skills. Similarly, Wren was very focused on being nice to others and being a good friend. As she explained, "I like to have a lot of friends. I like to be nice to a lot of people. I like to be known as a person you can talk to if you need a friend." Ella stressed the importance of being nice, a sentiment that was also reflected in a number of other interviews across the range of girls we talked with. These comments challenge the idea that being a successful smart girl requires a single-minded focus on school; being social and friendly are important, too. And these traits are imperative to supergirl popularity.

Ella had more of a challenge than some of the girls when it came to managing the social side of being a supergirl, primarily because she had skipped a grade. But with some careful thought about her situation, she was able to pull it off. She admitted that she had been embarrassed by her academic success her whole life. She worried about what other students would think about her skipping a grade and that they might consider it "weird" that she was younger than them. And occasionally, she did feel teased. While she did not regret her decision to skip a grade, Ella sometimes wished that she was older or that others did not place as much importance on age. This part of Ella's story highlights some of the real struggles smart girls have around acceptance, sociality, and popularity—struggles we examine further in chapter 3. That said, Ella explained that, while other kids at her school were "outcasts" because of their high grades, shyness, and dedication to school, these traits were not a problem for her because she was just as dedicated to her social life as she was to school. She was outgoing, involved, and ready to talk to people—she understood the importance of being willing to "put yourself out there."

Other research on popular, high-achieving girls has found that they prioritized relationships with friends and had the strong social skills necessary to secure a wide friendship network.[41] These girls were confident and comfortable with their high academic achievements, tended to be physically attractive and fashionable, followed conventionally gendered lines, and positioned themselves as mature.[42] Some of the supergirls in our study were, in a number of ways, similarly fulfilling popular versions of femininity because they were conventionally pretty and dated boys, but this was certainly not the case with all of them. Wren was a bigger girl, for example, but self-confident and clear about her successes. As she said in her first interview, "I like who I am. I like to be smart. I like to be successful. I like to be liked by teachers and people. I like to be good at music, and that's my hobby, and art and drawing, and writing. That all comes with 'smart' I guess." But girls like Wren were also very focused on being nice, another hallmark of femininity. Wren talked about how she tries to please everyone and told us that she gets very upset if she feels she has disappointed her friends because, as she put it, "[I don't] like to think that anyone thinks down on me." She carried an overwhelming pressure to always present herself as happy, positive, and fun to be around, keeping any sadness hidden.

The girls in this chapter seemed to fit the idea of the gender-flexible alpha girl celebrated by Kindlon.[43] They did not shy away from embracing their smartness and their pursuit of high grades. They were athletic, sometimes aggressively so. They sought out leadership roles in their schools. Some of them quite consciously eschewed dating in order to focus on other accomplishments, and they did not all embrace popular femininity.[44] Yet they were committed to being nice and friendly. This more cooperative, compliant form of femininity can be seen to soften the threat of girls' capacities and ambitions. It also prevents girls from fully exploring or outwardly expressing their frustration or anger in the face of inequality and overwhelming demands.

Those who appear to be supergirls make it seem effortless[45]—they exude confidence, juggle multiple commitments, and keep up a smile. But as we learned from the girls in our study, this identity is not always easy—neither to maintain nor to aspire to. These girls are involved in "onerous and consistent identity work"[46] as they try to meet the punishing ideal of being perfect at everything, especially when doing so really suggests fitting into a narrow range of what it means to be smart, involved, and social. But while a supergirl identity is challenging to keep up, there are also certain circumstances that make this ideal much more attainable. It helps to be in a context that provides a wide scope for what success might look like, for instance. It also helps to be a girl in that context who has supporting resources and privileges.

THE SCHOOL MATTERS

A significant pattern in our study was that certain schools provided an environment that was much more supportive of smart girls, including girls who might be considered supergirls. In other words, the possibility of achieving supergirl status seemed more likely for *some* girls in *some* school contexts. These schools often had programming for strong students, supported diversity, and did not seem to have rigid gender-role expectations.[47] In these schools, being smart was in fashion, allowing smart girls a lot more freedom and latitude than they had in schools where being smart was a potential social disaster. We explore the context of schools in relation to all the smart girls in our study in chapter 6, but in this chapter we focus on two relevant examples: Jordan and McLovin.

•　　•　　•

Jordan changed schools between her first and second interviews, and in the process shifted out of a supergirl identity. When Rebecca interviewed Jordan the first time, they sat in the dining room of her small, nicely decorated house, located in a fairly modest part of Secord. Jordan's mom, who hovered nearby during the interview, worked as an administrative assistant in a busy local office, and her dad was a contractor. Both parents were very supportive of her education. Jordan was pretty, without being flashy in her style. White and from a lower-middle-class family, she had long brown hair, braces, modest makeup, and a toned body that reflected a strong commitment to her jazz, lyrical, modern, and hip hop dance classes, which she attended two nights a week. She was also in the school musical, which involved rehearsing and choreographing before and after school. Like Ella, Jordan still found time for a bustling social life. In her first interview, she talked confidently about being popular at her Catholic middle school, St. Paul's, describing herself as outgoing, athletic, and involved. She felt that people were attracted to her friendly personality, although she also worried that some people might be friends with her simply *because* of her popularity.

Jordan was happy at St. Paul's, but because she was academically ambitious, her parents saved their money so she could switch to the "best" private school in Secord, Academy House. However, her parents were only able to save up some of the tuition, so she also applied for—and received—scholarships that enabled her to make up the rest. Academy House was an exclusive, historic, coeducational private school that focused on both athletics and academics. It was well known internationally, and families from around the world sent their children there as boarders. Some of the other girls we interviewed who also went to Academy House were happy there because of the smaller classes and academic challenges. When we interviewed her the second time, Jordan seemed content to be at Academy House, but she explained that some of the other students did not really want to be there and that this hindered a supportive academic environment. The biggest change for Jordan was that she was no longer at the top of the social hierarchy. The style at her new school was preppy, which did not really fit with Jordan's more casual way of dressing and her lower-middle-class background. She also felt uncomfortable sharing her academic talents, as it was always possible that the popular girls and the jocks would tease her, as they did not seem to care as much about school and sometimes put smart girls down. Jordan felt that there was a premium placed on being pretty rather than smart, suggesting that it was more important to cultivate a certain kind of femininity than it was to be a strong student.[48]

Jordan's experience of shifting social status emphasizes the precariousness of the supergirl identity, which depends on particular contexts, social locations, and peer and school cultures, as well as the personal resources and backgrounds girls bring to those cultures. We heard similar stories from other girls, such as McLovin, whose supergirl identity really opened up when she started at Blue Ridge High.

McLovin and her sister Caramel were among the very first girls we interviewed. Middle-class and white, they had enormous parental support, both financially and emotionally. The girls were voracious readers who were invested in school, enjoyed time with their friends, and were involved in a lot of extracurricular activities. McLovin was also an avid athlete. She talked about loving her high school, particularly because she felt uncomfortable with being smart in elementary school. Many of our participants went to Blue Ridge, a public high school with a well-attended French immersion program and other academic, musical, and athletic opportunities. It was located in a community with a higher average family income than other parts of Secord and, consequently, a reputation for having students who were "snobs." But for McLovin, Blue Ridge was an oasis for smart girls. As she explained, "If you're smart, you're in. [...] The guys always want the smart girls, and looks are a bonus."[49] At Blue Ridge, McLovin was in a place where she felt that she could really thrive: she was involved and popular and was acing her courses. She was also very clear that part of her success was linked to being at this particular school.

HEAD OF THE CLASS: RESOURCES AND PRIVILEGES

Not everyone can come close to fulfilling the supergirl promise, no matter what school they go to. Being a supergirl takes skill, confidence, resources, and parental support. The girls in our study who came closest to the media construction of the supergirl were all able-bodied, native English speakers, and white. Most also came from financially secure families. Girls like Brooke, McLovin, Julia, and Abbey all had parents who could provide an extra cushion of support by being able to pay for trips and lessons, for example. Brooke's dad was a computer systems analyst and a "really big boss" in his company; her mom had worked in a nursing home while Brooke was younger but was now a stay-at-home mom, "because there was no, like, financial need for her to be working." Despite this economic security, Brooke was expected to pay some of her way through university, so on top of her other activities, she had a part-time job. McLovin's family was also secure, with one parent working in municipal health care and the other as an employment consultant. Julia and Abbey's mom was a literary specialist, and their dad owned a successful business.

Other researchers have also found that girls from middle- and upper-middle-class families are overrepresented among popular, smart, high-achieving girls.[50] Some researchers suggest that middle-class students have a greater affinity for school because they are steeped in dominant cultural and social capital garnered in the home (we discuss this in chapter 5). In turn, their involvement in school generates more cultural and social capital.[51] Their parents tend to hold university degrees and support and encourage participation in extracurricular activities both by paying for lessons, memberships, equipment, and trips and by having the time and ability to drive them from event to event.

However, the girls in our study who might be viewed as supergirls did not all come from privileged backgrounds.[52] Ella's family, for example, was lower-middle-class. Her family's house was modest and her parents' income somewhat unstable. She was also one of six children. Wren came from a working-class background, lived with her divorced mom, and worked during the summers and took year-round babysitting jobs in order to save money. Ella and Wren both had a lot going for them, however, despite their socioeconomic backgrounds. They had exceptionally supportive parents who were committed to the arts and education, and they were at schools that provided them with many opportunities to excel. They had personal talents and a drive to succeed. Girls like Ella and Wren suggest that talented, supported people can sometimes beat the odds; they are exceptions that perpetuate the assumption of the meritocratic smart girl stereotype. But really, widespread patterns indicate that structural supports and class-based privilege play a significant role in supergirl success.[53]

THE TOLL OF BEING A SUPERGIRL:
WORK HARDER, TRY HARDER

A final component of the media-generated supergirl identity is the appearance of effortlessness. Some of the girls we talked to, like Ella, Jordan, and Brooke, seemed, at first, to actually be supergirls. But when we asked more pointed questions, like "How do you balance the activities you are involved in?" we began to hear stories that suggested stress, precariousness, underlying worry, and sometimes even mental health issues. These girls described themselves as perfectionists who needed to do everything just right, for instance. Grades could always be improved, projects polished, and more awards won. We noted this kind of perfectionism when Ella told us about staying up all night to finish a long-term video project. Her goal was not to finish the project so it was good enough to hand in but rather to perfect "every last detail" and edit it "down to the last millisecond." The next day, she kept falling asleep at school. Jordan described almost the same story, telling us that things had been stressful that term: "I know I have been staying up late finishing something. It'll be ten o'clock, and I'll be done, but I will stay up an extra hour to change sentences and make it sound better or look better." More generally, she frequently had trouble falling asleep. "The majority of nights, I'll be in bed maybe by 10:30 or 11:00 pm, but there's so much going on that I won't fall asleep until midnight or 1:00 am. Then I get up early in the morning to get ready. I'm up at like 6:00 or 6:30 am, then I have to do it all over again. I could use a few more hours."

Julia and Abbey also described themselves as perfectionists and talked about the toll of trying to do everything just right. In the face of worry about her grades, Julia said that she just had to "work harder, try harder, put more effort in." Janey—a very high-achieving, social, and engaged participant in her student council—was interviewed with her similarly involved, but shyer, sister, Margot. They talked about the pressure to maintain high standards, "because if you accidentally slip or do bad on a test, it's like, 'What happened?' You don't know what went wrong, and you get a million questions, and they want to know why you didn't do so well. And blah blah blah. There's definitely a lot of pressure." Janey added: "For me, [my stress] wasn't that exams were here, it was that I still have to commit myself to basketball, I still have to commit myself to dance, I still have to commit myself, like, there is a whole bunch of people I'd be letting down if I didn't go to practice or I didn't go to a council meeting. So it was just like all topping up and people were counting on me. It was just, like, a lot to handle, especially with exams."

During our discussions with Laney, Brooke, and Jamila, we started to get a deeper sense of the underlying stressors associated with intense school involvement and the pressures of perfectionism. When we first met with these three girls over lunch, we reviewed their extracurricular involvements. During the lead-up to the school musical, they were especially busy. Laney described her day: she started with choir practice at 7:45 am, had another practice after school, went home for dinner, and then came back to school for rehearsal for the musical, which lasted until 9:00 pm. Homework was done during her free period. The biggest hit, according to Brooke, was on her social life, as she had little time left for any interaction with friends outside of school. Laney agreed: "Yeah, it's like you have to decide between sleep and ... friends." Jamila said that spending time with friends usually wins. She joked, "When you're dead, then you have to sleep!"

This topic shifted into more serious territory during the second interview, this time at a small downtown bistro. The girls seemed a bit more at ease and were able to speak frankly. Even so, it was not until well after we had polished off our salads and pastas that the girls broached some of the more challenging issues. First, the girls talked confidently about how they skillfully balanced their many involvements. Brooke spoke proudly about how people should only take on what they can handle, but said that she was the kind of person who could take on "tons and tons and tons and tons and tons of extracurriculars and still manage to be okay." She explained that she could do so much because of her organizational talents and outgoing demeanor, although she did lament that her "social life got shot in the head this year." She did not have regrets, however, and discovered that her true friends stuck by her even when she was very busy. Besides, she added, "if you have to lose something, you kind of have to sacrifice the social life, because as much as, like, my friends are really important to me, like, okay, I can't lose my marks, I can't drop my responsibilities, I can't slack, like, I can't take less shifts because I have to make money for university, so I guess [I have] to, like, cut down on my social time."

At this point in the conversation, Shauna wondered aloud about how they were managing with so much on their minds and the stress of juggling so many activities, especially because they seemed so together and confident. "On the *outside!*" Laney answered quickly, and they all laughed. Then there was an awkward moment when they all seemed to want to say something but wanted the others to go first. Brooke finally pushed on. She was happy to know that she didn't seem stressed, because, she admitted, "I *am* stressed out to the max, all the time." She was surprised that she still had hair! Brooke talked about having difficult moments and difficult days, but she felt that she was in a better place than she had been when she was younger. Laney was feeling worried about making the right choices, "because you have your whole life ahead of you." She mentioned that she worried about her appearance but tried to put that aside to focus on what she felt were more important things. Like Brooke, Laney also talked about containing her stress: "It's not that we, like, don't have worries or don't have stresses, it's just, they're more controlled, I guess." Jamila added, "Yeah, and we hide [stress] well." These comments were telling. Not only were these girls attempting to excel at their schoolwork and in extracurricular commitments while also holding part-time jobs, they also felt they had to hide any stress or other negative consequences that might result—one more task to add to their overflowing to-do lists.

At this point in the group interview, things took another interesting turn. Brooke divulged that she had experienced a very difficult time a few years earlier battling depression, news that was a surprise to her two close friends at the table. Brooke talked about going to see a therapist to help her figure things out because she was feeling lost and confused. She also found that her faith in God helped her through that hard period. After the conversation had shifted into this very personal domain, Laney talked about having had a very difficult time when she was almost twelve and her parents had just split up. At this point, she suddenly became responsible for her brother, and she "completely, like, shut down" for a long time. She also found puberty challenging and struggled with her body image. Her parents suggested that she see a therapist, and that helped her face how she was feeling. These private stories were only shared after we had talked to the girls for many hours on two separate occasions.[54]

Most of the perceived supergirls we talked to spoke about missing sleep and food, some talked about being so stressed out that they were reduced to tears, and some told us stories that indicated anxiety and other mental health issues. These girls were not exceptions. We know, for instance, that in Canada, teenage girls are second only to young women in their twenties when it comes to levels of depression, anxiety, and eating disorders.[55] While we are not suggesting that successful young women are all suffering from mental anguish and debilitating stress, clearly the image of the successful, easygoing supergirl is not accurate either. The pressure on girls (and from within girls) to be hardworking, well rounded, and successfully self-inventing, the need to be good at everything, and the denial of challenges that they face on the way due to gender and other inequalities sets the bar very high, and not surprisingly, many girls have a hard time clearing it.

In their powerful study *Growing Up Girl*, Valerie Walkerdine, Helen Lucey, and June Melody[56] see this dynamic as part of the impossibility of middle-class perfectionism. Through their study of working- and middle-class girls in England, they found that successes that were celebrated as outstanding by working-class girls and their families were treated as merely ordinary in middle-class families. The middle-class girls were on a narrow path of high expectations and conformity that was presumed to lead to professional careers. This study suggests that it is hard to feel successful when incredible successes are treated as commonplace and that the constricted, high expectations placed on girls (by others and themselves) contribute to deep anxiety. The solution the girls sought, of course, was to work harder and harder, but this was never good enough: "This heady normality, this utopian success, hides the opposite: a defence against failure, a terrible defence against the impossibility that the supergirl identity represents."[57]

THE LIMITS OF THE SUPERGIRL STORY

Janey and Margot had almost finished high school when we interviewed them. They were at a point in their lives when they were reminiscing about their earlier high school years, and they suggested that, if they could do it again, they would not work so hard, because they were now feeling worn down and overly stressed out, just when it really mattered. As Janey summarized, "when it really starts to count, you're all tired and you just gotta get through it." Even in the face of this exhaustion, she continued to push herself to do her best, although she acknowledged: "It does worry me a lot. Then you think, like, it's not over yet because you go to university. It's a lot ... of work."

We can see why media commentators and popular psychologists have celebrated the rise of the so-called supergirl, who seems able to accomplish so much with such ease. The girls in this chapter were dynamos who impressed and inspired us with their multiple talents and social sophistication. We do not want to diminish their achievements. Yet this book is also about the complexity and context that goes into such stereotypes. While supergirls are viewed as being good at everything, this construction does not acknowledge the crucial small print, such as how high and elusive the bar of success has become, how much context matters for such success, how many girls do not easily fit into the supergirl trajectory, and the stress, anxiety, and perfectionism these girls experience by driving themselves into the ground. Indeed, most girls are not able to become supergirls, no matter how hard they try to prove themselves as worthy. In our study, for instance, many girls found that popularity and conventional femininity did not fit well with being smart in school. In the next chapter, we explore these stories, including those of girls who really struggled with the tension between prettiness, "hotness," and smartness, and who consequently downplayed their academic success in order to fit in.

CHAPTER THREE

Fitting In or Fabulously Smart?

I tell you, this year we're going to be popular ... even
if it kills us!

Lauren, Square Pegs

Friendly, talkative, and animated, Virginia nonetheless struggled with what she saw as a deep incongruity between her intelligence and the possibility of being a popular girl at school. Middle-class and white, Virginia's family lived in a midsize, nicely decorated house in a suburban area of Secord. Virginia traveled about fifteen minutes to school each day to attend the French immersion program at Blue Ridge, which she described as having a "partying and preppy" reputation and a lot of rich, gossipy kids.[1] This description signaled Virginia's outsider status. She was tall with roundish cheeks, wore glasses that she felt enhanced her look, and had her hair pulled back into an easy ponytail. Compared to her very smart sister, Virginia considered herself to be social and outgoing, but she wrestled with her lack of popularity—a situation that flummoxed her. She felt that she should have more friends but saw herself as trapped in her academic identity.

Virginia told Rebecca that there were smart kids and then there were popular kids, although she really seemed to be talking about girls specifically. "It's a very rare species of person who is smart *and* popular," she explained, and those people "pretend to be dumb!" She felt strongly that the popular group was largely off limits to her: "If I try to go hang out with these blondes that are super popular, they won't accept me because they know I'm smart." In much of her conversation with Rebecca, Virginia maintained this dichotomy between being smart and being popular. For example, she felt out of sync with the other smart kids at school because she was interested in airy TV shows like *Jersey Shore*. As she explained, laughing: "I'm basically a popular girl trapped inside a smart girl's body." That said, she did find that popular girls would sometimes treat her nicely in order to copy her work—and sometimes she would let them do it because she wanted their friendship. Even her best friend would copy her work "all the time." Virginia also felt that it was hard to be smart and attract boys, describing smart girls as "the bottom of the ocean. You want to be the top, and you're not. *They* [boys] don't want to date smart girls! If they did, I would have had a billion boyfriends by now!"

Yet while Virginia wanted to be popular, she wasn't willing to compromise her intelligence or her academic ambitions to get there. Although it seemed to her that popular girls were less likely to work hard, she put effort into school because she was committed to academic success. Touching on the relevant, interconnecting themes of academic investment, gendered peer culture, and physical appearance, Virginia explained: "[Popular girls] just care about hanging out, and going out at night, and friends, and sleepovers, and beauty, and hair. It's like, that might be normal for them to their priorities, [but] for me that is second. School comes first. You are going to need school in the future, but you can always flat-iron your hair another day!"

Though brimming with confident quips about her life, Virginia was actually in a difficult place. She desperately wanted to fit in with the popular girls at her school, but she also valued her smartness and investments in school far too much to let them slide, and these two priorities were at odds with each other. Like other girls in our study, Virginia talked about how being a popular girl required sociality, good looks, and fashion, but she also felt that, to have a chance at popularity, she would need to suppress a part of herself that she cherished and that held promise for the future: her brain.

*   *   *

Most girls are not supergirls, and most girls, like Virginia, navigate some tough tensions if they want to be both smart and popular—the supposedly smooth path of the smart girl is frequently complicated by the uneasy relationship between smartness and femininity.[2] For some girls in our study, finding a place in peer culture meant downplaying or hiding academic success to prevent themselves from being seen as "too smart" or from being negatively singled out as antisocial and undatable. Others felt they had to make a comfortable or lamented trade-off between popularity and embracing smartness in order to stay true to themselves and secure future gains. Then there were some girls, like Virginia, who vacillated back and forth. While the girls in our study told us many diverse stories about their experiences of being smart— both positive and negative—to one extent or another, they all had to navigate academic success in relation to being a girl.[3]

Boyhood and masculinity are inextricably linked to the story of smart girls. Like girls, boys must maneuver the expectations of gender, and the ever-present backdrop of masculinity complicates the possibility that boys can thrive in their studies and in peer culture at the same time. Like girls, boys must manage their smart identities, but with different challenges, resources, and effects, all of which interconnect with, and inform, girls' experiences. In our interviews with boys, we learned about how they saw girls, the distinction they made between being smart and working hard in school, the fact that they were more concerned with how they prioritized certain kinds of athletics over their looks, and their use of humor as a strategic tool. Their stories thus offer a fascinating counterpoint to the girls' stories.

In this chapter, we focus on the entanglement of gender, peer culture, and academic success within the post-feminist and neoliberal landscape, which places the individual at the center of all things and downplays gender as a relevant context or concern. And yet dominant gender norms and the inequalities they bring affect how girls and boys deal with academic success. If girls have achieved gender equality, why did some girls in our study feel the need to dumb down as a way to flirt with boys? Why was Virginia so frustrated with her own dating prospects? Why do terms such as "teacher's pet" and "class clown" get applied to girls and boys differently? And what does it mean when boys tend to position themselves as actively engaged in shaping the world around them, while girls are still expected to be accommodating and look pretty for others? Given these considerations, the girls in our study often seemed caught between the idea that being smart is a compatible, comfortable feature of girlhood and the experience of being on the outside of what we call "popular femininity" because of their academic success, deepening the context of what it is like to be a twenty-first century smart girl in the West.

GENDER AND THE ROCKY SOCIAL TERRAIN OF
ACADEMIC SUCCESS

In the 1980s cult classic sitcom *Square Pegs,* protagonists Patty and Lauren are intent on shifting their status from nerd to cool. Lauren's long-shot plan is for them to "click with the right clique," no matter what. Yet the best friends' scheme is consistently thwarted, as there is no tolerance in the popular clique for the looks, style, and brains of the two girls. A few decades ago, smart girls like Patty and Lauren were largely presented in film and on television shows as "nerds" and "losers": socially awkward and undatable, dowdy and bungling.[4] These smart girls were depicted as longing to be pretty, have dates, and fit in with the popular girls, for whom the smart girl was either irrelevant or an object of derision.[5] In the 1990s, this stereotype shifted slightly to the makeover nerd, which involved a smart girl like Laney Boggs in *She's All That* or Josie Geller in *Never Been Kissed* who gets transformed—often on a dare—into the most desirable girl in school.[6] However, in order to complete her transformation, the makeover nerd had to suppress her academic side and fully embrace popular femininity. More recently, the post-nerd—a smart girl who is intelligent, capable, and "hot" at the same time—has emerged in television and film.[7] Characters such as Veronica Mars from the eponymous television series, Rory Gilmore from the *Gilmore Girls,* and Gabriella Montez from *High School Musical* typify this new archetype, suggesting that girls can, and perhaps even *should,* be both conventionally beautiful and super smart.

Yet, despite the proliferation of a new kind of smart girl in popular culture, feminist researchers assert that there is still a tension between being smart and being a girl. For example, they argue that an "ideal" girl is typically compliant, nice, helpful, decorative, and passive, whereas smartness and academic success tend to be associated with more conventionally masculine traits, such as being assertive, outspoken, competitive, critical, confident, and focused on the intellect over the social.[8] Research from the 1990s and the early 2000s illustrates the consequences of this pattern: when girls are invested in being smart in school, they are often excluded from popular femininity.[9] We found that this opposition between smartness and popular femininity remains an ongoing challenge for numerous girls, as Virginia's story suggests.

· · ·

The girls and boys that we talked with explained that academically strong students were in danger of being seen as caring too much about school, and it was assumed that this meant that they did not have the time, energy, or skills to invest in a social life. We thought at first that our participants would worry about being labeled nerds,[10] and some did, but the ultimate danger was being thrust into the position of the outcast or loner.[11] Loners were isolated and quiet, and they hung out alone or with a very small group of loner friends. They were people who were outside of accepted peer circles, and not all of them were smart or strong students. Becoming a loner was presented to us as a worst-case outcome for being too smart. If someone was overly focused on getting high grades, was cocky and in-your-face about their smartness, or failed to invest in being sufficiently social, then they might be cast as a loner. Bella, an athletic Academy House girl from a financially secure family, was very careful to manage the balance between schoolwork and social life. She explained how academic success can take you down the loner road: "Like, there's some girls in my grade who are very single-minded in their academics, so they do freak out about their grades, and they maybe don't hang around as much with other people because they're studying [...]. Like, the boys for example, they might not talk to them as much because they're just more focused on schoolwork [...]. Like, I'm still focused on my work, but I'm not as single-minded on it as they are, which is why I'm less known as being smart as they are."

The dangers, pleasures, and consequences of academic success did not unfold in the same way for girls and boys, however, as expectations and opportunities were generally different and depended on gender dynamics. There are certain forms of masculinity and femininity that are idealized within the broader cultural context and which are, therefore, relevant to how girls and boys negotiate being smart. We use the terms "popular masculinity" and "popular femininity" to talk about these dominant forms of masculinity and femininity in the context of school peer cultures to acknowledge the overlaps between dominant gender norms and popularity in school. Popular masculinity is commonly linked to being athletic, muscular, attracted to girls, "hot," independent, and even aloof, whereas popular femininity is commonly linked to being pretty, thin, nice, attracted to boys, "hot," fashionable, and demure.[12] Popular masculinity and popular femininity also reinforce each other in an intimate hierarchy. It is frequently and problematically assumed, for instance, that, in a dating relationship, a boy's masculine strength, brashness, and rationality complement a girl's vulnerability, kindness, and emotional depth.[13] These are not rigid ideals, however. Gender expectations shift between situations, including across schools, racial- and class-based backgrounds, and religious contexts and through the multiple ways that young people "do" gender.[14]

In the rest of this chapter, we explore dominant gender ideals in relation to how our participants negotiated their peer relationships and academic success in school. First, we explore the various ways that the smart girls in our study reckoned with popular femininity. While some girls shifted between strategies and others challenged the dichotomy between smartness and popular femininity altogether, we discuss how certain girls acquiesced to popular femininity at the expense of school and how other girls despairingly, matter-of-factly, or sometimes happily embraced academic success at the expense of popular peer relations. We then go on to explore how boys navigated the gendered terrain of school. The commonalities and differences in girls' and boys' approaches illustrate the ongoing relevance of dominant gender norms and the interconnections and inequalities between the experiences of girls and boys.

POPULARITY AT A PRICE

When Shauna asked fifteen-year-olds Jenny and Agnes who was popular at Blue Ridge, they had no trouble providing examples. Agnes first suggested that it is a lot of football players, as well as "loud and obnoxious people." Jenny was more generous, adding, "It's people who are friends with everyone and have a lot of friends." Agnes then agreed with Jenny, "They can be anywhere in the hallway and be, like, 'I'm going to talk to these people.'… It's, like, how many people do they know?" The social side of school is significant to most students, and many of the girls we talked with were both aware of social hierarchies in their school and interested in being popular. These girls most commonly defined popularity in much the same way that Jenny and Agnes did—that is, as being social and well known. Frequently, these characteristics also linked popularity to fulfilling dominant gender and dating expectations within a heterosexual social world—such as when Agnes referenced football players.

It was because of aspirations to attain this kind of popularity—and fear of being labeled a loner—that girls reined in or masked their academic success. Many girls were reluctant to broadcast or even discuss their grades, and they felt frustrated if teachers did so. Some refused to put up their hand in class or ask questions. For instance, Christy, a poised perfectionist who attended a Christian public school, told us that she had to "tone it down a bit" and that "you really have to watch it. You don't want to be the know-it-all." Christy did not want to bring attention to herself, stand out, or appear cocky. Even during their interviews, some girls distanced themselves from being seen as being "too" smart by temporarily positioning themselves outside of the smart girl category. As Anna explained, "sometimes the smart kids are always talking about school, so sometimes it's nicer to not hang out with smart kids."

One specific category that girls can be placed in powerfully illustrates the dangers of being too smart in school: the teacher's pet. Typically girls, teacher's pets—also known as "brown-nosers," "suck ups," and "know-it-alls"—are individuals who are keen in class and seen as attempting to curry favor with the teacher. Teacher's pets were commonly described in our interviews as students who are brazenly committed to showing their smartness and who suck up to the teacher for marks—behavior that was considered more prominent in elementary school than high school. While many said there were no teacher's pets at their schools or that it was no big deal, there was a vocal subgroup of younger girls who had negative feelings about other girls whom they saw as teacher's pets. Joanne, a fourteen-year-old student at

Blue Ridge, found teacher's pets annoying: "They raise their hand for everything. They just have to answer and feel better than everyone else, and it's pretty annoying." Celeste, also fourteen, was in the French immersion program at Pinecrest Public School, and she similarly said that teacher's pets were "nerd girls" who "suck up" to the teacher and "always have that little smirk on their face." Quinn, who attended St. Helen's Catholic Elementary School, lamented, "I just don't think it's fair how they get special treatment just because they kiss up to [the teachers]. I wish it were more equal." Interestingly, it was only girls who condemned teacher's pets, and it was only girls who talked about trying to avoid being seen as a teacher's pet.[15] The term "teacher's pet" can thus be seen as a gendered and derogatory term for openly smart girls who try too hard, refuse to contain their intelligence, and reject a nice, passive, and demure identity.[16]

To dodge appearing cocky or like a suck-up, lots of girls avoided flaunting their smartness, and other girls took this effort a step further by dumbing down or intentionally pretending not to be smart. While a small number of participants talked about boys dumbing down, girls appeared to be much more likely to engage in this practice. Both the girls and boys in our study had observed girls dumbing down, and some girls also spoke about doing it themselves. Isabell and Kaitlyn, friends who were interviewed together, suggested that some of the popular people think it is cool to be "dumb" because it elevates their status. More frequently, participants said that girls dumbed down in order to attract boys.

While a few girls told us that boys were attracted to smart girls, more felt that it was just the opposite, and this left many smart girls wondering how to get dates. For example, Caramel overheard a group of boys on the bus say they would not want to date a girl who was too smart, and Christy felt that, "If you are the brainiac know-it-all, then usually you aren't that attractive [to boys]." In short, smart girls were seen as being too focused on school and also intimidating, which meant that they might upset the gender hierarchy of a dating relationship. Laughing, Smartypants explained, "maybe boys don't really generally like smart girls as much as normal [*laughs*] girls. [...] I think for a boy it would be intimidating, 'cause they would feel, like, dumb and stuff, but [they're] not!"

Haley and Luna went to St. Mary's High, the Catholic and sports-oriented rival of Blue Ridge. They also noticed girls dumbing down at their school, which led to a spirited conversation during their interview. Haley told us, "The girls that hang out with the hockey guys act dumb, and I know they are smarter than that." Luna agreed: "You can tell, sometimes they say their answers and it's really good. You know they are capable, but they are acting stupid." Haley thought that this was perhaps because "guys find it attractive." Luna agreed, noting that sometimes girls try to dumb down and "put their beauty on" to appeal to guys. Haley and Luna were not alone in their observations of girls dumbing down to attract boys. Anna, also a student at St. Mary's, talked about a friend who "goes around purposely acting dumb and will go around asking the guys if they know the answer even though she *just* told me the answer!" Michelle, a student at Emily Carr, also suggested that a girl would act stupid around a boy she cares about so that she can be the damsel in distress and the boy can save her. Thirteen-year-old Olivia, one of our younger participants, noted that girls acted dumb at her school, too: "The boys will act, like, 'Oh my gosh, oh you don't know *that?*' Then they will tell her and tease her playfully." But she saw this as an acceptable form of flirting and admitted that she also engaged in it. These examples illustrate how a number of girls strategically embraced popular femininity. Along with cultivating a social life that prioritized peers over school culture, they played down their intelligence to position themselves as inferior—and thus seemingly attractive—to boys.

BOYS DON'T MAKE PASSES

Of course, girls' appearances and bodily presentation were also highly important to acceptance and popularity, and the girls we interviewed often suggested these attributes were valued more than intelligence.[17] Sighing, Haley explained, "Our school definitely goes for pretty [over smart]." Participants told us that, to be considered pretty, especially by boys, a girl needed to be thin, care about her looks, have nice skin and long (blonde, flat-ironed) hair, wear makeup, and be fashionably dressed. Being skinny, in particular, was mentioned frequently as important for girls, and a number of our participants had concerns about their weight. Prettiness was thus connected to a certain body type, prep time, beauty skills, racial background, and class-based privilege that enabled girls to afford the latest fashions and the right makeup and hairstyles.

Elizabeth, a gregarious, white, middle-class girl at Blue Ridge High, who was herself fashionably dressed and had flat-ironed hair, suggested that smart girls might sometimes be unpopular because they do not do the work to make themselves attractive: "Sometimes, smart people become smart because they are so focused on the school work and, like, getting good grades and stuff," and because of this, "they don't spend as much time trying to like look like everyone else and, like, put makeup on and straighten their hair and everything." She was somewhat approving of these priorities, acknowledging that the girls were right to be so focused on school, but she was also critical of girls who took it "too far" but still wanted higher peer status. Elizabeth further explained it this way: "Some people, like, come to school with, like, their hair just tied back in a ponytail and, like, sweatpants and, like, a grubby T-shirt on and then they say 'Oh,' like, they think, 'Oh I wish I was popular,' then they don't really put the effort in, but that's because they are more focused on being, like, the best intellectually they can be."

Related to looks was the question of heterosexual dating. In our interviews, we asked if smart girls could also be seen as "hot" or sexy to boys, and again we heard about the need to invest time in looking good. Maggie, a middle-class, white student, was still in middle school when she was first interviewed. She was pretty, tall, not really into fashion, and not yet dating—but she was still highly observant of the social scene. To Maggie, "the people who get, like, the boys more would have to be people that don't get bad marks, but don't get good marks. [It's] people in the middle that kind of try and put together their clothes rather than doing homework." Many girls argued that the pressure to look good was far greater for girls than boys. Kaitlyn explained, "Girls try so hard to be perfect and spend so long on their hair and their makeup. I know some people who wake up at six in the morning even though they have to go to school at eight." She noted that girls have to put on their makeup and straighten their hair every day, while "a guy can just roll out of bed and no one will say anything. I know guys who will wear pajamas to school and no one will laugh. People will comment, but it's nothing. Girls wear pajamas and people will be like, 'What are you wearing? You're weird.'"

While a few of the boys suggested that the pressures on boys and girls to look a certain way are equal,[18] far more boys talked about the unique pressures on girls to be attractive. John, for instance, pointed out that girls are pressured about weight and fashion to a degree that just does not affect boys. Boys also occasionally referred to the role media played in creating unrealistic ideas of what a girl should look like. Noah, for example, told us, "Everything you see is pressure ... like, anything in the media, if you read a magazine, you see it advertised—there's a woman who is thin, right? And in TV shows, really there's always, the women always are thin, you know, etcetera, etcetera." For this reason, Noah felt there was a lot more pressure on girls related to their looks, as well as more general "social stuff ... like fitting in, like weight, like how you dress, how you look." Kurt made very similar observations about the role of the media in girls' lives, although he also felt that girls "put a lot of it on themselves." He was constantly telling his female friends, "You don't have to listen to the media!"

Louis, a popular boy who liked video games and sports, helpfully summed up the differences between pressures on girls and boys in his interview, explaining, "for girls, for the most part, if you're pretty, you'll be popular." In contrast, he said, boys do not always have to be good looking: "They just have to be kinda outgoing and funny and that kind of thing, mostly outgoing." Andrea, our research assistant, then asked him, "So if a girl were outgoing and funny, but she wasn't particularly good looking, could she still be popular?" Louis paused and then said slowly, "Maybe, if she was good friends with one of the popular kids." But then he reconfirmed that being good-looking was *the* most important thing for girls.[19]

Given this context, it is not surprising that one of the ways girls tried to manage or downplay their smartness was by devoting attention to their looks, including which fashions they wore. We saw a poignant example of this in Erin's story. On a shopping trip to update her wardrobe at Lululemon, an expensive leisure and yoga clothing store, Erin asked a friend to honestly tell her why she was not considered pretty and, thus, popular at her school: "We were talking about why some of the other girls make fun of me. She said one of the things was how you dress and the way you look. When I asked her what was wrong with the sort of stuff I was wearing, she was honestly saying, 'I don't know what to tell you.' […] She showed me what sort of stuff girls like to wear for their makeup. We went through my stuff and put … a pair of shorts and a pair of track pants in the bag [to donate to the thrift shop]." Erin, a lower-middle-class, white student, was one of the smartest girls in her class, but she was also one of the most ostracized in our study. The solution, at least according to her friend, was to fix her up with cosmetics and the latest fashions. This highlights the ongoing importance of popular femininity. British cultural theorist Angela McRobbie notes that girls can express themselves as being smart or accomplished only as long as they remain conventionally feminine by investing in their bodies and physical appearance. McRobbie calls this unwritten rule the "post-feminist masquerade"—excessive femininity is required to buffer and downplay women's success.[20] McRobbie suggests that the post-feminist masquerade is indicative of the broader post-feminist and neoliberal landscape, which assumes gender equality yet ironically prioritizes hyper-femininity. Like the heroines of makeover movies, who change their look and style to become popular, Erin felt the only way to fit in was to balance out her academic success by redoing herself according to a narrow, fashion-oriented definition of feminine beauty.

IT'S ALL ABOUT THE SOCIAL LIFE

Many of our participants, both boys and girls, talked about how it was important to have social skills in order to be popular, but for girls, this skill set took on a specifically feminine feel, as we discussed in chapter 2. Being social was all about vigilantly being nice and spending significant time on building and maintaining friendships, both of which are hallmarks of white, middle-class femininity.[21] Ella, Allie, Celeste, Lisa, and Nicole all acknowledged the importance of being nice, particularly in relation to popularity. Even playing down their smartness was part of being nice, because being pegged as having an obsession with schoolwork could be seen as throwing one's intelligence in other people's faces. As Agnes observed, "It's how socially willing you are. If you won't talk to people, and [you] study all the time, people will think that you think you are too good for them." Reflecting the dangers of being seen as a teacher's pet, Maggie made particularly cutting comments about smart girls who were perceived as mean because they were too focused on school: "Goody two-shoes, [girls who] try too hard, browners [brown-nosers]—most of them are fake. Once you get to know them, they just do it for marks and to be smart; they don't care about others' feelings. They are just fake so they can be smart, get grades, go to a [better] school."

Allie stood out as a girl who placed a lot of importance on congeniality and tied it firmly to a specific kind of popular femininity: "It just means that, like, you are [...] part of, like, the pretty girls and the small girls, the nice girls and stuff." White, middle-class, and a devoted Christian, Allie was well known for having phenomenal grades and working hard in her small-town elementary school. While she was popular among her peers, she had been called "smarty-pants" in the past, and this contributed to her ongoing concerns about being too blunt and, therefore, seen as uncaring about others. She also worried about her looks and wished boys thought she was pretty. But Allie, like all of our participants, was a multifaceted girl and was not willing to wholeheartedly compromise her academic success for social status. Later, she admitted her frustration with girls who focused too much on their looks, and she was confident that independence and smartness would take her further than hair and makeup. Allie went back and forth in her interviews in this way: was it better to be pretty and nice or independent and smart?

We also spoke with girls who were less invested in, or less successful at executing, the nice girl persona. Tony B. and Tony M. were white, working-class girls at Central High who were uninterested in joining the popular group, for instance, and did not mind that they might be seen as "awkward" or "weird." In fact, they embraced their outsider status—an identity they actively cultivated. Flowerpower was also a working-class girl, with a South Asian heritage. She had recently transferred to Blue Ridge to gain access to the more diverse possibilities for friendships she thought a large school could offer. At Blue Ridge, she gradually shifted from hanging out "with the party kids" to befriending students who, in the past, she would have considered too "quirky," including those who shared her interest in social justice. Flowerpower described herself as a popular girl who fit in with different groups of kids, but she also felt that other students sometimes thought of her as "weird and too vegan." She was occasionally teased because of her politics, and felt pigeonholed as "this angry little person." Unlike Tony B. and Tony M., who seemed not to care what others thought of them, Flowerpower blamed herself for giving off a negative impression and believed that she needed to have more control over her emotions. She was drawn to the nice girl ideal but could not attain it, in part because of her political stance as an activist, feminist, and vegan. As we argue in chapter 4, many girls felt that certain political beliefs, such as feminism, were at odds with being perceived as nice—and most, therefore, chose to pursue the latter. Flowerpower, however, was unwilling to give up that side of herself for the sake of popularity.

EMBRACING SMARTNESS, WHATEVER THE COST

Although students like Virginia and Allie cared about fitting in and being popular, they also placed great value on their intellect and were loath to entirely push it aside. They were not willing to hold back, dumb down, or reject school and were part of a significant number of girls who did not embrace popular femininity in its entirety, with its incessant focus on looks as a way of defining oneself or fitting in, the need to dumb down to attract boys, and the centrality of peer-oriented social lives.[22] They refused to play that game, even if some of them really wanted to be popular. For these girls, academic success was more important; it was part of their sense of identity, it earned them status and freedom, and in their minds, it was directly tied to future success. The demands of a narrow form of popularity had too great a cost. For example, Darlene categorized herself as "middle" in terms of popularity at Blue Ridge, and she put a lot of energy into getting good grades. She described her intellect as the primary source of her personal worth: "I think that you, as a person, just being smart, you feel better about yourself. I think you are more confident with yourself if you are smart, and other people look up to you."

Both boys and girls took great satisfaction in earning high marks. Their identities as smart and their school successes sometimes earned admiration and respect from their teachers and pride from their parents. They talked about the glow they experienced from doing well on tests, bringing home a strong report card, or getting awards. A few also talked about earning respect from other students. Joanne, for instance, knew that some girls would dumb down to gain popularity but said she enjoyed getting recognition for her successes: "You definitely get respected [by peers]. Like, if you aren't a total airhead or always goofing off, more people will respect you and want to talk to you." Participants also spoke about getting certain perks and freedoms at school because they were liked and trusted by their teachers. Overall, many students that we talked with appreciated their own intelligence and the admiration and independence it brought them. Students like Virginia acknowledged that there were trade-offs, but they also saw some immediate, valuable benefits, as well as future advantages, in choosing academic success over popularity.

For those who could not, or would not, achieve popularity, their imagined futures validated their skills, choices, and trajectories. They were confident that their intelligence and their grades would translate into future success, even if they were grappling with unpopularity in the present moment. As Haley put it, "It doesn't bother me if someone calls me [a nerd]. I'd rather be a nerd than not smart. [Being smart] will help me in the future. I'll get a good career and they won't." Kurt, a gregarious boy who sometimes faced challenges at school, similarly said, "If someone is bullying you because you're smart, then you can just think in your head, 'In twenty years, you'll be working for me!'" These responses suggest that some students thought about the hard work they did to cultivate high grades as part of developing their cultural capital.[23] In a way that fits well with the broader popular narratives of neoliberalism that favor individualized, school-based success and self-actualized futures, those students who looked to their futures for solace in the present assumed they would be able to convert their skills and qualifications into university enrolments and, later, well-paying jobs. Haley, criticizing some of her peers, said, "Yeah, right now, like, [...] some of them are really smart, they just don't care 'cause they are like, 'Oh, I'm going out to party tonight; I'll study later.' They just need to realize that in thirty years, I'm not gonna remember whose party you went to, what you were wearing, and you will remember that you didn't study and now you're working at a low-paid [job]!"

There were many overlaps in the commentaries of the girls and boys who focused more on future aspirations than on their present social life, mobilizing a narrative of individualized, middle-class success. However, there were a few differences in how boys and girls framed this focus on the future. The narrative of future economic success steered girls away from a more traditional and unequal form of femininity in their present lives—a form of femininity that encourages dumbing down or spending time and money cultivating a certain look—and towards a goal of economic independence. For certain girls, this desire for independence was specifically tied to the expectation of encountering sexism and the need for women to have autonomy from men, which we discuss in the next chapter. Boys were more likely to link success in school to being able to get a job in particular high-status, masculine occupations—for example as a doctor, chartered accountant, or aerospace engineer—and earn an income that would allow them to have a house, family, nice car, and even a boat. In this way, boys could mobilize a future-oriented masculinity in order to counter possible challenges they had with popular masculinity in the present.

The dream of future success was not the only thing that helped some participants prioritize their schoolwork; many kinds of support were also crucial. School cultures varied, some providing a context that better facilitated girls' commitment to academics, and girls' friendship groups also made a valuable difference—two factors that we return to in the last chapter of this book. Many girls also talked about high levels of parental support in their education, and while sometimes this support was experienced as pressure, parental commitment helped them negotiate the pulls of peer culture. An excellent example of this negotiation came from Erin, whose friend once asked her to "dumb it down" a little. Erin was mystified: "You want me to be dumber?!" She spoke to her mom about the incident afterward, and Erin found solace in her mom's advice to "never dumb it down.... If you need to dumb it down for your friends, that's not a good thing."

Some girls received added cultural or religious support. In chapter 5 we discuss the challenges some participants faced due to the widespread and problematic stereotype that Asian students must be smart. That said, some girls with Asian backgrounds attributed parental expectations that they would work hard to their cultural background and cited this as a valuable form of support. Unexpectedly, we also found that, for a small group of girls, religion was deeply connected to investing in school, even at the expense of popular peer expectations. For Smartypants, a South Asian girl and a devout Mormon, faith was integral to her academic focus. In her interview with Shauna, she referenced a booklet called "Strength for Youth," explaining that "Heavenly Father wants us [*laughs*] to, um, He wants us to get a good education, so I think that's motivation for me." She also felt that her religion gave her the guidance she needed to have good morals and standards that helped her do well in school. Among the eleven girls we interviewed who prioritized their religion, about half of them considered faith to be integral to their commitment to education.

BOYS' STRATEGIES FOR NEGOTIATING
ACADEMIC SUCCESS

John, the first boy we spoke with, began his interview by outlining some of the ways that boys negotiated their smartness in school. He met with Rebecca in the corner of a Tim Hortons coffee shop in one of the small towns outside of Secord. He was a middle-class, white student with a slight build, a close-cropped haircut, tanned skin, and big, brown eyes. Like many other participants in the study, he was committed to school and earned high grades. He was also one of the more involved boys we talked to; he participated in speed skating and volleyball, represented youth at the municipal government level, and was on his school's student council. He was proud of these involvements and his academic achievements but careful about the impression he gave to others. He wanted to make his parents and teachers proud, but he also wanted to be "part of the culture, to be the popular one." That said, if he had to choose between hanging out with friends or studying, he would take the same route as Virginia: "I guess it would be the schoolwork [...] over the friends."

In general, John explained, there are "stereotypical things people have with smart people [...], like the nerdiness thing they kinda think of." It is not that John was teased for being smart, but more that people had assumptions that made him feel uncomfortable. He was frustrated that people associated academic success with being weak at sports, so he would try to make a more "athletic" first impression. In this way, he aimed to bridge the gap between being smart and being popular—

something he said only "a few people" can achieve—by getting formally involved in athletics and student council activities, and this strategy seemed to work for him. He had a good circle of friends, including some who were more athletic and some whom he described as "low-ballers"—popular boys who just "float by," getting average grades.

Emphasizing sociality, John felt it was possible to fit in while being smart "as long as you don't just go in your shell and you're always open and you're always social." Like others, he noticed that the boys who were negatively labeled as loners were usually "techno-type people" who talked about video games, kept to themselves, or bragged. John added, "Personally, I don't go out and announce, you know, 'I'm smart! Look at me!'" He also confided that he had avoided being involved in the technical side of a theater production in order to sidestep the nerd label. Overall, he suggested that being a smart boy was the same as being a smart girl, even though boys were more likely to be cast as nerds or geeks. But later in the interview, despite this observation, he noted that it was girls, not boys, who dumbed down: "I guess they want to get more attention so, um, they don't want to make [being smart] a turnoff, I guess." He also talked about the pressure on girls to keep up to date with friendships and fashion in ways not required by boys. His own style was to dress casually to fit in with his friends, and he usually wore jeans and a T-shirt.

In chapter 1, we explored the corollary to girls' purported rising success: the narrative of the failing boy. A common trend in this narrative is indicating the so-called innate tendencies of boys that lead them to feel out of place in school, which is often criticized for better serving girls. For instance, some researchers and journalists have pointed out that the majority of teachers are female and noted that a large percentage of classes prioritize cooperative learning and seatwork, suggesting that education has been feminized in a way that turns boys off.[24] This form of analysis has, in turn, shaped policy, including the introduction of specialized boy-focused reading programs.[25]

Yet others[26] have raised significant concerns about this approach, consistently pointing out that, just as not all girls are academically successful, not all boys struggle in school. Often, it is specifically racialized boys from low-income neighborhoods who face more challenges, while other (for example, white, middle-class) boys flourish, illustrating how a uniform, innate masculinity is not the issue.[27] Expectations that are linked to dominant gender norms are relevant, however, to students' school-based achievement. Just as there are tensions between popular femininity and academic success, popular masculinity precludes certain aspects of academic achievement; if popular masculinity is premised on the denigration of anything feminine, this denegation includes presumed feminine studiousness, attention to detail, and obedience,[28] which all contribute to doing well in school. That said, as we pointed out above, there are also areas of strong resonance between certain aspects of popular masculinity and schooling. Smartness in school is often about individual competition for grades, for instance, and intellectual inquiry is frequently coupled with risk-taking, logic, and rational detachment, all of which correspond with popular masculinity.[29] So are academic pursuits more in line with popular femininity or popular masculinity? We argue that academic success in schools today is multidimensional, requiring attention to detail but also creativity and risk-taking; obedience but also critical engagement; cooperation but also competition; and emotion but also rationality. These features vary across subjects and the way they are taught. In other words, there are central features of academic success that conflict with popular femininity, but there are also features that sit uncomfortably with popular masculinity.

In this context, as we see with John, boys also managed their academic success in school, but they did so from a different location within gender dynamics. As we describe below, being smart was valued over being studious, for instance; athletics and humor were more likely to provide gender security for boys;[30] and looks were less essential. Despite many comments in our interviews that gender was irrelevant, these patterns came together to outline a peer-oriented, gendered terrain that shaped boys' (and, in turn, girls') engagements with being smart and studious—sometimes for the better and sometimes for the worse.

"LOW-BALLERS": BOYS JUST GETTING BY?

There were boys and girls who argued that it was easier for girls to be smart. Academically strong girls could garner popularity, they argued, while boys could not. Rory, a girl who fully embraced her own academic skills, even if it meant sometimes taking flak from other students, was particularly adamant about this gender distinction, suggesting that, if boys are smart, "no one likes them," and "they are instantly not cool at all, [but] when girls are smart and cool, it's okay." Sully, a fourteen-year-old girl, even told a story about a boy in her seventh-grade class who asked her to mark a few questions wrong when students were marking each other's work because he was embarrassed to get too high a grade. These arguments reinforce the common perception that the "nerd" label is more likely to be applied to boys—and this was an observation that the girls in our study were particularly likely to make. For example, Virginia, Isabell, Kaitlyn, and Lisa considered boys to be more typically nerdy. Lisa explained it like this: "For some reason, being smart as a girl often makes you more popular, but being smart as a boy makes you more of a nerd. I don't know why, but that's how it is a lot." Others, like Michelle, said that smart boys were nerdy, but she also noted, with a smile, that she found nerdy boys attractive.

Donovan, a smart, athletic, white student with a Beiber-esque hair cut, who was comfortable with his mid-range popularity at school, echoed these girls' observations, but he shifted the focus from smartness to school work, which resonated with much of the data we collected from the boys. "If you are a girl, you can be smart and really popular," he explained. "For a guy, I think it's harder. I think if you are smart, they won't make fun of you, but they will judge you and think you care a lot about school, and that might affect [your popularity]." Just as we heard from John, Donovan felt that there was an assumption that an academic focus thwarted social skills and told us, "The only thing you get teased about is that you try too hard for marks or care too much about school." For these boys, intelligence itself was fine, but working hard at school was not.[31] Donovan framed it this way: "People who are smart, in my opinion, are people who don't have to try. You can memorize a textbook, but you aren't necessarily naturally smart." Part of the failing-boys narrative is the argument that it is uncool for boys to show interest in school—an argument that certainly jibes with these comments.

Other things that boys said suggested that, perhaps, more boys were happy to coast through school as "low-ballers" in a way that girls were not. Semai, a sharp, somewhat awkward, middle-class, white student who was really into Japanese animation, explained that girls just care more, put more effort in, "and go above and beyond," while boys like him "go for the least work with the best mark." He wondered aloud why this might be: "Maybe boys are just more relaxed? Perhaps it's just laziness." Paul, a very athletic, working-class boy who described himself as "kind of popular," also noted this difference: "Girls try to be smarter, guys really don't care." And Batman, who aspired to be in the military when he was older, linked this pattern to future promising, nonacademic, masculine occupations: "I don't know, I guess [it's] the way we are taught, that we can do the manly jobs! You don't need a physics degree to chop down a tree!" With a few exceptions, the boys we interviewed presented themselves as having a laid-back approach, downplaying their need to study or saying that they certainly could study more but did not really feel the need. The intense perfectionism of some of the girls we interviewed was absent in all but two of the boys. These observations suggest that the stakes are lower for boys, who may feel less driven by the job market to go to university, and may also bolster the position that, while it is quite acceptable for a boy to be smart, it is less acceptable for a boy to work hard in school.

Indeed, a number of boys and girls contradicted the idea that it is not cool for a boy to be smart. They pointed out that it is easier for boys to publicly share their grades and compete in class than it is for girls. John and Paul enjoyed a bit of competition with their friends over grades, and Tim and Jason suggested that boys take pride in telling others what marks they got, while girls do not. As Tim explained, "I see a lot of guys who will show me their grades and yell them out, but the girls won't do that." Many also said that it is harder for girls than for boys to be both smart and popular, countering the stories that opened this section. They pointed out, for instance, that it is girls who tend to downplay their intelligence. Louis argued that girls hide being smart, while it does not matter if a boy is open about being academically successful. Smartness is not a pro or a con, it simply *is,* he suggested, and smart boys fit in regardless. Walrus, who seemed very blasé about his academic successes, argued that a negative "nerd" label was more of an issue for girls. Even Rory, who contended that only smart *girls* can be popular, later said that smart girls were "weird" and "can't get dates."

Interestingly, being called "geek" or "nerd" was not always an insult among boys. While there were boys, like John, who certainly felt that a boy who was very smart could be negatively labeled a nerd, many boys (and girls, too) talked about "nerd" being used in a positive, joking way between friends, and some even happily identified themselves as nerds. It seemed to depend a lot on how the terms were being defined between friends and within peer cultures. If being a nerd or geek meant that you were clever, then some boys considered it to be a badge of honor. It was not being smart that problematically made one an uncool nerd but rather being overly focused on certain activities, such as video games or *Star Wars,* and keeping to oneself—in other words, being a loner with limited or obscure interests. Adding to the complexity, a few boys suggested that being smart was actually a social bonus, remarking that academic success helped them make friends and naming popular boys who were both smart and popular.[32]

It is clear from these mixed observations that it is less difficult for a smart boy to fit in than it is for a boy who is seen as overly focused on school[33] or on other pursuits that are considered similarly antisocial. While being perceived as working too hard at school resulted in social risks for boys and girls, girls seemed more likely to soften or mediate their cleverness, while boys seemed more likely to downplay their studiousness. Reinforcing this observation, while Rory and Lisa felt certain that it was difficult for smart boys to be popular and were more likely to negatively portray these boys as nerds, the boys we interviewed were more circumspect, problematizing a focus on schoolwork rather than smartness. This can lead to some real challenges for boys. If they want to do well in school, most boys cannot simply wing it—they need to study. But doing so will leave them vulnerable to social risks in a climate where studying is considered anti-social and even a sign of weakness. Some of the boys who were interested in going to university managed this tension by focusing on the future successes that hard work would (hopefully) ensure. Other boys projected outward nonchalance but worked just enough to get the grades they needed. And, as we discuss in the next section, the boys were also able to balance these rival pressures with other interests, particularly if they could mobilize useful resources, such as athletic skills or humor.[34]

ON THE FIELD AND IN THE GYM

While, overall, boys were not as involved in extracurricular activities as girls were, particular activities were important counterweights to an academic focus, as we saw for John and Donovan. Athletics, especially certain sports like football, hockey, soccer, and wrestling, are central to popular masculinity in North American high schools.[35] Athletic skill can secure a boy's popularity[36] and provide a buffer to being considered too focused on school. Researchers argue that what allows some boys to be invested in an area that seems less masculine— excelling in reading, for example—is their specific capacities in (and knowledge of) certain sports.[37] Not unexpectedly, boys' involvement in sports came up frequently in our interviews and provided insight into how boys strategically located themselves, especially as involvement in sports was seen as antithetical to being too nerdy or a loner.[38]

Kevin, who did not hold back at all about being smart, was one of the boys who talked directly about the value of being both intellectual and involved in sports. He suggested that other kids did not bother him about his academic success because he was on the basketball team. It was not that he was great at basketball. "But I'm not horrible," he told us, adding, "I don't get picked on because I'm kind of an asset." Kevin suggested that playing basketball balanced out his academic pursuits. Kevin was a bigger boy, and he was particularly sensitive to the fact that his size was both helpful in sports and an armor against bullying, especially as one of his friends, who was small and smart, was picked on for not being as athletic as the other boys. Kevin also felt that playing basketball provided an avenue for building social connections and friendships: "I've tons of friends who do sports, we just all enjoy playing them, [it's] kind of really fun." Louis also talked about athletics as a common and valuable binding factor among his friends, all of whom were "kind of known for sportiness." He suggested, "If you play sports, it helps [your popularity]. A lot of people don't even know if you play sports, and they are like, 'Hey, do you play any sports?' 'Yeah, I play this.' 'Oh, cool!'" He said that being good at sports helped him along socially, although he contended, "It doesn't really matter [in the same way] for girls." Other boys were strong in athletics in a way that seemed to trump their academic success. Tim's heavy involvement in various sports, from hockey to soccer, meant that he was known mainly for being sporty, not smart, even though he was also very accomplished academically. Tim was one of the more popular boys in our study, and he saw this social success as directly tied to his athletic abilities.

Sports were not the only activities that could help boys successfully negotiate popularity and academics, however. While the girls in our study were more likely than boys to be highly involved in extracurricular activities, there were some boys who, like John, found that their participation in certain clubs and councils helped them shift away from being seen as just overly focused on studying. While involvement in activities like manga or robotics club might be considered a little too nerdy, playing music or being on the student council could counter an academic stigma. Jason's involvement in a band allowed him to be considered well rounded, and John's involvement in student council provided him with an opportunity to develop status and social connections. While researchers[39] have been rightly inclined to emphasize athletics as central to popular masculinity and, therefore, to boys' social standing at school, there are other ways that less athletic boys can enhance their status, and these should not be overlooked.[40]

ONLY BOYS CAN BE FUNNY

Like the girls, the boys emphasized the importance of sociality vis-à-vis being popular, although rather than being nice, building friendships, and holding back, they were more likely to focus on being easygoing, outgoing, and, especially, funny.[41] A sense of humor was mentioned frequently by the boys as a way of managing popularity and intelligence, and this was well summarized by Noah: "If you are, like, loud, if you make friends easily, if you are very outspoken, if you are funny in class, then I think it would be a lot easier to be popular [and smart at the same time], but if you are not, if you are quiet, if you just, like, don't talk, then I think you won't be popular."

Kurt used humor as a central strategy in navigating school. Kurt was a lower-middle-class, white student who was tall, slightly overweight, and wore short, curly blond hair. He was also outwardly gay at his Catholic high school. He was exceptionally strong in the sciences, not at all athletic, and though well known, had few close friends. Kurt would frequently speak out in class and was very generous in helping other students with their assignments. He was gregarious and confident during his interviews, although his comments implied that things were not always as easy for him as he let on. For instance, he said that he was accepted for being gay but also that he would not want to have children because they would be bullied for having gay parents. Similarly, he was one of the boys who suggested that looking toward future success was a way to manage bullying in the present. For Kurt, being funny and easygoing and laughing things off seemed to be a key strategy for making his way through the challenges of school: "I don't like things being overly stressed out. I, like, try to make a laugh out of anything 'cause [...], like, you have to be happy or you're going to eventually get miserable. So I just try to ... make people laugh."

The positive and negative possibilities of boys' humor and silliness sharpened when we asked about class clowns—those students known for joking around a lot, especially in the classroom. None of our participants had to ask what a class clown was. Rory nicely summarized this unique social role: "Every guy wants to be like them, and they want attention from girls. They sort of get in trouble and get to make the teacher angry and think it's funny."[42] Almost every participant said their school had class clowns, and almost all of the class clowns were boys. Not all class clowns were popular, however. Some were very popular and considered very funny, garnering attention and lightening the boredom of slow-moving classes, but others were less successful and described as annoying because they would go too far. Bella explained this fine line, saying, "If you're the kind who disrupts the class, you will be less liked than the people who know exactly when their humor is okay, they are kind of more loved." In other words, being a class clown was one possible avenue to popularity, but it could easily backfire.

While many of our participants spoke fondly of the more successful class clowns, some girls were very critical because the joking was often at their expense. Maria and Selena noted that class clowns named anyone who tried to stop them a "goody-goody." Flowerpower was quite blunt, calling class clowns "idiots because they are assholes, they say really offensive arrogant things [laughs], and ... that's how I feel towards them!" As an example, she told us about a time a boy said something racist toward her in an attempt to be funny, and even the teacher laughed. Many other participants made comments about class clowns wasting time or disrupting lessons. Darlene provided a concrete example of this frustration: "The teacher loves him [the class clown] and is always laughing at him and thinks he's hilarious, and I *hate* it. It also distracts the rest of the class, and we can't do our work, and it's hard to stay on track." Paul was similarly annoyed at how class clowns would break his concentration. He even tried, unsuccessfully, to address this with one of his friends, whose clowning was a distraction.[43]

A particularly interesting part of the class clown discussion was speculation on why class clowns tended to be boys and not girls, and it was in these observations where gender inequality became strikingly apparent. While some participants said that girls are not class clowns because they are more focused on doing well in school, a noteworthy number argued that girls are more self-conscious and less confident about making jokes in front of everyone, because, as Yasmin said, "the girls will do nothing to, like, do anything funny or embarrass themselves ever." Abbey reinforced this: "Everyone would be shocked if a girl was a class clown." Boys, however, were considered to be less afraid of saying what was on their minds, less afraid of what others thought of them, and less afraid of getting in trouble. A smaller number of participants said that, although both girls and boys sometimes *tried* to be funny in class, boys were funnier. For instance, Celeste suggested that, while she liked both girl and boy clowns, there was an edge to girls' clowning that felt unkind. Bella echoed this feeling: "Class clowns are the boys; loud and obnoxious people are mean girls. [...] They are doing it in different ways. The girls are doing it in a mean way, and the boys are just doing it to be funny. They are lighthearted, while the girls are mean and manipulative." The negative tone and content of these comments provides good evidence for why girls might be more self-conscious about clowning around in class and shows how boys' meanness may sometimes be overlooked or redefined as good-natured humor.

Overall, a sense of humor could be an asset to boys, unless they took it too far. It was one potential avenue smart (and other) boys could take to garner social acceptance—one that was less available to girls. Being funny in class also required brazenly putting yourself out there, which was risky, but this risk unfolded very differently for boys and girls. When girls tried to be funny, according to Celeste and Bella, they ended up being painted as mean rather than friendly or fun. There was little positive payoff. Boys also took risks—of going too far, undermining the lesson, and getting in trouble—although these risks did not seem to slow them down much, and the payoff could be very high.

GENDER DIFFERENCES AND GENDER INEQUALITIES

Being a smart, academically engaged student is not always easy, and the stories in this chapter show that this is true for boys and girls. We have highlighted myriad clashes between a focus on school and the gendered demands of peer culture. Within specific schools and friendship groups, and with specific family support and future goals, some young people in our study were able to fully embrace their own intellectual skills and interests—sometimes wholeheartedly and sometimes with regret—but most were actively and thoughtfully engaged in careful negotiation of their academic identities. How clashes between peer culture and academic demands play out can undermine both girls and boys in terms of school achievement, if girls hold back on putting up their hands, for instance, or boys do not want to be seen as studious. These clashes unfold differently and hold distinct consequences for boys and girls.

As noted in chapter 2, girls in our study came across as far more likely to be stressed out, expressing worries about the present, the future, their bodies, and popularity. Boys cared about peer relations and school, to be sure, but they did not appear to care nearly as much as girls did, or if they did, they certainly did not show it during their interviews with us. We also noticed that boys were often rewarded for being extroverted, a presentation of self that positioned them as active, public subjects. Girls, however, were more likely to be positioned and to position themselves as passive, or as objects, by playing down their intelligence, holding back, being nice and worrying about appearances. These gendered actions and consequences reflect and reproduce gender inequalities not just in the school but also in broader society, where such distinctions (girls as passive, boys as active; girls as objects, boys as subjects) continue to be reproduced. One other thing was very clear to us: girls will manage or contain their smartness to be attractive to boys and to be popular with other girls, but boys only felt the need to manage or contain their smartness to be popular with other boys. In both instances, the judgments of boys held the most weight.

The post-feminist landscape suggests to girls that gender inequality is a thing of the past, evidenced by girls' ubiquitous and easy success in school. Yet the examples in this chapter tell a different story. We have outlined ways in which narrow, dominant gender practices endure, which was abundantly evident in how smart young people talked about maneuvering through the social world of school. These stories betray ongoing gender dynamics and inequalities that are woven into everyday peer interactions. In the next chapter, we specifically explore our participants' perceptions and experiences of gender inequality in both the informal and formal spaces of school.

CHAPTER FOUR

Sexism and the Smart Girl

No one uses the word sexism anymore.... It has an
old-fashioned, almost quaint ring about it.

Judith Williamson, quoted in Rosalind Gill
and Christina Scharff, *New Femininities? Postfeminism,*
Neoliberalism and Identity

Post-feminism's current foothold in Western culture was made
abundantly clear during the summer of 2014, when a Tumblr
blog called *Women against Feminism*[1] gained international attention for showcasing hundreds of young women from around the
globe holding handwritten signs explaining why they no longer
needed feminism.[2] The sentiments represented on the blog
ranged from a desire for freedom from the "shackles" of feminism ("I don't need feminism because I believe in equality, not
entitlements and supremacy!"), to a refusal to take up the "victim" mentality so commonly associated with feminism ("I don't
need feminism because my self-worth is not directly tied to my
victim complex. As a woman in the western world I am not
oppressed, and neither are you!"), to an understanding of feminism as a hatred of men ("I don't need feminism because feminism is the irrational fear of men disguised as 'equality'!").

These refrains include all the elements of post-feminism: the valorization of individualism, the perceived link between sexism and victimhood, and a fierce belief that gender equality exists. In fact, any incidences of gender oppression described on the website were attributed to personal responsibility or completely denied: "I can take care of myself!" "I don't need anyone to fight my battles for me!" "Sexism is over! We have equality now!" As one sign read: "I don't need feminism because [a] victim mentality is a personality disorder."

Interested in why so many young women have turned away from gender politics, feminist researchers have analyzed the widespread perception that taking a feminist stance is tantamount to admitting weakness.[3] This link between victimhood and feminism seems to keep many young women from expressing any affinity for gender politics or from talking about gender inequality.[4] According to the *Women against Feminism* website, being able to take care of oneself demonstrates far more empowerment than relying on the help of others in the form of collective political action. Independence is associated with strength, self-control, and rational autonomy, while feminism is associated with fragility, neediness, and an inability to fend for oneself. And in the new global economy, only independence is valorized.[5]

But ironically, the pervasive belief that gender inequality should be treated as nothing more than the problems of individuals has enabled sexism to flourish through a catch-22: the postfeminist landscape suggests that girls have achieved gender equality, making feminism obsolete, while it in fact perpetuates a system of political inequality that makes feminism more relevant than ever. In other words, the very situation that makes feminism useful precludes the context that necessitates feminism. This ironically, in turn, limits girls' understanding of feminism as an important political stance that would help them identify and address sexism in their own lives.[6] This post-feminist feedback loop enables sexism to thrive under the guise of personal responsibility and free choice while simultaneously making sexism difficult for girls to name.[7]

Certainly, not all the girls in our study were unaware of feminism as a form of relevant political action in their lives. Indeed, while post-feminism is a highly influential force in Western culture, it is not the only persuasive narrative out there. Some girls were aware of feminist politics through social media and popular news accounts, which have helped crack open the individualizing narrative of girl power. Some various examples of high-profile challenges to sexism are: international Slutwalks, which protest a blame-the-victim mentality;[8] battles fought by students over sexist dress code policies in schools across North America;[9] young women demanding—and achieving—the end of Photoshopping in some teen fashion magazines;[10] the countless critiques of the *Women against Feminism* blog by bloggers of all ages and genders;[11] the outspoken feminism of numerous Hollywood actors;[12] the powerful global activism of young women such as Malala Yousafzai;[13] the huge number of postings to the Everyday Sexism Project;[14] and the radical resistances of Eastern European feminist groups Femen and Pussy Riot.[15] These and other highly publicized confrontations with sexism have poked holes in the individualizing elements of post-feminism, and they also highlight the contradictory messages about feminism that girls and others must navigate in the West.

While we acknowledge the power of the post-feminist landscape, which proliferates through media, popular culture, and educational accounts of gender equality, we do not wish to suggest that this climate has turned girls into cultural dupes without a clue.[16] Rather, in this chapter, we explore the ambivalent and complex interplay between girls' strong belief in gender equality and their everyday experiences of sexism, something that at times challenged the individualism of girl power rhetoric but also created confusion for girls as they came face to face with their own bewilderment over what gender inequality is and how it might be affecting their lives. In this way, the girls in our study were very much caught between post-feminism and feminism, which caused an unnamed tension to ripple through our interviews as these girls sought to articulate what it means to be a smart girl in the twenty-first century.

In this chapter, we also continue to contrast the stories of girls to those of boys, who had their own tales to tell about gender discrimination. While girls felt overlooked and underappreciated by teachers, some boys felt the same way—unfairly judged by teachers for being untrustworthy or cast as jokers who did not get their work done. The girls felt that boys received the bulk of their teachers' attention, while the boys felt that girls received the bulk of their teachers' praise and trust. These gendered layers inject contradiction into the dominant stories of successful girls and failing boys, showing these narratives to have far more depth and breadth than standard media and popular psychological accounts suggest. They also help highlight the complexity of post-feminism as the backdrop against which girls live their academic identities. After all, the individualizing narrative of girl power runs through most of the girls' stories about what it takes to be a smart girl, as well as their opinions on whether sexism still exists.

The presumption of gender equality in the West is what has enabled the smart girl stereotype to flourish, establishing a common-sense link between girlhood and success in school. But this presumption is also what has rendered sexism invisible,[17] making the very notion of gender inequality seem outdated, whiny, and weak. For example, if girls are outachieving boys in school, what could they possibly have to complain about? Girls' perceived high achievement trumps the possibility of any other problems. The new assumption is that boys are now the ones experiencing gender inequality, and this inequality is thought to be a result of girls' skyrocketing academic success. Ultimately, it is far easier to believe that girls' triumphs in school are indicative of a radical shift in the gender order than it is to believe that girls still experience gender inequality—especially when their report cards seem to suggest otherwise.

HAVE YOU EVER EXPERIENCED SEXISM?

During our interviews, we asked girls if they had ever experienced sexism—either in relation to their academic success or more generally, out in the world. While some girls gave us examples of sexism, often followed by a qualitative "but," many girls responded with a resounding "no!" While these girls had a vague sense of what sexism meant,[18] few saw it as a relevant concern in their lives. When asked if she had ever experienced sexism, for example, Anna vigorously responded, "No! We are in the *twenty-first* century!" This was a common response, often coupled with the idea that, while sexism does not exist in North America today, it does exist in countries where people are "less enlightened." When we asked Julia if she thought girls were equal to boys, she responded, "I think so. They weren't a long time ago, but they are now in some places of the world. I know in other places, it's harder for women to live day-to-day, and I'm glad for where I live." Her sister, Abbey, agreed and added, "I guess we are lucky to live in Canada." Interestingly, while Julia and Abbey were able to recognize gender inequality in other parts of the world, they were unable to see it in their own lives. Similarly, Olivia said she had never experienced sexism before but explained that it occurred in other countries: "Yeah, like sometimes there might be a guy who thinks he is better and girls should be low. Especially in Afghanistan and places like that, that's bad for sexism, and boys think girls are like animals. But around good places, like Canada and North America, I don't hear much about it."[19] These responses bolster the post-feminist belief of gender equality while also romanticizing a democratic and liberal West.[20] Everything is fine *here,* but girls and women definitely struggle *over there.*

Most of the girls who did identify sexism in their lives generally explained it away as "just joking around,"[21] refusing to take any of it seriously or suggest that it might be rooted in broader forms of systemic discrimination. Bella, for example, said that she had experienced sexism, noting that the boys "sometimes say stuff, and there's, like, ongoing jokes between boys and girls, like, 'Make me a sandwich!'"[22] But in the next breath, she defended such remarks, explaining that the boys were just having a bit of fun: "But they don't mean it. It's not a big deal, it's not taken seriously, it's not noticeably there." After a moment's thought, however, she offered a somewhat unrelated anecdote that suggested she was not as comfortable with the idea of joking around as she initially claimed: "We have girls' hockey and boys' hockey and [the girls] are just as good. [However,] there have been situations where the boys say, 'Oh, you won't beat us,' because they think they are *so* strong." Bothered by this sexist claim, she then added, "If it was a house Reach competition on knowledge, the *girls* would win!"[23] Unlike the joking around we described in chapter 3, where girls generally seemed to take little to no offence when they were called "nerd" or "geek" by their friends, Bella's addendum suggests that, in fact, some girls do take offence to sexist jokes. While willing to excuse the recurrent "make me a sandwich" line, Bella became defensive over the idea that the boys thought they were stronger (and, therefore, better at sports) than the girls. Her need to distinguish girls' abilities in the house Reach competition hints at her anger, yet she does not directly acknowledge her discomfort with some boys' more blatant dismissal of girls.

Throughout our interviews, many girls vacillated between taking sexist jokes lightly, feeling angry about them, and downplaying their budding critiques of them. As in Bella's story, athletics often provided girls with a flashpoint of recognition: girls got the worst rink times, cheapest uniforms, smallest audiences, and least administrative support, while boys got everything, including glory, resources, and attention.[24] As Rory stated: "Yes, guys are very sexist. I was trying out for basketball and I got up to sign the sheet and everyone was like, 'Oh, get back in the kitchen!' I was like excuuuuuse me?" But then her anger turned to acceptance: "Guys are like that, and you get over it. It doesn't bother me, it's stereotypical. We read these books [all the time] where women are in the kitchen." Such contradictory statements highlight how girls were sometimes frustratingly caught between post-feminism and feminism. While girls experienced sexism, they ultimately did not want to—or felt they could not—name it as such, opting instead to retain an easygoing attitude that did not earn them the potentially socially damaging label of "feminist."

Linked to our discussion of popular femininity, calling boys out for sexist behavior might cause girls to appear unattractive or ugly to boys, as well as to other girls.[25] After all, the common caricature of a feminist is the opposite of popular femininity: bitchy, outspoken, and unsexy.[26] Similar to girls' complex negotiations of academic success and popularity, girls also had to be careful not to compromise their popularity or social standing by being labeled a "feminist," "man-hater," or "bitch." Related to this fear, the girls seemed to be careful about maintaining a nice persona, and coming across as someone who could not take a joke would jeopardize this important feminine quality.[27] As we have discussed, niceness is seen as a valuable trait that is associated with idealized middle-class femininity.[28] Though expressing masculine traits can sometimes have a payoff for girls—particularly in bids for certain kinds of popularity[29]—the complex negotiations between successful girlhood and academic success were further complicated by girls' careful management of their anger in relation to boys' sexist behavior.

For all of these reasons, girls seemed reluctant to name feminism as relevant to their lives. Interestingly, however, girls sometimes expressed concerns that boys were victims of gender discrimination. Elizabeth offered this example: "Like, it was really cool, because our school is very focused on football. There has been a girl on the football team for the last two or three years. If there's any teams, there is almost always a boys' team and a girls' team. But if there is only a boys' team, girls are allowed to go out for it. However, if there is only a girls' team, guys aren't allowed to go out for it. Sometimes it's almost opposite [i.e., there is sexism against boys]. I don't think guys are allowed to be on the gymnastics team." Similarly, during our first interview with Wren, she explained that boys were disadvantaged at her school because girls had more options: "There's more opportunities with your hair or with makeup or with clothes that you don't get when you are a boy." She then added: "If you're a girl, you're allowed to do sports *and* instruments *and* be pretty, but if you're boys, there's no pressure except to be a jock." Wren later asserted that girls had more opportunities in the job market, too, and that this disparity was sexist against boys: "You can't be a boy cosmetologist; you'd get made fun of [...]. If a girl wanted to be an architect, though, [that's] fine." Wren raises an interesting contradiction: on the one hand, she feels that boys have less pressure in their choices, actions, and looks, but on the other hand, she observes that boys have fewer options because they are pressured to adhere to popular masculinity.

McLovin also described a power imbalance between girls and boys at her school, in which the girls definitely came out on top: "The girls kind of control the guys, but at the same time we are equal." When Shauna asked her to elaborate, she continued: "Uh, we can get them [boys] to do whatever. You can be like, 'Oh, so-and-so, grab that from the top of my locker. Can you pick that up please? Can I have a hug?' We just kind of ask for anything, and they do it. We don't control them, it's just that we, in a flirtatious but serious way, can have them do something."[30] While Elizabeth, Wren, and McLovin depict different kinds of girl power (physical, economic, sexual), they all suggest that girls today have it easier than boys and that boys are somehow disadvantaged due to girls' newly minted social status. This post-feminist stance makes it easy to see why the word "sexism" feels outdated to some girls—it has become obsolete or been made to seem redundant.[31] And for some, it has even become manipulative, because they feel that it is boys who are truly disadvantaged.

HARD WORK = SUCCESS?

As many of the girls in our study did not feel an affinity for the collective political action that feminist politics entails, it is not surprising that they relied on individualism to explain their academic success in the form of hard work. Invoking post-feminist sentiments of gender equality and neoliberal accountability, most of the girls in our study represented themselves as "can-do girls"—girls who can (and must) make things happen on their own.[32] In relation to academic success, this belief means that girls will succeed if they try hard enough and do their absolute best. Candace, Magda, and Hayden offered some complex examples of this can-do, girl power attitude. White and middle- to upper-middle-class, all three girls received an enormous amount of economic and parental support. Though they attended different schools, they had known each other since elementary school and were good friends. They were not media-hyped supergirls, but they had enough of a friendship group outside of their respective schools to feel socially connected and enough confidence to not really care if they were popular.

Tucked away in a corner booth over fries, salads, and pops, we asked them what it took to be academically successful girls. They talked about the importance of being independent and taking care of things themselves. Magda then explained that hard work was the quintessential ingredient for academic success: "I feel that I have to work hard 'cause I'm always never really happy with my grades. So, like, I always just want to do better, then better, then better." The other girls agreed. Trying hard and doing well in school promised a good life down the road.

When we asked Magda why she thought it was important for girls to be academically successful, she zeroed in on the idea of unrestricted choice and the increased freedom of young women, tying together post-feminist and neoliberal attitudes: "Umm, I think it is important ... because now girls have *all* these options. You can, you know, if you want to grow up and have a family and stay at home then that's, you know, it's *your* decision. And now, you know, you're kind of faced with a lot of decisions. And even probably more, well, I don't know, just as many decisions as men, but probably even more, and so I think that it's, it's important to be able to make decisions, and all *that* fun stuff." Magda's sarcastic overemphasis of "all *that* fun stuff" caused Candace and Hayden to laugh nervously, perhaps because the neoliberal concepts of free choice and individual determination are fraught with pressure, risk, and fear. Will good grades really be enough to ensure future success? Does hard work actually guarantee a good life? Or will unknown life and structural issues get in the way of these future plans? There seemed to be a fuzzy understanding that the road ahead would be neither straightforward nor simple, but these unclear thoughts were hard to express. The girls undoubtedly did not want to sound bitter or angry. But at the same time, although post-feminist promises of gender equality kept them hopeful, deep down, Candace, Magda, and Hayden seemed to recognize that they would have to fight for their place in the world, not just because hard work is what it takes to succeed in today's neoliberal economy but also because sexism exists as a very real threat to the myth of choice.

Vacillating between the post-feminist belief that girls have the world at their fingertips and the feminist understanding that gender inequality still exists, Candace, Magda, and Hayden were better able to communicate these concerns a little later on in our discussion. When we asked them if they thought girls and boys had the same options in the world, all three clearly stated that boys had more opportunities for success than girls. Candace explained it this way: "If a boy isn't as good at school, they're like, 'Don't sweat it, the world is at your finger-tips,' right? 'You've got so many other options, especially if you're well rounded.' But, with a girl, even if you are, like, way more well rounded than any guy, it's still kinda, like, 'You're in it to win it, so do well at school,' right?" The understanding that girls had to put in more effort than boys in order to achieve the same level of success was pervasive across our interviews. The general consensus was that girls work hard, while boys coast along. Candace made this observation explicit when she explained that, even if a girl and a boy had the same grades, a girl would still need more accomplishments on her college application in order to get the attention of an admissions officer—because girls are expected to be smart, they needed to sweeten the pot a little. Agreeing, Magda added, "Yeah, 'cause there are still, like, some sexist people, and it's, like Candace was saying, if it's, like, either a boy or a girl, if the girl kind of has that extra little bit [on her CV] then, you know [it will help]."

The stories of girls' concern for their future success offer an interesting point of contradiction to the earlier comments girls made about having it much easier than boys vis-à-vis their physical, economic, and sexual power. Such discrepancies between empowered optimism and frustration based on sexism were common across many of our interviews, making it impossible to position most girls as either entirely post-feminist or feminist. Instead, they were clearly enmeshed in both lenses—caught in an often-confusing space where there were no clear-cut answers to challenging and unexpected questions.

SEXISM IN THE CLASSROOM

As we have discussed, the shift away from concern over girls' education is a direct result of the post-feminist landscape, which has helped to foster the belief that girls today no longer experience sexism anywhere, let alone in the classroom. While a number of well-known studies emphasized the sexist nature of classroom dynamics in the early 1990s,[33] in recent years, the common refrain has been, "What about the boys?" This well-documented catchphrase contributes to the smart girl stereotype and the common belief that there are no longer any impediments standing in the way of girls' success—particularly not gender discrimination.

Yet when we asked the girls in our study if they had ever noticed a difference in the way teachers treated boys and girls, their answers sometimes disclosed both obvious and subtle examples of sexism. Earlier, we noted that many girls denied or did not recognize sexism in their lives, but a more specific focus on everyday experiences seemed to make it easier for girls to identify their frustration with gender discrepancies. Even so, their allegiance to girl power individualism still made them hesitant to make these acknowledgements. For example, when we asked Candace if she thought teachers ever treated girls and boys differently in a way that favored boys, she clearly stated that they did. But instead of calling it sexism, she commiserated with the teacher: "Like, sometimes, what if [the teacher is] having a bad day or they overheard you say something that you didn't think anyone heard and they're a bit annoyed at you that you keep talking [in class] today, or you failed your last quiz. Like, there's so many things that could be riding on that. But I would never say, 'He hates me because I'm a *girl*,' I'd say, 'He hates *me*,' you know, 'My teacher hates *me*.'"

Yet later in our discussion, Candace offered a very different take on one of her teacher's differential treatment of girls and boys. She angrily explained that boys who received high grades garnered far more praise than girls, whose grades were often even higher. Candace, Magda, and Hayden described this unspoken rule: girls were expected to do well (and, therefore, did not receive much praise for doing what they were supposed to do), while boys were expected to do poorly (and, therefore, received loads of praise when they surprised a teacher by doing well). Candace offered a poignant parody of this incongruity, mimicking her history teacher announcing the two highest marks on a recent test: "It's like, 'John got 98 percent [*very loud and exuberant voice*]! And Magda got 100 percent [*very quiet and uninterested voice*].'" Hayden and Magda burst into laughter at this spot-on impression. They all seemed to recognize the validity of her critique, and after the laughter died down, everyone was quiet for a moment. Then Madga brought us out of the silence: "Well, it's maybe not always to that extent, but, yeah, it's definitely there. Like, if a guy's good, like, *as* good [as a girl], it's kind of more, like, '*Ohhhh!*' Right?" The other two, sipping their drinks, nodded vigorously.

Similarly, the examples of the teacher's pet and the class clown continue to be important in relation to girls' and boys' perceptions of teachers' favoritism. Many of the girls in our study maintained that teachers favored boys because they had easy, jokey, and laid-back relationships with them. As Magda explained, some of her teachers—both male and female—liked to goof around with the boys, constructing what she felt was an exclusionary rapport, and Magda angrily questioned this perception of special treatment. She wondered, why favor the boys when girls "try so hard and get really good grades and are *much* more deserving of attention?" Agreeing, Candace admitted to hating when teachers "go off topic and start joking with the guys and everyone else can hear. I'm kinda, like, 'Okay, we're all sitting here, trying to learn! We only have an hour and a half, let's go—I need this class!'"

Yasmin was an upper-middle-class, first-generation Canadian student whose parents had emigrated from South Asian to give their children the best education possible. She attended the posh private school, Academy House, where she maintained that girls and boys were treated equally. But during her second interview with Shauna, she countered this earlier observation, suggesting that girls had it way harder than boys, particularly in relation to gender assumptions about work habits. "Our math teacher doesn't [treat boys and girls the same] because our math teacher likes girls 'cause they work and they're quiet, and the guys don't work and [they] run around. They [teachers] mostly focus on the guys 'cause the guys don't want to work in class." While Yasmin felt that her teachers liked girls better because of their studious class-room demeanor, she also noted that teachers tended to give boys more attention because they were rowdy. Echoing Candace and Magda, Yasmin said she was frustrated by class clowns who took up the teachers' time. But interestingly, in the next breath, she became nonchalant about such disruptions. She refused to acknowledge that it really bothered her when teachers became easily sidetracked by the boys and told Shauna she would simply ask her tutor for help if she needed it—she was used to fending for herself and had the resources and parental support to get assistance elsewhere. Who needed teachers, anyway?

Consistent with the idea that girls do not want to associate themselves with feminist critiques for fear of being perceived as victims or not nice, many girls were reluctant to name teacher favoritism as sexist. Caramel offered a powerful example of this disinclination. When McLovin suggested that women were still discriminated against due to the gender wage gap, Caramel exclaimed: "It's not exactly true! We might get paid or treated less at times [...] [but] it's not noticed as much anymore, which is why we don't see it so badly anymore. [...] We still see it, but we don't want to be, like, the *underdog*." While Caramel saw sexism, understood sexism, and even experienced sexism, she was not willing to let it get her down. She felt that being the underdog was tantamount to failure, and so she wanted to avoid that, even if it meant accepting that women "get paid or treated less at times." Caramel preferred to rewrite the story as a narrative of success in which girls are *not* victims.

WHAT ABOUT THE BOYS?

While some but not all of the girls had strong opinions about the favoritism teachers showed boys in the form of jocular rapport and lowered expectations, some but not all of the boys had strong opinions about the favoritism they felt teachers showed girls. The stories of these boys help to complicate the straightforward and simplistic narratives of successful girls and failing boys, and they also offer some insight into boys' experiences of schooling. While these anecdotes do not negate girls' experiences of sexism, they are important in their own right and help to paint a picture of school life as contradictory, complex, and context specific. The day-to-day challenges they describe may not make for interesting headlines, but they offer a far more honest portrayal of young people's lives.

When our research assistant Andrea interviewed friends Lebron and Lattrel, white students from middle- and lower-middle-class families, respectively, who were both popular and athletic, they emphatically explained that teachers discriminated against boys. Lattrel stated, "Yeaaah, last year, our teacher, oh my God! I swear it was sexist. She liked girls way better than boys." Lebron continued, "She would flick our ears when we were working." Lattrel added, "If we leaned [back in our chair], she would kick our chair down. A girl did it, and she was just told to put the chair down. She hit Lebron in the head with a book, and he flipped out on her and went to the principal's office." When Andrea asked them if anyone complained about this appalling behavior on the part of the teacher, Lattrel explained, "We got Lebron's mom to talk to her." Similarly, Noah noted that his English teacher from the previous semester "seemed to treat girls better all the time, and I thought she was a bad teacher. She was more strict to guys, and she would, like, if I was talking, she would yell at me. She wouldn't yell at a girl." A number of the boys who had had such experiences suggested that teachers were more likely to assume boys were automatic troublemakers and thus treated them as such right off the bat. While the girls frustratedly described some boys as class clowns who received teachers' positive attention, the boys described this attention as negative, suggesting that they were categorized right away as "shit disturbers" who needed to be strongly disciplined. Just as the girls felt disadvantaged by their gender when teachers offered them less praise because they were just doing what girls were "expected" to do, boys felt that this common practice of gender stereotyping was a form of discrimination against them, and they sometimes felt overly persecuted simply because they were boys.[34]

It is interesting to note that, while the girls struggled to name sexism, the boys seemed far more comfortable with the language of structural critique, even though they also reproduced sexism—often without realizing it. For example, Paul explained that, in his old elementary school, "All the girls got better grades than the guys, which was so stupid. I didn't like the teacher at all; we always had to do gymnastics. I don't understand why guys would do gymnastics at all. It was a *guy* teacher." While Paul clearly articulated his concern over unfair grading practices, the last part of his statement carried a sexist undertone. He questioned why a male teacher would force male students to engage in what he considered to be a female activity. In his second interview, Paul's commentary included an example of sexism against girls. When asked why he thought girls tried harder in school than boys, Paul sympathetically suggested that girls probably had to try harder in order to counteract the belief that girls are less smart than boys. Suggesting to Paul that this ingrained impression created an unjust understanding of girls' abilities, Andrea then asked, "Is that maybe sexism?" Paul carefully replied, "A little bit, yeah." Here, Paul notes that girls experience sexism, but paired with his earlier anecdote, we also see just how complicated recognizing gender discrimination can be. He was able to name sexism against girls, but he did not see his own complicity in maintaining oppressive constructions of gender vis-à-vis his anger over being made to do gymnastics—a "girl activity."

In an interesting twist, John, a middle-class, white student who was soft spoken and confident, invoked a post-feminist stance when he refused to acknowledge that sexism was relevant to girls' lives. When Andrea asked John who he felt tried harder in school, he responded that girls and boys tried equally hard, explaining, "I think [sexism is] changing now. I think girls have as many, you know, open fields as guys do. I mean, obviously [it] wasn't always that way, but I think now, you know, especially in the schools, you know, teachers will push for gender equality and all those kinds of things, so I don't think that's the case anymore." On the one hand, John's belief in girls' ability to thrive is supportive and feminist, but on the other hand, his post-feminist stance contributes to the refusal to acknowledge the sexism that girls still face, not just in school but also in the workplace. While girls in the West do have more opportunities than ever before,[35] the post-feminist landscape also perpetuates overt as well as subtler forms of gender discrimination that may go unnoticed.[36] For example, John suggested that, because teachers recognize gender inequality, it must no longer exist. John's remarks are thus a part of the catch-22 that post-feminism enables: the very condition that makes feminism necessary has rendered it irrelevant.

While John proposed that girls and boys try equally hard because the playing field is level, a number of other boys submitted that girls try harder because they are more uptight than boys. Jason and Tim, also middle-class, white students, were both popular athletes at St. Mary's High, and they believed that girls put in more effort than boys because girls thought about the future too much. As Jason explained: "I want to have a comfortable life and a good job. I want two or three kids, and that's basically it. I don't know how my wedding is going to be or where I'm going to live." Jason and Tim considered girls to be overly obsessed with the future and noted that girls put more time and energy into thinking about their lives after high school, while they saw themselves as living more in the moment. In the opening story of chapter 1, Wren, too, noted that girls thought more about their futures than boys. But rather than call this pursuit frivolous, Wren suggested that girls *had* to do this if they were going to figure out how to juggle children and a career without compromising either. We explore girls' beliefs about what future success might look like, as well as how sexism might interfere or interact with these plans, in the next section by looking at the concerns academically successful girls voiced about careers, economic stability, and equality within relationships. Interestingly, this is when girls became the most political in their understandings of gender inequality. The not-too-distant future played heavily on their minds and, in some instances, so, too, did sexism.

WHY DO GIRLS NEED TO BE SMART?

While some of the boys put effort into appearing nonchalant about getting good grades, many of the girls emphasized their hard work and linked it to a future payoff. Like Wren, Brooke suggested that being smart was more important for girls: "I think we see the big picture easier, you know? We know how important marks are because we need to get into a good university, to get a good job, you know?" While Brooke did not articulate why girls needed these things, another girl in her group interview, Jamila, offered a reason that pointed to her neoliberal positioning as a flexible, can-do girl but also to her understanding of changing times. Jamila suggested that, as gender roles continue to vary and families continue to shift, girls have to be ready for anything—they have to strive to be smart in order to have as many options as possible, "because the man is no longer the main breadwinner in the household. You know, you have women who aren't the typical stay-at-home moms; they are working and they are highly educated. So, I think that's really a driving force behind young women wanting to be smart."

Donovan similarly articulated why he thought girls needed to try harder than boys in school. While Donovan felt that having a good education was important for boys, he could not see himself ever stressing about doing well: "I don't think it's crucial to have the 93 [percent] average." But he felt it was different for girls because "the jobs women get are more so through education than males." When Andrea asked why, Donovan replied, "The things [boys] do straight out of high school are more male-oriented," such as "trades and apprenticeships—especially plumbing—[those jobs] are mostly for males." Donovan's comments verify the belief of many of the girls that boys do not try as hard as they do in school and that boys have an easier time after graduation. Donovan's views also serve as a sharp reminder that women are frequently discriminated against in particular fields, such as blue-collar work in trades that are categorized as male.[37]

Donovan highlighted a number of concerns that many girls also articulated. Boys' feeling that they don't have to try as hard as girls is linked to their expectation that they will still be able to get good jobs and pay, while girls are more concerned about what their futures will bring. As Caramel angrily described: "Like, so, I have some guys in my English class that were always goofing off, being like, 'Oh, I don't care, it's grades—who needs them,' and it [makes sense] because they will get paid better and they won't need better grades than us." The knowledge that men were paid more than women for the same work incensed the girls more than any other gender disparity that was raised. While sexism in the classroom and the school's social world seemed somewhat defensible, most girls were unable to justify the pay gap between men and women, and, as a result, it became the foundation of their frustration. Nicole added to this critique when she explained why it was important for girls to do well in school: "Well, apparently guys get paid more for the same jobs than girls do ... so ... I guess [girls need to try harder in school]." When Andrea asked her if this inequality in the workplace bothered her, Nicole replied: "Yeah, 'cause we're the same [...]. We're just different. But the same [...]. I *still* don't understand that part." Nicole struggled to understand why such a glaring inequality as the gender pay gap still persisted. It defied explanation and thus lent itself to fueling girls' nascent feminist critiques.

Jenny-Po also asserted that girls had more reasons to do well in school than boys because they had more concerns about their futures: "Not that boys don't, but they like to think more short term. Girls worry more." When Shauna asked why girls might worry more about their futures, Jenny-Po noted that girls were concerned "about when they grow up, if they will be able to survive, paying bills and stuff. Boys think they will be single forever. They don't even have to make their bed if they are single!" This sentiment was echoed by McLovin, who perceived that boys and girls had an unequal concern for the future: "The guys don't really think that far.... And girls are given more competition because they want to prove that they are, like, 'I want to be something, and I want to prove I am as good as all those people, so because of that I'm going to try harder.' Because of this, they try harder, and guys have that thing in their mind like, 'Oh, I'm a guy, I can get this because I'm a guy.' They don't [say it], but it's a subconscious thought."

Some girls spoke directly to their worries about the double duties of work and parenting that disproportionately fall on women's shoulders. During their group interview with Shauna at a local donut shop near St. Mary's High, Audrey, Emma, and Mauve, three white students from middle- and lower-middle-class backgrounds, were quick to agree that there was no sexism at their school. But when Shauna asked about sexism outside the classroom, the three girls opened up about some of the pressures they felt girls experienced that boys did not. Audrey, for example, observed that girls were pressured more by their parents to do well in school: "Sometimes they might expect more from a girl to be more smart and, like, into school work, and maybe they aren't. They would expect boys to be into sports, so it's different." While a few other girls in our study also suggested that parents put more pressure on girls to excel in school than boys, Emma felt that girls and boys experienced unequal pressure after graduation and that this created an unfair advantage for boys: "I think later in life, you have different pressures. You have to have a job and be a mom, and the dad is more there for support and not raising the children. Moms have to feed the children, take care of them, drive them around like a chauffeur." Audrey and Mauve nodded in agreement. Emma continued more tentatively: "Sometimes I think dads should take care of the children [...] more, but then it's like dads are there for financial support and other kinds of support, like parenting support." Here, Emma tries out a feminist critique, although it then becomes a justification: fathers are breadwinners; mothers are primary care givers.

These justifications for sexism were influenced by girl power individualism, as girls might allow their early feelings of frustration and confusion to melt into personal responsibility, accountability, and free choice. Jenny, middle-class and white, and Agnes, upper-middle class and South Asian, offered a perfect example of this when they spoke with Shauna and Andrea at the local public library one day after school. Sitting at a tiny table in the well-worn lobby, Shauna asked the girls if they expected to face sexism in the workplace. Agnes confidently replied, "I don't. I want to go into business, and there are a lot of powerful women in business now, so I think it's getting better." But a few moments later, after giving it further thought, Agnes offered a powerful critique of gender inequality: "No! Actually, I read an article that, like, thinner women get up to $28,000 more [in salary] than overweight women. And then overweight men make more than underweight men." Then Jenny jumped in: "So, you have to look good because you're a *girl!*"

However, Agnes undermined these bold statements by offering a justification for this sexist behavior. Her rationale was both post-feminist and neoliberal: "People have always treated better-looking people better. And there is always going to be, like, you have to be thinner because you're a woman. And so you put those two things together, then [that is what is expected]." Shauna asked Agnes if she thought this kind of pressure on women to look good was fair. Agnes responded by focusing on personal preference: "Not so much pressure, like, I wouldn't not make an effort [to look good] ... . I like doing it, because I wouldn't be happy with myself if I didn't. It's not, like, about other people as much [as myself]. I'm really picky with how I look." While Jenny and Agnes enthusiastically stated that sexism in the workplace was unfair to women, they rapidly recuperated the right to look good by associating it with personal choice and individual responsibility. Even though they acknowledged that there was unfair pressure on women to look a certain way, Jenny and Agnes would never *choose* to remain ungroomed. In a way that coincided with girl power rhetoric, the girls framed maintaining their good looks as a fun-filled pleasure that they did for themselves rather than for others. And by insisting that it was their choice to conform to popular femininity, they safeguarded themselves against any accusations of playing the victim or acting not nice that might arise from their earlier feminist critique.

"I JUST DON'T THINK IT'S THAT FUNNY"

The can-do attitude was visible in girls' refusal to be underdogs, which made it challenging for them to name sexism and call it out as a hindrance in their lives. The influence of the post-feminist landscape thus loomed large in the way the girls talked about gender inequality in the classroom and in their imagined futures. The girls felt that boys took it easier but still got attention from teachers and moved towards promising futures, while the girls saw themselves as constantly working to stand out in order to be successful later on. Fear of being labeled a complainer seemed to obstruct girls' access to feminism, as did the more pressing fear of being seen as a victim, which appeared to be the least attractive position for a girl. These fears, coupled with a lack of social support needed to offer deeper structural critiques, speak up against sexist behavior, or wage a collective battle, left girls vulnerable to gender discrimination. Being caught between post-feminism and feminism created some confusion—girls understood certain things to be wrong but did not know why these things happened or how to protest them.

As we have discussed, it was far easier for girls to acknowledge the persistence of sexism in the lives of girls and women who lived far away, in countries deemed to be less enlightened than their own, than it was for them to recognize it in their own backyard. Chanel, a working-class, black student who was one of the more political girls in our study, pointed out this irony and the difficult consequences it produced. When Shauna met with Chanel at a local coffee shop in downtown Secord, she asked Chanel why she thought girls might get picked on more than boys for being smart. Chanel replied that people still did not associate girls with intelligence and, instead, continued to associate them with looks, bodies, and "hotness." Girls, she reiterated, were generally depicted as less important than boys and men. She then recounted this story:

> I saw a picture once, I think it was meant to be a joke, but it really, really aggravated me. It was an animated picture of a woman, and it said [...], "You can't do work as much as men, you don't produce as much as men, you're constantly complaining about equal rights, da, da, da. The only use you can be of is cooking, cleaning, and

bearing children, and if you can't do those, then you're useless." That really, really frustrated me, because I find that sometimes people can tend to associate Third World countries with sexism and, umm, barbarism, and just general ill will toward women, and yet they would completely ignore it if it is, like, right in the back door, right? Whatever. And that picture, to me, seemed to be the perfect example of that 'cause, like, that same mentality is the same one that people in the same Third World countries [...] used to justify [the killing] of women who are barren, who can't bear the children, and I just think that that's sick and pessimistic at the same time. It's like, you want to shun those actions and yet, in the same breath, you are justifying it as jokes! [...] I just don't think it's that funny.

Chanel's powerful critique of sexism, both at her own back door and in other parts of the world, shatters the common perception that gender inequality is just a joke. In our interviews with boys, we heard references to sexist jokes fairly regularly. Kurt explained that there were a lot of jokes made at the expense of girls. However, in keeping with his own style of letting cutting remarks roll off his back, Kurt acknowledged that a sexist joke might make a girl feel badly but it was her own problem if she let it get her down: "Like, if you're insecure with who you are and someone were to say a sexist joke—even though they're joking—you'd still take it personally." Here, Kurt is somewhat sympathetic, yet he takes up a neoliberal attitude in his assessment of the injurious nature of sexist jokes. Instead of admitting that a girl has a right to feel badly about being put down, he suggests just the opposite—it is her own fault for not being thicker skinned.

John, too, took a neoliberal approach to how girls should deal with sexist jokes, suggesting that, while these jokes were common at his school, girls did not need to take them so seriously: "Yeah, I've definitely heard [sexist comments] before," he said casually. "It's kind of one of those joking things, too, though, right? It's, uh, I don't think it's meant to be hurtful. It's just a way to joke around, I guess." When Rebecca asked John for an example of this kind of joking, he explained that his school had a cooking program, "and um, you know, girls would be more regarded to go do the cooking than the guys would, right?" Puzzled, Rebecca asked, "[So] if a guy wanted to do a cooking program, he would get harassed for it?" John explained, "It wouldn't be a problem [for a guy to do it, but] it'd be the girls that would get singled out for that, and [they would get reminded that girls belong in the kitchen]."

Though Kurt and John suggested that girls needed to be less sensitive in relation to sexist jokes, not all of the boys we spoke to were oblivious to the damaging nature of these jokes. Jason and Tim, for instance, were also aware of the sexist jokes that floated around their school and told Rebecca a story that exemplified gender inequality. "There's this common joke," Tim began. "About women in the kitchen," Jason continued, "and even the teachers—one of them—well, this one guy I know wrote on his history test that asked, 'Where did women work in the '70s?' and he wrote, 'In the kitchen, where else?' and he actually got it right!" Rebecca then observed that such thinking about girls was linked to an old fashioned view that women did not need to be smart because they could be housewives and mothers rather than career women. But, Rebecca noted, "[that] seems to be changing." Interestingly, Jason disagreed: "It's changing—but then again, it's not!"

Lebron and Lattrel reinforced Jason's last comment. When Andrea asked Lebron if he would ever date a smart girl, he replied, "Okay, so a smart girl is somebody who's good in school but doesn't excel, you know what I mean. And a brainiac is someone who's smarter than me and makes me look dumb. So then, like, I date girls who have book smarts and street smarts [but who aren't brainiacs]." Confessing that it would definitely bother him if his girlfriend were smarter than he was, Lebron also acknowledged that it would likely *not* bother his girlfriend if he were smarter than her. This double standard did not seem to trouble the two boys—who saw it as simply a matter of fact. Asked to clarify why a brainiac girl would be unattractive to them, Lebron simply repeated, "Because it makes us look *dumb*, that's why!" Like Paul, who called out sexism yet reproduced it at the same time, Lebron and Lattrel seemed willing to concede that smart girls are acceptable to date only as long as they are not *too* smart. Aware that they were engaging in a double standard, yet unbothered by the fact that they were doing so, Lebron and Lattrel provide a powerful example of why some girls struggle with being both academically successful and noticed by boys.

FEMINISM AND THE SMART GIRL

Girls' lack of affinity for feminist politics is certainly not just a result of girls' misunderstandings of feminism. They—like all of us—live in a culture where feminism is routinely caricatured and disparaged, even as high-profile, emboldening movements seem to be redefining feminism for a new generation. There is a large disconnect between the everyday struggles of girls and the prevailing post-feminist culture, which continues to gather strength even as young women push back. But rather than feel pessimistic about the girls' refusal to acknowledge the existence of sexism in their lives—or their inclination to excuse it—we are encouraged by their ambivalent struggles. Many of the girls—in spite of their incredulity toward gender inequality—

still saw feminism as a positive force. Magda, for example, proclaimed, "Women and men should be treated, like, completely equally, and they're not!"

Some of the girls overtly recognized the importance of feminism for continuing to level the playing field between girls and boys. Acknowledging that girls were shut out of higher education not that long ago, Brooke was thankful that feminism had made it possible for young women to pursue education and new career paths: "I think we should take full advantage of [these opportunities] because it wasn't always like that." Brooke was "proud of being a woman," partly because of "how far we've come." She continued: "It is important to recognize that we have made all those advances from where we used to be, even just from, like, our moms' generation." Smartypants, another one of the more political girls in our study, felt that the feminist revolution was what "encouraged girls to do well academically" in the first place. When Andrea asked her why she thought everyone was talking about how well girls are doing these days, Smartypants replied: "Maybe girls feel more empowered and more encouraged to succeed, and then guys are just, like, they are just the same. I don't know ... things are *still* working out for them."

A small number of girls were outright in voicing their feminist politics. Lisa, for example, had no trouble calling herself a feminist: "I think a lot of people now associate feminism with hating men. I think that's really stupid. Obviously that's not the same thing, it's completely different. [...] I consider myself a feminist. I want equal rights and to be thought of equally, and kind of, well, there's so many stereotypes, and that's part of oppression, especially in a society where we do have more rights, but we are kind of bogged down by these ideologies." Lisa's feminist declaration is a good place to end this chapter.

Given the post-feminist belief that academically successful girls prove that gender equality has been achieved, this chapter offers much food for thought about how sexism acts as an everyday hindrance in smart girls' lives, how it plays out in the classroom and in girls' understandings of future success (or failure), and how girls might be working to tease it out from the pervasive girl power rhetoric that tells them to stop complaining and start enjoying all their newly acquired options. If sexism were a part of everyday conversations with girls and boys, and if feminism were constructed as a useful and relevant force in young people's lives, what would that mean for girls' academic success? What hidden obstacles might be challenged? What possibilities might emerge?

CHAPTER FIVE

A Deeper Look at Class and "Race"

Belongings and Exclusions

Asian-American students tell me that they feel
ashamed of their identity—that they feel viewed as a
faceless bunch of geeks and virtuosos. When they
succeed, their peers chalk it up to "being Asian."

Carolyn Chen, "Asians: Too Smart for
Their Own Good?"

There were lots of things that made Flowerpower stand out. At
eighteen, she was our oldest participant and the only person we
talked with who had already left home—she moved out when
she was sixteen and, at the time of our interviews, was living with
a roommate in downtown Secord. To pay her rent, she worked as
a waitress and a babysitter while going to school. Her mom had
dropped out of high school as a teenager and now worked at a
hair salon and at the local casino with Flowerpower's stepdad;
both of them had immigrated to Secord from Southeast Asia
before Flowerpower was born. Flowerpower explained to Andrea
that she had a fair bit of conflict with her parents. She suffered

from depression and left home partly to escape the pressure she felt from her mom and stepdad, who interpreted her behavior as stubbornness rather than a mental health issue. In consultation with a school counselor, Flowerpower decided to move out.

Reflecting her chosen pseudonym, Flowerpower told Andrea that she was dedicated to supporting social justice causes, including the environment, feminism, LGBTQ+ issues, and veganism. In school, she was drawn to classes in sociology, global inequality, and English. Even though she was a smart girl, she sometimes had trouble prioritizing her schoolwork—this was largely because she was often tired from and busy with her other commitments, but it was also because her classes did not always interest her. She was much more invested in "what's going on in the world." For this reason, she saw herself as politically smart, with a capacity to see through ideologies in a way that other students could not. Her schoolwork also suffered somewhat because she had made the decision to focus on her mental health by choosing to be "happy" rather than "stressed out." She described herself as emotional and intense, and talked about her ongoing challenges with depression and low self-esteem. That said, she was also positive and forward thinking. At the time of her second interview, Flowerpower was completing extra twelfth grade credits. She had a renewed focus on her studies, as she wanted to attend university in order to make the world a better place.

Flowerpower wrestled with many challenges. She was dealing with depression and self-esteem issues; she came from a family that had difficulty making ends meet, whereas many students around her came from privileged backgrounds; and her Southeast Asian heritage was sometimes a source of discomfort in her predominantly white surroundings. Sometimes other students' racist assumptions and jokes created awkward and unpleasant social experiences for her. She was also overtly political in a way that was very different from what was accepted within popular peer culture and popular femininity.

.   .   .

We asked all of our participants about their social and cultural locations. Just as when they discussed gender and gender inequality, many of the young people we talked to reflected a neoliberal ethos as they described their racialized and classed worlds as neutral and contended that everyone was treated equally, diversity was accepted, and social and cultural categories made little difference. But just as they had when they spoke about gender, participants made contradictory comments that complicated these statements, reinforcing the power of gender, class, and "race" and highlighting the way these locations significantly shape young lives and interweave across peer cultures and classrooms.[1] A smart white girl will have different experiences than a smart black girl or a smart Asian girl. These intersections are, in turn, dramatically shaped by class background and myriad other interwoven identity contexts. Such intersections are not always simply positive or negative, and they certainly complicate what it means to be a smart girl in the West, making it challenging to digest sweeping statements about what it is like to be a girl today.

Sexuality, disability, and mental health also arose as important identity locations in a number of our interviews. We had conversations with participants who suggested that some schools were much more welcoming than others for LGBTQ+ students, for instance. We also learned that participants had a good grasp of why certain students received accommodations for exceptionalities and that some, like Flowerpower, faced mental health challenges that made their experience of schooling different from those without this particular circumstance. In this chapter, however, we focus on the two most prominent and powerful intersections that seemed to shape our participants' experiences of belonging and exclusion at school: class and "race." Dedicating a specific chapter to these important contexts of inequality is tricky because we do not wish to suggest that they can be dealt with in isolation from all of the other issues we talk about in this book. We have indicated how class is relevant to the media-hyped concept of the supergirl, how girls feel they need to be nice, and how narrow definitions of prettiness are invisibly rooted in white, middle-class perceptions of popular femininity such as "blondness," high-end styles, a particular body shape, and flat-ironed hair. Yet we feel that it is important to dedicate this chapter to the relevance of class and "race" in girls' negotiation of smartness and peer culture to ensure that each of these prominent forces receives the unique focus that it deserves.

Class positioning and inequality shaped how girls described, lived, and negotiated the tension between academic achievement and peer culture. Girls could mobilize class resources to navigate pressures and downplay their smartness, for instance, and girls who lacked such resources were vulnerable to exclusion. We also found that assumptions and stereotypes about Asian students complicated how academic achievement was framed in some schools, as being too smart could be equated with being too Asian, which, in turn, was equated with being an outsider. In this way, whiteness came to be positioned at the center of peer culture.

We have examined how post-feminism produces an illusion of gender equality, and this popular position has been joined by the argument that we live in a world which is "post race" or that "race" is no longer relevant as a vector of social inequality. Like claiming "colorblindness"—not seeing "race"—this position denies the experiences and effects of racial inequality and under-cuts our ability to talk about racism.[2] These ideological positions dovetail with neoliberalism and the meritocratic contention that we are all competing equally, as individuals, on a level playing field. The structural inequalities relating to gender, class, and "race" are consequently denied. In this chapter, we foreground some of the crucial relevancies of class and "race" in relation to smart girls' negotiations of their academic identities.

CLASS: SNOBBY SCHOOLS AND "GHETTO" HOUSING

Because her family was not well off and she now supported her-self, Flowerpower drew a direct connection between success in school and class-based advantages. We asked her if other smart girls at Blue Ridge also worked after school and on weekends. With frustration, she explained, "The majority—not all—are privileged. They are the ones that have their own car that they drive to school everyday [...]. There are people who have never worked before." To Flowerpower, being a smart girl appeared easier for the girls who did not have the same kinds of demands on their lives that she had. She said that it was hard to see how fortunate everyone was while, in contrast, she had to work to pay her own bills. In spite of her frustration, she offered a positive framing of her situation, noting that she had gained money-man-agement skills and self-sufficiency. Yet at the same time, she rec-ognized that financial security and plentiful resources help girls flourish in school.

Flowerpower also wished her parents could prepare her for university, but instead they were satisfied with the possibility of her graduating from high school and going to a technical college. She explained that, once she had moved out, they no longer gave her even this encouragement, so she had to find the impetus within herself to go on to university. It becomes clear how powerful class is in both hindering and facilitating academic achievement when we contrast Flowerpower's position to McLovin's. McLovin's parents were both university educated and had jobs in municipal government. McLovin explained that she wanted to go to university and that her parents would support her by paying her tuition. She added that they had also provided good moral support for her and her sister Caramel by teaching them to prioritize their homework over other activities. McLovin then mentioned, "When it comes to math, my dad just kind of teaches me because he used to [teach courses at university], so I don't know, that's good." McLovin's experience confirmed the advantages of having parents who were able (and willing) to pay for university, teach study skills, and even help with advanced homework, making her confident that she would excel in school.

.   .   .

Class powerfully shapes young people's lives.[3] Class is anchored in material conditions and is often associated with how much income and wealth[4] a family has, the time the parents spend working outside the home, the kind of work the parents do, how secure that work is, and where and how the family lives. But class is also about culture, which includes values and dispositions that arise from a family's or community's material conditions, the ways of being that are most important and rewarded within a specific society, how closely a family approximates those ways of being, and how they are judged as a result.[5] It is clear that, on multiple levels, class is deeply relevant to a discussion of young people's success in school. Despite a ubiquity of narratives that focused on individualism, our participants frequently touched on class inequalities in their evaluation of schools, assessments of each other's clothing, determination of cliques, and appraisal of other students' scholarly success or failure. These observations were largely about material resources, but they signified so much more. Our analysis showed deep class biases, with class markers used to indicate social success, popularity, smartness, and even cleanliness. In this way, class sharply intersected with smart girlhood to reward privilege, create boundaries, and produce exclusions.

The girls considered certain schools "rich." Virginia described Blue Ridge as a "very rich" school, for instance: "[There are] Bentleys and BMWs and Lexuses in the parking lot. Everybody wears Abercrombie, Hollister, Bench—all the brand names. Almost everyone has an iPhone, or the new iPod touch, and everybody you know is rich and has lots of clothes and pretty hair and sparkly shoes, and oh, everyone wears the real brand Uggs." Though Virginia was able to keep up with the fashions, she still felt like an outsider in this school culture. Elizabeth agreed that there were a lot of designer clothes at Blue Ridge, explaining that American Eagle was "almost the unofficial uniform. Instead of it being The Gap and Old Navy, it's a little bit higher." But she also said that you don't really notice it as much when you are there, a statement that betrayed her own middle-class position as someone who is comfortably able to fit into such an environment. Haley and Quinn made similar observations of their school, St. Mary's High. Haley said that the school had a lot of wealthy kids, but she did not include herself among them: "You can just tell by, like, what they wear and what they talk about, and all, like, all these things they do. A lot of them go on vacations quite a bit, yeah. We have to buy the uniforms [...]. So the majority in our school is not exactly rich. But we are pretty wealthy."

Schools in affluent neighborhoods had reputations for being stronger academically,[6] while schools that served less well-off families were considered, at least from the vantage point of Blue Ridge students, to be 'ghetto' schools.[7] Sara explained that, at Blue Ridge, there were a lot of people from "pretty good family situations." She went on to point out that one of the differences between Blue Ridge and Central Secondary was teen parents: "It's, like, 'Whoah, that does not happen here!' Like, [at Central Secondary, they say,] 'We have daycare at our school.'" Sara's friend Basil piped in, "Yeah, we *don't* have daycare at our school. *That's* not happening here."

Interestingly, two girls who went to Central High also commented on the daycare program at their school, but they treated it as a point of pride. Janey explained that she had gone to a local board meeting of students from various schools, and when she mentioned that her school had a daycare, other students were shocked. But Janey noted that her school's daycare serviced students from other schools as well, *including* Blue Ridge: "Yeah, Blue Ridge High doesn't allow pregnant women to stay at their school, so they come to our school. [...] I was just kind of, like, 'What are you guys doing? It's an issue that is reality!' People are hidden from it, but at Central it's, like, reality and this stuff happens, you know what I mean?"

While the above story depicts how class was used to make judgments between schools, it was also used to make judgments between students within a school. Disputing some of the commentary on peer culture in chapter 3, we found that fitting in is not just about how social or friendly one is. Like Flowerpower's story, Rory's experience is a strong illustration of how a student's class background can shape her sense of belonging, which, in turn, affects both her social and her scholarly success in a particular school. At the time of our first interview, Rory went to Pinecrest Elementary, a feeder school for Blue Ridge. Rory's parents had her when they were young, and she was proud of them for doing so well; but they lived near government-funded housing, and her dad had recently been laid off from his greenhouse job. Her mom was an accountant, and the family was renovating their house so that she could start a home daycare. Rory explained that Pinecrest's reputation as a "snobby" school was "pretty accurate, considering we have rich snobby kids," and she pointed out that they would likely "think my house is a ghetto." She added that, since she lives near government-funded housing, other kids think that she lives in a "bad" area and, except for her close friends, no one comes to her house. She said she tried not to care but admitted that she did care "a little." In her second interview, Rory talked about preferring her new high school, Great Lakes Secondary. It was closer to her house and did not seem to have the same pretentions as Pinecrest. She said she loved it so much because she "actually fit in." She could bring friends home and not feel embarrassed because, "for all I know, they could live in the [government-funded] complex over *there,* that's kind of run down."

The girls' judgments about schools and neighborhoods that were linked to observations about wealth and disposable income were reflected in the way that some of our participants talked about fashion, particularly name brand clothing. Fashion was clearly important in most schools: different styles marked out the boundaries around cliques, certain brand names helped to secure popularity, and other kinds of clothing was for loners. Given that fashion and looks were considered particularly important for girls, money was a resource that enabled smart girls to thrive socially, as well as academically. American sociologist Julie Bettie looks at how high school girls understand class through interaction and performance rather than through a class-consciousness directly arising from their parents' sources of income. According to Bettie, class culture is symbolized by consumption, which she notes is traditionally associated with the feminine sphere. Class markers and group membership are, therefore, frequently about purchases, especially of clothing and accessories.[8]

Caramel and McLovin were keen to talk about the relevance of name brand clothing at Blue Ridge. Even though McLovin said that she and her sister hung out with everyone and did not "divide people by their class," McLovin argued that the ability to buy certain clothing brought higher social status. For instance, it was prestigious to wear clothing with the school's name embroidered on it: "If you see people walking around with school sweaters and track pants and bandanas, it's like that person's cool because they can afford to wear our clothes." Erin—the girl whose friend took her to Lululemon for wardrobe help—went to a smaller elementary school in a fairly well-off community. In preparation for the expensive shopping trip, Erin saved up $200 to spend at the store, a prospect that she found "scary." But Erin said it *had* to be Lululemon—or Hollister or Aeropostal—because it might help her counteract the stigma she felt that being smart had at her school. She already knew that wearing clothing with such brand names was effective because she had received a Bench jacket for her birthday: "I really didn't know what it was, I didn't think people really cared. Then I got to school and everyone was, like, 'Ooooohhhhh, you've got a Bench jacket.'"

Another girl who talked about the challenges of name brands was Smartypants, who went to Bethany High, a public Christian

school, and was far from wealthy. She lived in subsidized housing, and her parents' jobs were precarious. At her school, Coach
bags were the trend, and she explained that pretty much every
girl had one. Smartypants did not tell us whether she had a
Coach bag, but she did talk about the pressure to look a certain
way: "You don't want to be the girl in the corner not wearing
certain styles or not wearing proper makeup." When she was
younger, she insisted on buying clothes at Garage so she would
fit in, but she also noted that, often, the trendy clothing is very
expensive, like Lululemon. "It's frustrating," she lamented. "I
wouldn't spend that much, but they are very nice pants." Smartypants felt that the kids who were able to be both smart and
popular were those who had the cash to dress a certain way.
Consequently, she explained, "the ones who are less fortunate
are most likely the ones who are less popular."[9]

The idea that financial insecurity can hinder a girl's popularity was echoed in Jordan's observations about the local Catholic
school she went to before Academy House. She told us about two
girls in her school who were not as well off as everyone else and
who, therefore, did not have the "right" look. She would sometimes stand with the two girls at recess, but she said that it was
hard to be associated with them because of other kids' negative
comments. Rory talked about being on the other side of this
dynamic as a girl that was judged for her less trendy style. She
said that there was a popular group in her school that she did not
like dealing with because of their judgments regarding her looks.
With annoyance, she noted: "People say I'm gross because I wear
Roots track pants or my bangs are too long." That said, there
were also girls in our study who talked about choosing comfort
over style, alternative clothing over brand name items, and sec-
ondhand shops over retail stores in a way that rejected fashion as

the be-all and end-all of peer hierarchies.[10] Girls such as Tony M. and Tony B. indicated that, while some students really prioritized fashion and the status it represented, others were less able to participate, less concerned, and/or pushed back against an ethos that they did not share—a point we return to in chapter 6.

The school a girl attended and the clothes she wore were assumed to indicate access to financial resources (or lack thereof), and these observations frequently came with judgments about families, too. It was around these material issues of schools and dress that discussions moved from the status of disposable income to deeper, class-based judgments, including about who is smart and functional. We saw this in a discussion with friends Sully, a middle-class, white student, and Joanne, an upper-middle-class, East Asian student. The two girls went to an elementary school that they positively described as having "rich, nice kids," as if "rich" and "nice" were interchangeable. They both felt that the students from wealthier families and schools were smarter than others, in part because these students could afford the extras, like textbooks, technology, and tutoring, that would produce higher grades. Sully noted that the parents of these students were "successful, like teachers and doctors and stuff." In contrast, Sully and Joanne noted that the kids who went to the local "ghetto" school were not considered smart: "The ghetto kids have good parents, but sometimes they feel like they aren't good enough or something."

In this exchange, Sully and Joanne rightly noted some of the direct and hidden injuries of class inequality, something that not many of our participants talked about. They saw that practical resources can help students be successful and that poverty can sometimes negatively shape people's expectations and self-efficacy. But they also problematically privileged wealth by equating "rich kids" with "nice kids" and assumed richer parents were smarter parents. They also generalized "ghetto" kids as lacking in certain ways. How might working-class young people negotiate such assumptions? Furthermore, Sully and Joanne expressed a typically neoliberal view in that their nascent class analysis focused exclusively on individual families' choices and inclinations rather than on the deeper structural issues, such as unemployment or an insufficient minimum wage, that foster these inequalities.

Sara and Basil also noted that class is linked to academic performance. Sara was part South Asian and keen on computers and gaming. Her dad was a computer consultant and her mom was a homemaker. Basil was upper-middle-class and the only white girl in her circle of friends. Her mom was a doctor, and her dad was starting his own business. She was an avid reader and also involved in a local Jewish organization. Both girls came from financially secure homes, and while they did not place themselves among the rich students at Blue Ridge, they did see themselves as wealthy compared to students at other schools. Within a wider conversation about class, Shauna asked them whether they felt that it is the rich kids who are also known as smart kids. Nodding, Sara said yes, explaining that parents with a higher education expect more from their children. Basil added, "Usually [with] higher class parents, it's like if you don't get a high mark it's not acceptable. They expect a lot. There's a possibility it's genetic too." On the one had, as Sully and Joanne had pointed out, Sara and Basil rightly noted that there is a link between parents with more education and the educational performance of their children.[11] But on the other hand, Sara and Basil primarily focused on expectations, without acknowledging the possibility that expectations are a consequence of certain conditions rather than a cause. Such an interpretation, based on individualism, is again typical of neoliberalism, which easily shifts toward blame, holding working-class people responsible for their own (presumed) lack of success without recognizing the structural challenges they may face. Basil's final comment reinforces this position by suggesting that rich kids may be smarter due to genetics.

A final example is offered by Isabell, a lower-middle-class, white student, who laid out the hierarchy of popularity at her school, Lester B. Pearson High. According to Isabell, the popular group was rich, pretty, and smart, while the "average" people were "alright looking, kind of smart, but they aren't rich," and "then there's the umm, kind of, like, the scrubby people, I guess. People who don't exactly have an extremely good quality of life." Shauna asked Isabell what she meant by "scrubby people." Isabell explained: "Like, they didn't grow up in a stable family. Like, maybe their parents did drugs or were alcoholics or something like that. They tend to kind of go to the lower part of the cycle, I think, just because their parents let them get away with stuff." The "scrubs," she then clarified, were the poor kids. The school hierarchy, in this telling, is all about class, with rich students enjoying an attractive synergy of looks, smartness, and wealth and the poorer students condemned to hardship. Even though Isabell herself was not well off, her story presents a troubling portrayal of poor families as inherently dysfunctional and rich families as competent and successful. The girls did not question how rich families became rich, how structural forces and private resources preserve that wealth, how children from richer families may be advantaged in schools, or what kinds of broader social challenges and resiliencies poorer families negotiate.

In most of our interviews, girls said that popularity was about being well known or well liked and that some smart girls just had the charisma and the skills to attract others. But clearly, popularity and acceptance are not just about being friendly, outgoing, or kind—the class context of a school, class inequality between students, and class prejudices and stereotypes play an important, but largely unacknowledged, role as well. Very few of our participants noted that inequalities are embedded in our institutions, including the dynamics of peer cultures. Furthermore, there was little recognition of the broader structural issues that are reflected in economic inequalities, such as the difficult consequences of a low minimum wage, unemployment and underemployment, the lack of social supports for challenges such as mental illness, and the ways that schools favor more privileged children. Instead, most girls individualized troubles and successes. Yet there is a vast body of literature about the blunt and more deeply hidden injuries of class differences within schools.[12]

At a practical level, when families have difficulty making ends meet, it often means that parents are working long hours with low wages, and this makes it difficult to prioritize a relationship with the school.[13] A lack of income also makes involvement in school trips and fundraisers difficult and prevents students from having the extra resources that they may need, such as tutors or Internet access at home. And of course, class-based judgments and discrimination from peers and teachers, including judgments about what kinds of people are smart, shape students' (and parents') feelings of belonging within the school.

At a deeper level, researchers have drawn on French sociologist Pierre Bourdieu's work to suggest that schools reflect and reward middle-class culture.[14] As we have discussed, some of our participants gave up peer popularity in the present in order to focus on school, with the hope of translating their high grades and academic skills into good jobs (and economic capital) later in their lives. But cultural capital is not only for the future; it is also present in rewards and accolades that are bestowed in the present for certain ways of being a student.[15] For those students who come from middle- and upper-middle-class backgrounds, there tends to be a "natural" familiarity between school culture and home culture, given the dominance of middle-class culture in schools.[16] Meanwhile, students who do not have such an affinity for middle-class culture will not feel as comfortable[17] and will be more likely to clash with the school, whether it be in terms of curriculum, disciplinary issues, or peer hierarchies.[18] The concept of cultural capital provides a useful explanation for the experiences of students like Flowerpower, who felt disconnected from both the curriculum and her peers. Flowerpower's exposure to inequality allowed her to see through ideology in a way that a lot of her classmates could not. She wanted courses that recognized these inequalities and provided opportunities to talk about social justice. Flowerpower blamed herself for being angry at the injustice around her, but her anger made a lot of sense when it was contextualized in a school environment that did not resonate with her own experience and concerns.

Class is not just about fashion, holidays, or houses—it is also about ways of being and belonging. Where a girl lives, how she looks, and where she goes to school can shape who she can hang out with, whether she will be considered popular, and consequently, whether she will find comfort in both academic and social success. The wealth of students' families even shapes the "fit" they feel between their school environment and their own ways of being. As we have seen in the above examples, a student's class positioning can even influence whether they will be considered *able* to be smart.

THE "SMART ASIAN" STEREOTYPE

When Flowerpower was a child, she asked her mom to give her an English name that she could use instead of her Chinese name, like some other Asian[19] students she knew had. This story exemplified Flowerpower's past discomfort with her racialization and cultural heritage, but when we spoke with her, she was moving toward embracing her roots. This acceptance was clearly a difficult journey for Flowerpower, one that was directly linked to challenges she faced in school. She explained, "[At my previous school], everyone referred to me as 'the Asia,' and I was also referred to as 'the Asian,' or I would walk into a party and people would be, like, 'Oh, it's Asia.' Even though it was kind of, like, a friendly gesture for their intentions, I was offended. To be honest, I couldn't accept my ethnicity, so being reminded I'm different hurt me." Flowerpower attributed the hurtfulness of these comments to her own embarrassment over her "race" and ethnicity,[20] internalizing and individualizing the interaction. However, such "joking" singled her out as different from her classmates based on how she looked and also suggested that there was little difference between her and billions of others who are homogenized by the term "Asian."[21]

Sociologists and antiracist scholars have analyzed how "race," as a social category, plays out in schools, focusing particularly on anti-black racism in the attitudes and actions of school staff. For example, teachers' and administrators' evaluations of student performance and behavior can be laden with discrimination against black students.[22] Less research has been conducted on racism within school peer groups, however, but some of this research indicates that Asian American students are particularly vulnerable to peer discrimination.[23] Even so, we heard stories about black students that raised concerns. Chanel, our only black participant, told a frightening story about being called racist names and chased outside of a busy supermarket in Secord, and she also talked about the ubiquity in her school of lesser racist incidents. Allie, who was white, was bothered that some students at her school offensively used the "N-word." And Yasmin, who was South Asian, noted that certain students at her school were called "dark chocolate," "milk chocolate," or "brown bunny," which she described as a joke. Together, these troubling examples suggest a strong undercurrent of peer-based anti-black racism in the Secord area.

While a number of the girls described their schools as multicultural, Secord and its surrounding area is limited in terms of racial diversity, and most people are of European heritage. Despite our many attempts to locate diverse participants, the majority by far of those who signed up for our study were white, and while these boys and girls had a lot to say about "race" and ethnicity, it was primarily about Asian students and the "smart Asian" stereotype—which also points to the perception that whiteness is invisible.[24] Across our interviews, the "smart Asian" label was repeated over and over again.[25] There were two key threads to this discussion. First, participants frequently claimed that their social worlds were full of diversity and equality. And second, through a wide range of comments, cracks appeared in this neoliberal narrative as it became clear that Asian students were understood through a narrow stereotype that reproduced a relationship between being smart and being on the outside of peer cultures. Most commonly, the "smart Asian" stereotype assumes that Asian students are good at school, hardworking, and especially gifted at math and science.[26] While some of our participants were able to critically recognize this pattern as a stereotype, most presented it as a social truth that Asian students, much more than girls specifically, were the ones they assumed would try hard and succeed at school.

On first thought, the characterization of Asian students as inherently smart appears to be positive, because being smart is valued and promises rewards. Jenny-Po, who was East Asian, explained that her friends "are called 'the Asians,' because Asians are always smart." When Shauna asked if this stereotype bothered her, she replied, "No, because it's usually good, like, [being] smart. Or I can play an instrument. This one time I did a chin-up in gym class this girl was, like, 'Whoah! She's smart *and* strong! One of those.'" Smartypants, who was South Asian, also considered the "smart Asian" stereotype to be a compliment. Rory, who was white, observed that people poked fun at a group of Asian students at her school, but she then quickly rationalized that it was "not in a mean way, but they just, like, sometimes say, 'Oh, you are so Asian' instead of 'so smart.'"

But while the assumption of academic success appears innocuous enough, there are significant troubling effects of this kind of supposedly "good racism."[27] The "smart Asian" social category generalizes across enormous diversity, reduces people to an assumed set of narrow traits, and is the basis for other exclusionary assumptions. The girls in our study with Asian backgrounds included immigrants and second-generation Canadians, and their families came from such diverse places as China, Korea, the Philippines, and Cambodia. They included girls who were religious and nonreligious, and girls from wealthy families alongside girls, like Flowerpower and Smartypants, from either stable or precarious working-class families. A positive stereotype does not prevent students from experiencing discrimination or what Canadian anthropologist Dan Yon terms "cultural racism"[28]— they must still grapple with the homogenizing assumption that they have inherent traits based on how they look or where they come from.[29] Furthermore, the expectation that all Asian students are thriving can magnify feelings of incompetence when Asian students struggle to learn certain material and may make Asian students less likely to ask for, or receive, the kind of instructional support they need.[30]

The fact that her peers denied any possible struggle she may be having in school was an issue for Flowerpower, who both perpetuated and defied this stereotype. She observed, "Asian parents have a reputation of being really strict and pressuring students to do well." But she explained that her parents did not pressure her at all "because they were busy with work and stuff. My mom would ask me if I had homework but never offer to help." She continued, "At Blue Ridge, all the students that are Asian are really involved in school and sports and have good grades. I guess with me ... no." Yet people continued to assume she was super smart: "They would say, like, 'Oh, you must be good at math'!" She described instances where other students asked her for help with their schoolwork because they presumed that she knew the answers because she was Asian: "When they ask me, I just go, 'I don't know,' and it makes me feel like an idiot, you know [...], because I don't know, because they ask me these questions and I have no answer for them [...]. So it's just kind of like a reminder, like, almost, you know, that you are not that smart [*laughs*], yeah."

Joanne also felt misrecognized. She told us that people saw her as a genius because she was Asian and automatically went to her for help. Joanne's co-interviewee, Sully, who was white, added, "In math class, everyone is, like, 'Oh, just ask the Asian'!" Despite being a very strong student in other subjects, Joanne struggled in math and could not answer their questions. But she said that these assumptions did not really bother her and were not necessarily racist, explaining, "It's a good part [of being Asian]." Yet she also noted that other kids did not see her for who she was: "Like, I'm *not* who you think I am." These racialized expectations thus foster the frustrating experience of being not only misjudged but also misrecognized.[31]

The use of stereotypes, such as that of the "smart Asian," enabled white students to exclude others by emphasizing cultural differences or social incompatibility without seeing themselves as racist.[32] Within Canada, multiculturalism and diversity are claimed as core values, and racism is widely considered socially unacceptable. That said, racism is defined narrowly, leaving subtler forms of racism, broader institutional racialization, and the centering of whiteness largely unexamined.[33] In our study, for instance, one of the ways that participants talked about the "smart Asian" stereotype was as a joke they used to tease each other about being smart or geeky. Joking can be complicated and powerful, creating both in-group bonds and exclusion. Sometimes, the joking seemed playful, especially when Asian students teased each other about embodying the stereotype, but this type of joking also suggested deeper discrimination and exclusion, such as the pain Flowerpower felt when she was called "Asia." As we discussed in the previous chapter, our participants talked about sexist joking. Some of the stories we heard about students using the "smart Asian" stereotype as a "joke" evoked in us a similar degree of discomfort and concern as did the sexist jokes, especially as the joking, and the reactions to this joking, masked discrimination.

For example, Andrea asked Maggie, one of our white participants, if she had ever seen racism at her school. Maggie explained, "No, obviously the racist things are the people of different races making fun of themselves. It's just a joke. It's not racism. They are just joking and having fun with each other." Andrea then asked if there were a lot of Asian or black people at Maggie's school, and Maggie said, "I think more black than Asian, but most of the people are Canadian." These contradictory statements have troubling connotations. First, Maggie suggested that there is no racism, and then she said that racism does exist but turned the idea on its head by saying that it is people of color who enact it against each other. Maggie then confidently noted that it is not actually racism, as the people of color are just joking around. In her final statement, she conflated black and Asian students with new immigrants, suggesting that they are not Canadian.[34] Together, these accounts presented a vision of benign and yet exclusionary Canadian whiteness, while portraying racism as something non-white students inflict on each other for a laugh.

Another example of this thinking was given by Elizabeth, who was white. She said that the "smart Asian" stereotype circulated at Blue Ridge but claimed that it was only used as a joke: "It's more a joke, not an actual ... There's a lot of Asians, like, a lot, like, half our student population. The jokes made are completely random, but it's that you're Asian, so you must be smart. It's not necessarily true." Elizabeth's comments were somewhat critical, as she perceived that the stereotype was not always accurate, yet her other statements drew attention to how the narrative of "just joking" needs to be examined more closely. She said the jokes are "completely random," but they are not; they are specifically aimed at and name Asian students. She also suggested that Asian students make up half the student population of Blue Ridge, which is out of sync with other students' description of the school as mostly white.[35] She also explained that, because the Asian students joke around with the stereotype, too, there is no racism at her school. Yet, later in the interview, she countered this observation, noting that some people take the joking "in a very negative way [...]. They will say, 'Oh, that was really offensive, I didn't like that.'" To her, however, this reaction was an example of a person who was just looking for something to criticize: "They want a reason to complain rather than they are actually offended by it." To support this observation, Elizabeth explained that "everyone" makes jokes about Asian smartness, "and, like, *everyone* knows they're joking, but there are certain people [...] that actually take offense to them just to get attention to get an apology kind of thing." In suggesting that students should not complain about "smart Asian" jokes, Elizabeth demonstrated how ubiquitous—and pernicious—such joking can be and how both joking along *and* complaining about such joking can be used to dismiss the seriousness of the issue.

Maggie and Elizabeth were far from the only participants to suggest that, because Asian students participate in the joking, it is not hurtful or racist. While they have a point in that peer culture is based on insider jokes that may not always *feel* offensive and that students can playfully engage with stereotypes, the flip side is that rigidly policed peer norms make it difficult to speak up in the face of subtle (or even overt) discrimination, as Elizabeth's comments make clear.[36] In fact, when students with Asian backgrounds participate in their own teasing, they may be working at being included. Given the pervasive narrative of acceptance that is central to Canadian identity and the positioning of Asian students as "perpetual foreigners,"[37] Asian or other students naming such joking as racism could, ironically, feel like too much of a challenge to the dominant Canadian ethos of tolerance and diversity.

While many participants saw the "smart Asian" stereotype as teasing and nothing more, some girls did not dismiss it as just joking.

Flowerpower named racism specifically when calling out the racist joking of the class clown. Similarly, Rory was concerned when students were saying that a girl in her class got very high marks only because she was Asian: "I think it's racist, just not as racist as people can be to, like, say, black people. […] Teachers say, 'Ignore [such comments] […].' They say, 'If you see someone being bullied, step in,' but if they are saying remarks that are rude, [they tell you] to walk away." Rory felt that such a response was insufficient—more needed to be done! Lisa noted that Asian students were categorized as smart through "stupid" jokes that "generalized." She then added, "Someone once told me I might as well be Asian [because I'm smart]. It wasn't a name or hurtful, but I would feel bad if I was Asian and was stereotyped the way they are."

While many girls recognized and celebrated multiculturalism and diversity in their schools, comments about "smart Asians" were clearly exclusionary. Being "too Asian," for example, was equated with being too focused on studies and being antisocial. In this way, it separated Asian-ness from dominant peer culture: being both Asian and smart meant that you could be seen as overly Asian. Caramel, who was white, outlined it this way: "Yeah, it's true at our school, there's Asians and then there's *Asians* […]. There's a kid at our school with a 109 percent average or something, and they spend their time doing homework and I can't.... I have a life outside of my school. I can't spend every moment of my life looking at a paper." For Caramel, this level of studiousness and consequent Asian-ness was undesirable. But she also framed these students' exclusion from peer culture as *their* fault—others are not actively excluding them, it is their Asian-ness that makes them unpopular. Again, a division was reinforced between smartness (in this case, being "too Asian") and being social. Like Elizabeth, Caramel also suggested that a focus on academics was, in itself, foreign: "More English people are slack about grades. People who came here from anywhere are all grade imperative." Seen another way, then, when Asian students try hard in school, they are sometimes seen as failing to be fully Canadian, which creates a quandary for Asian students who are invested in their academics but also in the social life of their school and the imagined idea of what it means to be a Canadian.

INTERSECTIONAL COMPLEXITIES

Jacqueline went to the same school as Flowerpower and was also subjected to the "smart Asian" stereotype because she was East Asian. But Jacqueline's experience at Blue Ridge was notably different. She was well supported by her academic parents, ambitious in her goals, and involved in a number of extracurricular activities, including engineering club, debating club, and drafting the school newsletter. She and her friend Cindy, who was also East Asian, said that, although they both encountered the "smart Asian" stereotype, they had not experienced racism at their school and felt that it did not really matter what their "race" or ethnicity was. While Flowerpower struggled at Blue Ridge, Jacqueline seemed comfortable with her social position. For Jacqueline, a certain configuration of class background, ethnicity, peer involvement, and personal context shaped a trajectory through Blue Ridge that ensured a degree of ease and promised ongoing success. The intersections in Flowerpower's life shaped a significantly different trajectory.

There are numerous intersections in girls' lives that shape how smart girls see themselves and others, experience and negotiate peer culture, and navigate the institution of the school. Of these intersections, class and "race" are pivotal, as they are embedded in historical and structural forms of inequality, deeply connected to family and community, fraught with problematic stereotypes, and loaded with long-term repercussions. Sometimes they significantly intertwine, and sometimes they diverge.[38] Yet, as with gender, neoliberal individualism masks these significant social divisions and inequalities. We—students, educators, parents, and researchers—need more stories about smart girls' diverse and complicated experiences in schools.[39] In exploring some of the complexities of these intersections, we have sought to illustrate the relevance of key aspects of identity and structural inequality as they interact with each other and play out in each smart girl's unique life, thus shattering the gender-only narrative that dominates media and popular psychological conceptions of successful girls and failing boys. In our final chapter, we offer two more ways of contextualizing the lives of smart girls: microresistances and school culture. These glimpses into how smart girls resist popular femininity and how they might be better supported in schools and beyond open the door to different configurations of academic success—and possibilities for social transformation.

CHAPTER SIX

Cool to Be Smart

Microresistances and
Hopeful Glimpses

I'm so glad that I'll never fit in,
That will never be me.
Outcasts and girls with ambition,
That's what I wanna see.

Pink, "Stupid Girls"

Tony M. and Tony B. answered the door together when Shauna rang the bell to Tony M.'s home in a mixed socioeconomic neighborhood in downtown Secord. Best friends attending Central Secondary, they agreed to be interviewed because it was "something to do." Both girls were dressed in what they later described as "alternative" fashions, including black Converse high tops, ripped leggings, baggy cardigans, and smudged makeup. Tony M., the more talkative of the two, sported a nose ring and long, brown hair with short bangs; Tony B. had a nose ring, a facial stud, and short, curly, blonde hair. While almost all of the girls in our study wore popular fashions from well-known stores, Tony M. and Tony B. took pride in looking different. Even their chosen pseudonyms reflected their resistance to conformity, and they roared with laughter when they picked such "hilarious" (and confusing) aliases. When Shauna asked how they would describe themselves, Tony M. was quick to respond: "I'm kinda weird... I'm different, I like different things. I'm crazy sometimes." Tony B. concurred: "I would say I'm kind of weird, too. I like to do different things than other people, I guess." Tony M. shouted, "Yah, *not* Hollister and Lil' Wayne!"[1]

While many girls in our study used their social skills to offset negative side effects of being smart, Tony M. and Tony B. labeled themselves socially awkward, which Tony M. tried to describe: "I can't really carry out a conversation, it's like 'Ahhhh!' I'll say something weird, then leave." But popularity was not particularly enticing to either of the girls anyway. While Tony B. mentioned that she was known as "the drummer" due to her participation in numerous school bands and said "hi" to a fair number of people in the halls, Tony M. was decidedly less popular and seemed happy to be out of the fray. Tony B. jokingly explained that it was better to be unpopular "because you don't have to listen to [popular kids'] music" or do the things "they like to do [...] like [taking] Facebook pictures and posing and stuff."

Tony M. and Tony B. were in eleventh grade at Central Secondary. "To me, [the word 'smart'] doesn't mean anything as far as grades go," Tony M. explained. "I don't need crazy good marks for what I want to do later. I try harder in arts stuff." They took courses in visual arts, music, percussion, photography, and fashion, and they shuddered at the mention of their academic courses, such as math, French, and science. But both girls were clear: they could do well if they wanted to. As Tony B. admitted, "If I do bad on a test and everyone else does good, I just think, 'I should have studied more.' It's not like I don't have it in me, I just didn't do it."

The girls described being bored in most of their classes, and Tony M. explained her classroom routine for dealing with this problem: "I usually, like, pull out some paper, and start doodling, I doodle *really* hard." But while the girls were unmotivated in their academic classes, the things that really piqued their interest inspired them to great heights. Aside from the arts courses that garnered them their highest grades, Tony B. was extremely invested in extracurriculars, including jazz band and soccer. And Tony M. suddenly became animated when Shauna asked about her musical taste. She eagerly explained that she liked "independent music and, I don't know, stuff that isn't really all over the radio all the time. I like Interpol, Peter Bjorn and John, and Animal Collective." Tony B. added that she liked "Green Day a lot; I like '80s music, like Joy Division and a lot of old vinyl stuff."

Sitting at a tiny table in Tony M.'s cluttered, incense-filled kitchen, both girls told Shauna that they lived with their moms and had very little spending money. Tony M.'s mom was an artist who also did odd jobs, and Tony B.'s mom cleaned houses, which Tony B. helped her with sometimes to earn a bit of cash. When the girls had money in their pockets, they would spend it on "concerts and bands and stuff." Though underage, they would see shows at a downtown bar that featured local bands on the weekends. Tony B. explained, "We don't drink or anything, we just go see the music, so it's not a big deal." This pastime also offered some much needed stress relief. Shauna wondered what got left to the wayside when the girls became too busy. "Homework," said Tony B. matter-of-factly. "I'll shower and watch TV when there is still homework." Tony M. had a different way to relieve stress: "[*Roars loudly*] I punch holes and get angry [*laughs*]!" But whatever they were stressed about, it was definitely not the future. Recall Wren's story at the beginning of this book and her concerns about juggling motherhood and a career. But when Shauna asked Tony M. and Tony B. if they were worried about acquiring jobs or having a family, Tony B. replied, "Sometimes. It's not something I think about a lot. I just kind of like to take it as it goes, kind of." For Tony M., the future was too far away to worry about now: "I don't think about marriage, but when I think of the future, I hope there's a nice apartment, maybe in Chicago."

CHALLENGING DOMINANT STORIES
ABOUT GIRLS

Tony M. and Tony B. are about as far away from the image of the media-hyped supergirl as you can get. With their punk aesthetic, laid-back attitude, admitted social awkwardness, and lack of interest in trying hard in academic courses, they represent another kind of smart girl—one who does well enough in school but is not particularly motivated by high achievement or its future payoff. But like all the girls in this book, Tony M. and Tony B. help to dispel the dominant story that media and popular psychological accounts put forward about girls: that they experience uncomplicated academic success at the expense of boys. A part of this narrative includes the idea that girls today are able to handle the kind of stress that is typically associated with high levels of extracurricular involvement and intensive studying—all while looking good and staying fit. But as Tony M. and Tony B. make clear, girls experience academic success in a variety of ways. The two girls highlight a very different kind of engagement with school and coursework: they refused to try hard. They also did not adhere to notions of popular femininity or feel the need to negotiate their academic success; they did not hide their grades or dumb down, and they did not care what anyone thought of them.

The smart girl stereotype is pervasive in Western culture, but as we asked in chapter 1, what stories are left out or made invisible by the smart girl story? And what interesting facets of smart girls' lives have been rendered unimportant as a result? The perception of easy academic success has become one of the most recognizable pieces of official knowledge about girls in the West, helping to sustain other powerful stories, such as failing boys and the overarching belief that girls now live in a gender-neutral world where anything is possible as long as they try hard and maintain a positive attitude. But as we, and many others, have argued, this postfeminist and neoliberal environment has created profoundly confusing and challenging circumstances within which girls negotiate their gender and academic identities. While, overall, the girls in our study were enormously proud of their academic success (whether they downplayed it at school or not), they were also constantly entangled in the interplay between post-feminism and feminism—trying to justify or make sense of things that often made no sense at all, such as sexism, racism, and classism.

Each chapter in this book has sought to bust a part of the smart girl myth and speak back to the dominant story that girls' skyrocketing success in school today means that they are taking over the world. The media-produced construct of the supergirl, for example, places enormous pressure on girls to be perfect at everything, including school, sports, extracurricular activities, and social life. We explored the supergirl as a cultural fabrication that holds influence over girls', parents', and teachers' expectations of what is considered "normal" for girls, and we also scrutinized the parental and economic supports that go into trying to live up to these impossible standards. It seems that not just *any* girl can be a supergirl; this category is generally only accessible to white, middle-class girls—who often pay a price for aspiring to such great heights. We followed this discussion with an exploration of the difficulties of being a popular girl and a successful student at the same time and looked at the challenges that this division places on girls to downplay their academic success in order to subscribe to popular femininity. This was far from uncomplicated, and the girls in our study reported intense negotiations that took place around their academic identities, many of them dumbing down, hiding grades, or accentuating popular femininity in order to offset the potentially negative effects of being smart. Boys, too, struggled to manage being smart in relation to popular masculinity, using different tactics, such as being the class clown or playing up an interest in sports. Exploring boys' experiences of academic success helps to shed further light on gender dynamics in the school and the powerful interplay between popular forms of masculinity and femininity as they are held in tension yet support each other.

Post-feminism and neoliberalism provide the backdrop for the smart girl stereotype. According to these ideologies, girls' perceived unbridled success is seen as evidence that girls now live in a gender-neutral world without the need for feminism. To question this mainstream assumption, we asked girls if they had ever experienced sexism, either in relation to their academic success or in general. Most girls first struggled or refused to name gender oppression, opting instead to focus on gender equality and a neoliberal construction of individualism. But in their stories, we heard a number of contradictions to this belief in gender equality, including narratives of teacher favoritism toward boys who clowned around. When we asked about these inconsistencies, some of the girls agreed that they *had* experienced sexism. We also heard from a smaller number of girls who named sexism in their everyday lives from the start.

Complicating the post-feminist narrative even further, some boys made no bones about telling us that they felt teachers favored girls and assumed boys were automatic troublemakers. These contradictory stories highlight the complexity of gender dynamics in schools. Further challenging this simplistic dichotomy, we explored intersections of class and "race" to demonstrate the complexity that diversity brings to the smart girl category. The lack of such context in media and popular psychological accounts is a gross oversight that hides other oppressions while privileging white, middle-class identities as the norm for girls. These diverse narratives poke holes in the dominant story about girls' perceived academic success and boys' perceived failure—an assumed division that holds enormous sway in educational policymaking and common-sense thinking about young people in school. They also poke holes in the broader story that Western girls are living free of inequality in a post-feminist era.

In this final chapter, we turn our attention to two other themes that emerged in our data that offer hopeful glimpses into smart girls' lives and places where possibility for change may be percolating. First, we more deeply explore ways that the girls in our study were contesting popular femininity through microresistances, as many of the stories we have told already illustrate. These small yet potentially influential challenges to dominant gender and other norms shift the landscape of girlhood by subtly expanding who and what a (smart) girl can be.

Second, we return to a topic that we have touched on throughout this book—the importance of school culture in fostering girls' comfort with academic success. Some school settings, while certainly not perfect, seemed to offer smart girls more supportive environments where they felt less encumbered by sexism and where microresistances that challenge popular femininity could flourish. Both supporting girls' microresistances to popular femininity and developing open school cultures are ways that teachers, administrators, and parents might continue to encourage smart girls. We conclude by broadening the discussion of where supports might be found in order to make more space for girls to take up academic success without apprehension.

MICRORESISTANCES TO POPULAR FEMININITY

Within feminist scholarship, there is an established tradition of examining girls' resistance to the rigidity of popular masculinity and popular femininity[2]—the most culturally validated forms of gender. These include, for boys, rugged strength, talent in sports, and toughness, and for girls, thinness, deference to boys, and looking sexy (yet being nonsexual).[3] While much of the research on young people's resistance has pinpointed consciously organized political action, some has concentrated on less obvious microresistances, which are harder to detect.[4] Writing about gender and education in the United Kingdom, Emma Renold and Jessica Ringrose take the latter stance, arguing that we often miss moments of subversion when we focus only on large-scale, more politically organized forms of resistance.[5] Instead, they suggest focusing on the everyday activities of girls to map "significant spaces of girls doing girl differently."[6] They also note how quickly such tiny ruptures can dissipate, which leaves them as brief moments in time rather than sustained forms of social change.[7] It is thus difficult to see how microresistances in girls' everyday lives might work to undermine popular femininity. But Ringrose argues that these minute movements can open up "spaces of possibility" for girls.[8] Spaces of possibility are opened, for instance, when small disruptions of the status quo echo across webs of relationships, such as those between girls, boys, schools, teachers, parents, and media. In chapter 5, we explored the complexities of Flowerpower's life, for example, and her unpopular stance as feminist, vegan, and activist. While she considered herself to be "weird" and said she was ignored by many of her peers, she was implicitly a part of various chains of connection in her school, such as with her small group of friends, her teachers, and those who knew of her. Her politics ripple across this web of relationships, and who knows what the effects may be?

Because we all affect each other in imperceptible ways all the time, new ways of thinking about and "doing" girl become possible through girls' everyday critiques of dominant gender. And while transformation is never a certainty, the potential for change lies in the possibility that these disruptive moments might grow into something bigger.[9] Below, we offer two of many examples from our study to show how the smart girls we interviewed were challenging popular femininity in their everyday lives, making space for new ways of doing (smart) girlhood.

. . .

Sporting a punk aesthetic and a less positive attitude toward academic success than most girls in our study, Tony M. and Tony B. saw themselves as "alternative," "weird," and "different." They refused to participate in a culture of girlhood at their school that was based on wearing mall brand clothing, posing for pictures to post online, and listening to pop music. But their critique of popular femininity also centered on their own unique understanding of being smart. While they did not see academic (as opposed to artistic) success as hugely relevant to their futures, they did see intelligence as an important part of their everyday lives. As Tony M. explained: "In a world where Snooki is a role model, we have to really put ourselves apart [by being smart]." Snooki was a popular personality on the MTV reality show *Jersey Shore* who was known for her fake tan, big hair, and ditzy personality. A party girl who used her body to get what she wanted, Snooki came to represent the stereotype of the Italian Jersey girl, or "guidette," a term she helped to popularize.[10] As Tony B. clarified, "[We want to] be better than that, kind of. 'Cause you don't want to be, like, that one person who, like, wears club wear to school! [...] Yeah ... *those* pumps at *our* high school!" Laughing, Tony M. added, "We have four floors, come on!" Then, in a more serious tone, she continued, "Like you don't want to fall into that 'average' category, you know, with everyone else, and, like, there is, like, that media portrayal of women. I don't even think that's necessarily so strong anymore, but the whole, you know, 'dumb blond,' type, like, a lady goofing around being bubbly, like, it's not something that I'd want to be."

Snooki represented a kind of femininity that Tony M. and Tony B. would never want to emulate—one that was silly, uncritical, and unintelligent. She was an example of how women dumb themselves down in popular culture; being ditzy garnered her attention not only from men on the show but also from viewers watching at home, earning her the distinction of being the most popular personality on *Jersey Shore*.[11] As a way of signaling their distaste for Snooki's performance of popular femininity, Tony M. and Tony B. positioned themselves against her unflattering persona, noting that being smart set them "apart" from girls like Snooki, who were "average" and "like everybody else." Their criticism of popular femininity thus included a negative view of Snooki's (working-class, ethnic) hyper-sexualized femininity.¹² But it also opened up a powerful critique of popular culture, where they saw frequent sexist representations that unfairly and gratuitously compartmentalized young women as dumb. While Tony M. was quick to note that this kind of negative portrayal may "not be so strong anymore," suggesting that popular culture is becoming less sexist, both girls understood that being smart was a powerful way of resisting the popular femininity of celebrity culture.

Continuing this critique later in the interview, Tony M. explained that the curvaceous 1950s pin up model Betty Paige was a much better role model than any of the über thin women in celebrity culture today. For Tony M., there was "nothing sexy about the anorexia thing." Tony B. added, "Yeah, I feel like now it's all big boobs, butt, you know, you've got to have all that kind of thing to be [perfect]." Getting angry, Tony M. pushed the point further: "It's like an unachievable idea of perfection from, like, the Photoshop, and, like, the celebrities, the way they're done up and everything. Like, none of it's real! […] Not *one* person can pull that off." She was also angry that boys were pressured to be "masculine and muscle-y types." Acknowledging that they were not into this particular look at all, Tony M. noted, "There are tons of girls who are, like, 'Oh, look at their rippling abs; I can't handle it!' It's not my variety of thing. […] [*laughs*] Meathead types."

Gesturing toward heavily policed gender norms, Tony M. and Tony B. challenged the media's focus on "perfection" that dominates not just popular culture but also their school's culture. Their anger over the admiration of unrealistic physiques extended to boys and girls, whom they felt were both negatively affected by limited body ideals, which maintain that girls must be thin and have "big boobs" and boys must be ripped and have "greased muscles." Tony M. positioned herself against not only the girls who find popular masculinity attractive but also the boys who embody it, calling them "meathead types," which conjures up images of young men who are into bodybuilding but struggle to carry on a conversation. The stance of Tony M. and Tony B. suggests that popular gender performances frequently portrayed in celebrity culture leave little room for valuing intelligence. Yet the two girls considered being unintelligent a highly unattractive characteristic.

While we do not interpret Tony M.'s and Tony B.'s critiques of popular masculinity and femininity as part of large-scale, collective resistance, we do view these challenges as opening up spaces of possibility for girls and others who either know Tony M. and Tony B. peripherally or are part of their social world. While Tony M. and Tony B. were outliers who existed on the social borders, they were also enmeshed in their school's culture, their own localized social world, and the broader working-class community in which they lived. These webs of relationships may continue to ripple with the critiques that Tony M. and Tony B. lived daily. While we cannot be sure of any lasting impact, we can gesture toward their strong disruption of dominant gender norms as an example of how "doing girl" can be done differently.

. . .

While Tony M. and Tony B. saw being smart as a way to guard against being perceived as "average" and "like everyone else" who was into celebrity culture, McLovin used to hide her academic abilities so that she would be left alone. "In grade six, it was kind of, like, 'You're smart! Ohhh, okay, the rest of us are smart, but you're *smaaaart*, so you must be some genius nerd or something.' [But] that was completely different from what I was. I was interested in the arts and sports and stuff." Her friends pigeonholed her as extraordinarily intelligent and were constantly asking for answers, which she found stressful. "If I got it wrong," she told us, "it was, like, 'Oh my gosh, you don't have the answer?' [...] I was, like, 'Back off! I love you guys, but I'm not your dictionary!'" So McLovin worked at letting her marks fall to around 60 percent.

McLovin did not want to be known for just one thing, but she was also up against the common assumption that sports and intelligence are distinct from one another. As she put it, "It was, like, 'McLovin is the smart one and not the athlete one,' or ...'" Her sister Caramel jumped in, "the Bear!" Putting her hand to her brow, McLovin moaned, "The Bear! Oh my God, I can't get rid of that one either." When McLovin stopped focusing on academics, she put all of her energy into being athletic—a tactic we discussed in relation to the boys, who used sports to mitigate their academic identities. As her grades fell, her athletic prowess increased, earning her a nickname that stuck throughout elementary school and into high school: the Bear. She acquired this moniker in seventh grade—almost a year after she started dumbing down—when a teacher gave her the nickname in front of the class. Pretending to be her teacher, McLovin imitated the remark: "'Not everyone is shaped the same way. Take McLovin, for example, she's a bear! She could pound half of you guys!'"

Initially, being the Bear brought McLovin a cachet that academic success never did. Her teacher called her a bear because she was tough, aggressive, and muscular. McLovin's classmates admired her for her strength, and being the Bear also enabled her to avoid the trappings of popular femininity. Instead, she got to be the boss—in charge, assertive, and dominant. No one pushed McLovin around, and when they did, she fought back. When Caramel was bullied for being a teacher's pet, McLovin defended her. With admiration in her voice, Caramel turned to her sister in their wood-paneled basement and exclaimed, "Actually, you beat them up!" McLovin nodded. "I didn't take anything from anybody," she explained. "The first time somebody tried to start a fight with me, I didn't want to, and he punched me, and I went home with a bleeding nose, and I was, like, 'Whatever, just ignore it.' [...] The second day he tried to fight me, I sent him home [all bruised up] [...], and no one ever messed with me since."

Yet McLovin's pride at being the Bear was not without ambivalence. Later in the interview, she explained that, over that summer, her goal was to lose muscle mass to trim down. When Shauna asked why, McLovin explained that, when her teacher had called her a bear, she started to feel done with being muscular. She expressed anger about the comment, and her pride in being strong took a back seat: "Really? It was supposed to be a compliment, but come on! I didn't say anything [about it], but it was my nickname for a long time." Sympathizing, Caramel continued to praise her sister's strength: "She can knock out all the guys!" Her teacher similarly thought McLovin's strength was something to brag about, but he paradoxically also sometimes suggested that girls were weaker than boys, which made McLovin feel uneasy about the way he positioned her as a bear. Was it a compliment or an insult? Was she being praised for her power and strength or ridiculed for her lack of typically feminine traits? She tried to put her finger on the tension: "The ironic thing was he was extraordinarily ... not *sexist*, but he would say girls can't be strong." "So that's *not* sexist?" Shauna asked. "It *is*," McLovin sighed. "He is kind of old, so it was okay to think that way. I wouldn't say he is sexist because of that, he doesn't think girls are lower [than boys]."

McLovin's ambivalent feelings toward being the Bear and being "the smart girl" shifted yet again when she entered high school. When she started the French immersion program at Blue Ridge, it was clear that being smart was valued in this new context. "I started getting back into the whole smart stuff," she told Shauna. "I noticed there were other smart people, and I was able to compare with them, and it made it a lot easier." The academic culture of the school meant that being smart was respected. Free from the pressure she felt in elementary school, McLovin worked to balance her academic side with her athletic side, and it felt mostly comfortable. At Blue Ridge, she was not known as *the* smart girl because there were lots of smart girls around her, so she could ace her tests and place high in her classes without attracting undo attention to herself and without the expectation that she had to help her friends. While athletics had always offered McLovin a way to fit in, she came to see the advantages of being smart as well, as both of these identities positioned her as strong, confident, and capable.

Proudly, she explained to Shauna that, in high school, she was still known as the Bear: "I'm the Bear because I'm the fastest runner on my rowing team and my basketball team. I can shoot from behind the half line." McLovin explained the shift in her thinking: "I [used to] think of [a bear as] a big scary animal that will eat you in the middle of the night." After a moment's pause, she continued, this time more positively: "I am a bit stronger than an average girl. It's in my character, and I have grown to like it. I *own* that name!" McLovin once again took up the Bear as a symbol of pride. The name challenged assumptions about girls' weakness and second-rate abilities at sports, and by being the Bear, McLovin could smash such stereotypes. The Bear had become more than a nickname—it had become a lived experience of both challenging popular femininity and struggling to fit in as a smart, strong girl.

But in keeping with the pressing demands of popular femininity, McLovin still expressed concern about being "too" muscular. At the end of her second interview, she said, "For me, I'm happy with my body, but you know, if I could lose ten pounds, I'd be completely happy. I weigh 130 pounds, but you know, that's fine because I'm muscle. At the same time, it'd be kind of cool to be, like, 'Yeah, I weigh 120.' Which is kind of funny when I can carry my boyfriend, like, all over. He can hardly carry me from, like, around the block. *He's* a pretty big bear actually. He's the strongest rower on the guy's team!"

McLovin's story of her shifting feelings about being the Bear highlights the intricacies of gender resistance in a post-feminist culture. While she took great pride in her athletic abilities and powerhouse strength, she also lamented her larger size—even though she was all muscle. While her boyfriend *could* be "the Bear," suggesting that she appreciated his ability to embody popular masculinity, McLovin was also pleased that she could carry him without any trouble, while he could barely carry her. And although she was angry with her teacher for assuming that girls are weaker than boys, McLovin experienced an ego boost when, ironically, he called her a bear because she was stronger than anyone else in the class. Throughout this complex exchange, McLovin wrestled with her contradictory desires to be smart *and* athletic, feminine *and* masculine, thin *and* fierce, and pretty *and* powerful. This story thus showcases the complexity of both participating in and resisting popular femininity. Spaces of possibility emerged around McLovin's refusal to "do girl" in an expected fashion, but these microresistances also dissipated in the face of pressures for girls to look and act a certain way. Caught between post-feminism and feminism, McLovin's challenge to popular femininity was both visibly on display and quietly lamented.

. . . .

While gender norms may still prevail over such microresistances, spaces of possibility can also open up across the webs of relationships in which girls like McLovin are interwoven. A significant component in girls' lives is school, which is not only a physical environment in which to "do girl" but also a particularly powerful location for the learning and policing of gender norms.[13] During our study, we were repeatedly made aware that there is no ideal setting for girls—no perfect refuge where they did not have to struggle in one way or another with the complexities of being a smart girl. But we also came to understand that some conditions make it easier than others for girls to challenge the status quo, making it possible for microresistances to grow into something more palpable. In schools where being smart was considered cool—or was at least not seen as a social catastrophe—concerns over academic identities were minimized. Girls reported feeling more comfortable in these schools, as they were less concerned with living up to a particular feminine ideal. Being popular was not as much of a priority as having a small group of loyal friends. We thus came to see school culture as an essential component for supporting girls' academic success and increasing spaces of possibility where girls might begin to challenge popular femininity while also enjoying their academic success.[14]

Below, we offer three examples of schools that, for various reasons, seemed to make being a smart girl easier. Each context is different, though similar threads run through the girls' narratives:

all three schools were said to have amazing teachers who cared deeply about their students; each occupied a unique niche in Secord that invoked pride in the student body; and all had fairly large student populations that were diverse culturally, economically, or both. While there were no guarantees, these contexts seemed to allow many girls in our study the space to escape the rigid confines of popular femininity.

ROOT FOR THE UNDERDOG: CENTRAL SECONDARY

Central Secondary was an inner-city school with a reputation for gangs, drugs, and dropouts. It was often considered a "last chance" high school, and students at Central felt the burden of their school's low academic and social standing in Secord. Margot and Janey, sisters who attended Central, were well aware of what other people thought. But Janey explained that Central's reputation was actually "the complete opposite" of how she experienced the school, and as a school leader, she was very vocal about this. "People think it's a really violent, ghetto school, where there are problem kids. *Every* school has problem kids, and Central has a bad rep, but people don't give it a chance. A lot of people that switch [to Central] from Blue Ridge say they would never want to go back. Central is not really a school; everyone knows each other, and the teachers are just like family."

Though Janey saw her school as full of warmth and kindness, from the outside, the school seemed full of troubled kids without promising futures. For the most part, however, the students loved their school and named the laid-back attitude of the diverse student body and teachers as the reason they thought their school was the best in the city—even better than schools in affluent neighborhoods. As Margot explained, "I think, at our school, since there are so many different races and stuff, no one really stereotypes." Janey continued: "Everyone is friends with everyone, there's no bullying or anything. It doesn't matter what color you are or where you come from, people accept you." While it is easy to dismiss this view of Central as overly utopian, Tony M. and Tony B. gave a similar account, telling Andrea that Central offered room for diverse identities in a way that other schools did not. It was this setting that helped Tony M. and Tony B. comfortably push back against popular femininity. Tony M. proudly explained that Central was "not really judgmental. [...] I've noticed everyone is pretty laid back about certain things, and, like, there's no one big group of, like, these girls, like, probably terrible." "Mean girls!" Tony B. clarified, referring to the type of girls showcased in the popular 2004 film of that name. Tony M. affirmed, "Mean girls, yeah, that's a good example [...], because there isn't that specific group of people who just like command the school. Like, we all kind of exist."

This positive assessment also extended to teachers, who were viewed by Margot and Janey as caring and friendly. "Yeah," Janey described, "sometimes it's, like, [they're] not even teachers. It's like good friends you are talking to. Sometimes I'll just go say 'hey' to a teacher and have a conversation. It's like they don't judge you. If you need advice or anything, you always feel like you can go to them." Margot explained that, if you had a reputation for being smart and you needed a little more time with your homework, a teacher might say, "It's okay, I know you are working hard, so if you need another day, I'll give you another day." Janey added, "And [the teachers] will help you get there. It's not like, 'If you don't do well, then too bad.' It's like, 'How can we help you fix this?' They are really great teachers."

Awareness of their school's socioeconomic status was a point of pride inside Central's old and discolored walls. In the face of criticism, the students saw their school as streetwise and caring. The negative reputation that proliferated outside of Central fostered an inside culture of acceptance where anything was possible.[15] The supportive teachers understood the demographics of the school and tried to build connections by talking to students on their own terms and listening wherever and whenever they could. It was not that Central focused on high achievement as its defining characteristic (as Blue Ridge did)—it was that the overall feel of the school was one of tolerance and acceptance, including of girls who happened to be smart.[16]

A VERY ACADEMIC SCHOOL: BLUE RIDGE HIGH

If Central had the worst reputation in Secord, Blue Ridge had the best. As Agnes said, "I'm pretty proud [of our school]. We have the music program, football is good, and the engineering club is good. We are well rounded." While we learned that Blue Ridge also had a reputation for being snobby, overall, the girls we spoke with who went there were less likely to mention girls' looks and bodies as key to being popular, less likely to mention girls who dumbed down in order to be noticed by boys, more likely to take pride in their academic success, and more likely to suggest that being smart is cool. As Elizabeth told Shauna, "It is a *very* academic school, so it's not a bad thing to be smart." Tellingly, we drew far more participants for our study from Blue Ridge than from any other school in the area.

With its mix of French immersion and English programs, advanced academic and applied courses, music programing, and diverse clubs, Blue Ridge seemed to offer girls multiple avenues to academic success. The competition between the French and English programs did create a hierarchy where girls in French were seen as smarter (and snobbier) than girls in English, but overall, most of the girls we interviewed found Blue Ridge to be lacking in overtly ostracizing cliques. Jenny noted that, while other schools struggled with divisions between more and less popular girls, "I was thinking, like, our school doesn't really have that because there are so many people, and not everyone will look up to the same people." Agreeing, Agnes added: "It's so mixed together you can't tell. There can be, like, a huge group of popular kids and a huge group of not popular kids, but in between there's a huge mix." "Yeah," Jenny laughed, "There's so many people I don't even know in my grade!"

Blue Ridge boasted a popular engineering club, to which a number of our participants belonged, including best friends Jenny-Po, Basil, Sara, Jacqueline, and Cindy.[17] While not the most popular girls in their ninth grade class (they said they were "in the middle"), they felt comfortable with their small friendship group of six or seven girls and with their unbelievably high marks. Jenny-Po's overall average was a whopping 95 percent, though, as high as it was, she confessed to Shauna that she had a secret rivalry with Cindy, who had the highest average in the ninth grade French immersion program: "It's 97 percent! It makes me upset [*laughs*]." But this friendly competition was part of what enabled Jenny-Po to feel so comfortable with her academic success. She never felt embarrassed about doing well because, as she put it, "I'm not [seen as] that smart around my friends [...]. We are all the same." Basil, too, thought the idea of being embarrassed over one's smartness was "not an intelligent thing to think; it's kind of a I-know-a-lot-of-things-so-that's-bad thing, [but] I never found [being smart], like, a hindrance to me at all."

Basil and Sara had similar averages, hovering around 94 percent. Both girls not only took pride in doing well but also truly enjoyed the accolades it brought them. It was essential to Basil to get high grades because, "It makes you feel special and important in a way, receiving awards, things like that. [...] I honestly cannot think of anything in my life that, if I hadn't been smart, that would have happened." Pausing for a moment to reflect on Basil's statement, Sara added: "I am so thankful that I'm smart. I've never been, like, 'Ah, I can't believe I'm smart!' I'm, like, 'Yes, I'm smart!'" Laughing, Basil was quick to concur, "Yeah, I'm, like, 'Yes, I got this, I did this!'"

All five girls were devoted to the engineering club, which was a major after-school commitment of seven or more hours a week. Though the club could have made the girls targets for nerd bashing elsewhere, the academic culture at Blue Ridge made being smart cool, even for girls passionate about STEM fields, which are generally characterized as male oriented.[18] Basil explained, "There's a certain amount of respect, actually. We have been to the championships; we are really good. It's the same as if a sports team went to [the finals] or something." Blue Ridge offered these five girls space for the expression of academic success because it was big enough to offer a little something for everyone and because its culture signified high achievement as a good thing that was admired rather than scorned. It was in this context that these friends flourished as smart girl engineers. Their involvement in the engineering club also offers another example of microresistance to popular femininity: while their participation in the club was not a risk to their social status, their orientation to this intellectual pursuit rippled across webs of relationships and generated recognition and acceptance of "doing girl" differently.

These stories of social comfort are sharply juxtaposed to the stories in chapter 5 of girls who felt that Blue Ridge was an exclusionary environment in relation to class-based privilege. But for Jenny-Po, Cindy, Jacqueline, Basil, and Sara, Blue Ridge was quite the opposite. Its culture of intellectualism meant they could participate in the engineering club without fear of nerd bashing, strive for sky-high grades without needing to hide their pride, and disregard popular femininity as a direct link to acceptance because there were other avenues for social success. Such freedoms were not always possible at other schools, or even at Blue Ridge, depending on whom you asked. But more often than not, Blue Ridge was seen as a relative haven for academically successful girls because being smart was a part of the school's high-achieving culture.

BAND GEEKS RULE: EMILY CARR

Emily Carr was known for being artsy. Located in the south end of Secord, the school drew in anyone seriously interested in drama or music. Though a public school, it had the feel of a fine arts institution, where things like the school play dominated students' lives for weeks on end. Brooke, Laney, and Jamila were pretty enthusiastic about their school's positive attributes. When, during a lunchtime group interview, Shauna asked them what Emily Carr was known for, they stopped eating and started speaking over each other in excitement. Brooke managed to be heard above the others: "Well, they are really known for their musicals. Every other year they do a big musical, and, like, a lot of the community comes out to support it. And, uh, our bands and choirs have competed and won and played all over the place!" During rehearsals for the musical, everything aside from theatrical preparations ground to a halt. More or less everyone was involved in some way. Jamila explained, "Like, with the show, it's either that you're in the band or you're in the show or you're doing tech for it or your doing stage for it. Like, everyone—" Brooke interrupted to add, "Or hair or makeup [...]! So there's always some way to get involved with it."

Carr's artsy status was further amplified by its reputation for having a unique or alternative student body. "I think, like, people from other high schools look at us like the *weird* school," Brooke explained. Jamila and Laney nodded vigorously. Jamila added, "I think it's because we all tolerate each other." "Yeah," Brooke agreed. "Like, we have different groups, like, every school has groups. Like, there's the athletes, the music kids, the tech kids, there's all different groups, but all of them kind of respect each other. [...] Like, everyone just accepts that we're all different and that everybody can get along." Given this description, Shauna wondered what made the school so "weird." Brooke was quick to answer: "Like, [...] we don't have a football team, and our cheerleaders, are like—" Jamila, laughing, interrupted: "Not the best cheerleaders!" Brooke continued, "It's just not like a school where the football [players] and the cheerleaders are at the top. Like, that's not how it is. And the band geeks aren't at the bottom. Like there's no—" Jamila, laughing again, interjected, "It's, like, we actually sometimes take pride in being a band geek. Like, we'll go around and be like, 'Oh, I'm a band geek. Yeah!' It's not a bad thing!" In fact, geek pride was a huge part of Carr's alterative status, marking them as a very different kind of school than ones where the pathway to popularity was determined by just the opposite. Brooke explained, "At our school, they don't really have that filter of, like, 'I've gotta pretend to be, you know, to be, like, cool.' [...] They're just always, like, 'Ahhhh!!!'

[*screams with excitement*]." "Yeah," Laney enthused, "we'll have things at our school, and we'll look at each other and go, 'Only at Carr … would this happen!' Like, you see things that don't phase you anymore, because you get so used to it." Prompted by Shauna to offer an example of these things, Laney continued, "Well, people will just break out into song. And, be, like—" Jamila finished her sentence, "In four-part harmonies, you know?"

The girls also explained that their school was "weird" because of its predominantly female population—Carr's student body was about two-thirds girls.[19] Shauna asked if having so few boys affected how girls at Carr engaged with their academic work. Jamila felt that it definitely did, "Because […] there's not as much of a distraction, I guess. Also, because, it sounds funny, but there are, uh, like, there's a number of gay boys at the school, too. So, I think that also plays a part, too, because it's just one more person that you don't have to worry about, I guess, and the fact that you don't have to impress them or anything like that." Brooke drew in a big breath and then added, "A lot of girls think they have to act a certain way around guys. And, I'm not sure, like, how it started, how girls think, you know, they can't be smart, they can't show their intellectual side around guys, so they try to dumb themselves down. Um, but, because at our school there's so few guys, they don't really have to worry about that kind of, like, pressure, you know? They can just be, you know, they can live up to their full, uh, intellectual potential. [*pause*] That sounds smart! I wasn't trying to!" Everyone at the table laughed. But Jamila and Brooke had offered powerful critiques. In their opinion, it was easier to escape popular femininity when there were fewer boys to impress. As a form of microresistance, it is easy to miss such a challenge to gender norms, but this particular school context allowed the girls an opportunity to reflect on why their school felt so different—and this opened up spaces of possibility for further insight and critique.

The example of Emily Carr suggests that acceptance of a broader range of gender and sexuality performances allows smart girls to thrive without fear of ridicule or the need to hide. The artistic focus of Carr may have also opened up possibilities for different kinds of skills to shine, risk-taking to be valued, and the disruption of gender norms to be accepted.[20] At Emily Carr, just as at Blue Ridge, popular femininity was not the only way to be a successful girl, nor did it sit in opposition to being a successful student. In her study of masculinity in three elementary schools in the United Kingdom, Emma Renold found similar results.[21] While popular masculinity was the most prevalent way to be a boy, one school emphasized academics over sports, opening up opportunities for less macho forms of masculinity. Renold thus advocates for schools where different kinds of masculinities and femininities are made available, as she believes that these environments increase the number of identities that are accepted for both boys and girls. Adding to this argument, our study suggests that one of the most significant factors in encouraging girls' academic success, as well as increasing what counts as normal for girls more generally, is a school culture that actively promotes (and not merely tolerates) multiple performances of gender and sexuality. In such a culture, it seems possible for girls to push the boundaries of girlhood, helping to change who and what a smart girl can be.

SUPPORTING ACADEMIC SUCCESS, SUPPORTING GIRLS

There were many points in our interviews where girls struggled with the expectations of popular femininity, the mixed demands of peer culture, the intersections and contexts of their lives, and their sense of self as strong and smart. We encountered numerous instances where girls resisted, contested, negotiated, and compromised as they confronted a messy social world that involved both the acknowledgment and the denial of gender inequality; a celebration of smartness alongside a warning that you should not be *too* smart; and a pressure to get along juxtaposed with evaluations and judgments based on how social you are, what fashions you wear, how much you study, and how much money you have.[22] Having discussed ways that certain schools seemed to create space for girls' academic success, we end this book with some concluding thoughts on how we might better support girls.

The young people we talked with did not have easy access to a language of analysis and change. Powerful terms like "sexism" and "racism" seemed difficult for many of them to accept or use, and they would frequently default to attributing any failures or problems they experienced to their own and others' individual choices and responsibilities rather than considering structural inequalities that shaped their lives. Talking about these issues in schools and beyond opens up greater opportunities for girls to recognize such disparities, embrace a critical voice, and engage with allies who might support that voice in becoming louder. We thus agree with the growing number of advocates who suggest teaching feminism and gender studies in schools,[23] which offers girls and boys a language of analysis and change that they can use to understand the challenges they face and to speak back to sexism and rigid gender norms that undermine diversity (including being smart). As we have illustrated, these gendered analyses also need to consider other forms of inequality embedded in girls' lives that powerfully shape their encounters with peer and school cultures, such as those based on "race" and class.

Similarly, we need to attend to the injuries of gendering education—from academic performance to specific subjects—as if certain forms of schoolwork are only relevant to girls or boys. When girls are dumbing down in order to be attractive to boys and boys feel that it is "unmanly" to study, we have a problem. As our discussion of school culture helps to demonstrate, it is important to embrace a breadth of acceptable possibilities for what it means to be a boy or a girl. When the possibilities of what being normal looks like are multiplied, more girls and boys can exist comfortably within peer culture rather than sitting on its periphery, or further afield, experiencing alienation and isolation.

To this end, we also make a renewed call for greater care in making broad statements—in media outlets, academic research, schools, and families—about girls and boys in school. It is certainly imperative that gender be a key part of analyses of young people's lives, as it has been in this book, but not as a singular, unanalyzed, and decontextualized variable. For example, analyses of academic success and other school-based experiences need to move beyond looking at exam results and admittance statistics simply through the variable of gender. One way to shift out of this superficial view is to focus on broader contexts that link schools and young people to wider ranges of culture and social dynamics, including the ongoing relevance of sexism and other oppressions. It is crucial to consider intersections of identity, such as gender, "race," class, sexuality, age, religion, and nationhood, and the privileges and disadvantages that cut across these categories. Interpretations of girls' experiences in school need to recognize the influence of post-feminism on girls' and boys' understandings of individualized, rather than collective, problems. In this book, we have explored how we might begin to think outside of the neoliberal self, which has been made popular by the girl power narrative. We have looked to an understanding of girlhood and academic success that considers both the unique texture of girls' lives and the crucial backdrops that shape those lives.

Peer groups also emerged as powerful systems of support for girls, who—no matter how hard things got socially—were sometimes able to rely on friends to help them concentrate on what really mattered to them. Jenny-Po, Basil, Sara, Jacqueline, and Cindy offer a strong example of the power of the peer group to create strength in numbers. While not terribly popular or noticed by boys, these STEM-focused girls operated with relative comfort at Blue Ridge because they did not need to look outside of their group of friends to feel included. They were content with one another's approval and, therefore, could push one another to greater heights. Within their small gang of friends, being as smart as possible was the most important thing—and no one else made them feel otherwise, likely in part because they did not wonder what other people thought about them.

And, of course, the influence of the family emerged as a significant node of support for girls' academic success. While some girls, like Flowerpower, experienced limited parental encouragement, most of the girls in our study spoke of the deep investment of at least one parent—someone who championed them to study and excel. As we have discussed throughout this book, parental support is impacted by class-based cultures, where middle- and upper-middle-class parents are often able to give more time, offer social connections or capital, and afford extras (such as tutoring, class trips, foreign exchanges, the right clothing, and devices). This established link between economic success and high achievement might explain why so many of our participants came from financially secure families in an area that is predominantly blue-collar. But even where there were few economic resources, family support seemed a crucial link to a girl's ability to weather any storm and feel resilient in her stance to pursue high grades—especially if this pursuit came at the expense of popularity and social comfort.

It *is* cool to be a smart girl in the West today. At least we think so after spending time with the amazing girls we met over the course of our study. And perhaps a number of our participants would agree. But for many, the risks of being a smart girl were challenging. Girls are not the hands-down winners in education that they are purported to be. They struggle in ways that do not make for good headlines and, quite simply, cannot be measured by statistics. The only way to know about such struggles is to ask girls to tell their stories and, importantly, to locate these stories within historical, social, and cultural contexts. It is only through this contextual reading and telling that we might begin to link together post-feminism, neoliberalism, the stress of trying to be a supergirl, the intensive social negotiations of gender expectations and inequalities, the power of "race" and class in relation to academic success, ambivalently felt moments of feminism, and those moments of joy and pride that continuously flow through the lives of smart girls. Crucially, while the stories girls tell—like all of our stories—will be shot through with inconsistencies, this messiness needs to be retained so that the complexity of girls' lives can be reckoned with rather than denied or ignored.

Lastly, we must be careful not to overlook the hard-to-detect microresistances which girls live every day simply by being smart—a social position that is often at loggerheads with popularity and heterosexual desirability. To this end, smart girls are already participating in shifting the landscape of girlhood toward positive social transformation. And in telling intricate stories about smart girls, we—adults, teachers, journalists, academics, feminists—can help shift this landscape, too.

Study Participants

Participants, in order they were interviewed	Age at time of first interview	School at time of first interview[1]	Class[2]	"Race"[3]	Religion[4]	Style of interview
			Girls			
Candace	16	Central High	Upper-middle	White	Not religious	Group of three
Hayden	15	St. Hilda's Catholic Secondary	Upper-middle	White	n/a	Group of three
Magna	16	Blue Ridge High	Upper-middle	White	n/a	Group of three
Laney	17	Emily Carr High	Lower-middle	White	n/a	Group of three
Brooke	17	Emily Carr High	Lower-middle	White	Christian	Group of three
Jamila	17	Emily Carr High	Settled working	Middle Eastern	Christian	Group of three
Caramel	15	Blue Ridge High	Middle	White	n/a	Pair
McLovin	15	Blue Ridge High	Middle	White	n/a	Pair
Erin	12	King Public School	Lower-middle	White	n/a	Solo
Margot	17	Central High	Middle	White	n/a	Pair
Janey	16	Central High	Middle	White	n/a	Pair
Wren	14	Agatha Benchley Public School	Lower-middle	White	n/a	Solo
Ella	12	Agatha Benchley Public School	Lower-middle	White	n/a	Solo
Virginia	16	Blue Ridge High	Middle	White	n/a	Solo
Luna	14	St. Mary's Catholic High	Settled working	White	Catholic	Pair
Haley	14	St. Mary's Catholic High	Lower-middle	White	Catholic	Pair
Yasmin	13	Academy House	Upper-middle	South Asian	Hindu, not central	Solo

Name	Age	School	Class	Race	Religion	Type
Christy	14	Bethany High	Settled working	White	Christian	Solo
Olivia	13	St. Luke Catholic Elementary	Upper-middle	White	Catholic, not central	Solo
Julia	16	Small Town High	Upper-middle	White	Not religious	Pair
Abbey	12	Orchard Park Public School	Upper-middle	White	Not religious	Pair
Tony M.	17	Central High	Precarious working	White	n/a	Pair
Tony B.	16	Central High	Settled working	White	n/a	Pair
Anna	14	St. Mary's Catholic High	Lower-middle	White	Not religious	Solo
Isabell	15	Lester B. Pearson High	Lower-middle	White	Catholic	Pair
Kaitlyn	15	Blue Ridge High	Middle	White	n/a	Pair
Elizabeth	14	Blue Ridge High	Middle	White	n/a	Solo
Audrey	14	St. Mary's Catholic High	Middle	White	Catholic	Group of three
Emma	14	St. Mary's Catholic High	Lower-middle	White	Catholic	Group of three
Mauve	15	St. Mary's Catholic High	Lower-middle	White	Catholic	Group of three
Sully	14	Blue Ridge High	Middle	White	Not religious	Pair
Joanne	14	Blue Ridge High	Upper-middle	East Asian	Christian, not central	Pair
Rory	13	Pinecrest Public School	Settled working	White	Christian	Solo
Jenny	15	Blue Ridge High	Middle	White	n/a	Pair
Agnes	15	Blue Ridge High	Upper-middle	South Asian	n/a	Pair
Jenny-Po	15	Blue Ridge High	Upper-middle	East Asian	Atheist	Solo
Maggie	12	Agatha Benchley Public School	Middle	White	n/a	Pair
Darlene	14	Blue Ridge High	Middle	White	n/a	Pair

(continued)

Participants, in order they were interviewed	Age at time of first interview[1]	School at time of first interview[1]	Class[2]	"Race"[3]	Religion[4]	Style of interview
			Girls (continued)			
Jordan	12	St. Teresa Catholic Elementary	Lower-middle	White	Catholic, not central	Solo
Chanel	15	Emily Carr High	Settled working	Black	Not religious	Solo
Smartypants	17	Bethany High	Settled working	Southeast Asian	Mormon	Solo
Nicole	12	Pinecrest Public School	Precarious working	Southeast Asian	Mormon	Solo
Allie	12	Orchard Park Public School	Middle	White	Christian	Solo
Chuchos	15	Blue Ridge High	Upper-middle	White	Jewish	Solo
Marie	13	Religious Private School	Settled working	White	Dutch Reform	Pair
Selena	13	Religious Private School	Settled working	White	Dutch Reform	Pair
Jacqueline	15	Blue Ridge High	Upper-middle	East Asian	Christian	Pair
Cindy	15	Blue Ridge High	Middle	East Asian	Christian	Pair
Celeste	14	Pinecrest Public School	Middle	White	n/a	Solo
Michelle	14	Emily Carr High	Lower-middle	White	n/a	Solo
Bella	14	Academy House	Upper-middle	White (grew up overseas)	n/a	Solo
Lisa	15	Academy House	Upper-middle	White	n/a	Solo
Sarah	15	Blue Ridge High	Middle	White	Not religious	Solo
Sara	15	Blue Ridge High	Middle	Part South Asian	n/a	Pair
Basil	15	Blue Ridge High	Upper-middle	White	Jewish	Pair

Flowerpower	18	Blue Ridge	Precarious working	Southeast Asian		n/a	Solo
Quinn	13	St. Helen's Catholic Elementary	Lower-middle		White	Catholic	Pair
Boys							
John	14	Sunnyside High	Middle		White	n/a	Solo
Kurt	15	St. Bernice's Catholic Secondary	Lower-middle		White	Catholic, not central	Solo
Semai	15	Lord Bing High	Settled working		White	Christian	Solo
Ben	14	Blue Ridge High	Middle		White	n/a	Pair
Samual	14	Blue Ridge High	Middle		White	n/a	Pair
Jason	15	St. Mary's High	Middle		White	Catholic	Pair
Tim	16	St. Mary's High	Middle		White	n/a	Pair
Kevin	13	Father Francis Catholic Elementary School	Upper-middle		White	Atheist/agnostic	Solo
Walrus	15	Blue Ridge High	Precarious working	Southeast Asian		Mormon	Solo
Noah	14	Orchard View Secondary	Middle		White	Christian	Solo
Lebron	13	Loyalty Heights Public School	Middle		White	Not religious	Pair
Latrell	13	Loyalty Heights Public School	Lower-middle		White	Not religious	Pair
Batman	14	St. Peter's High School	Middle		White	Not religious	Solo

(continued)

Participants, in order they were interviewed	Age at time of first interview [1]	School at time of first interview [1]	Class [2]	"Race" [3]	Religion [4]	Style of interview
			Boys (continued)			
Paul	14	Green Trees High	Settled working	White	Catholic, not practicing	Solo
Donovan	16	Blue Ridge High	Lower-middle	White	n/a	Solo
Louis	13	Pinecrest Public School	Settled working	White	n/a	Solo
Raghav	13	Apple Park Elementary School	Settled working	South Asian	Hindu	Solo

[1] All school names are pseudonyms.

[2] We categorized our participants' class location by drawing on parents' employment and education, neighborhood of residence and kind of house, family configuration (e.g., two parent, single parent), extracurricular opportunities, and comments in interviews regarding class. We thus drew on concrete information about parents' jobs but also on a cultural understanding of class as fluid. Following Julie Bettie (*Women without Class*), we developed gradations of class: precarious working class (households in which parents had precarious or infrequent work, low income, and no benefits); settled working class (households in which parents had jobs with some job security and benefits but low income, e.g., in stable service industry or manual labor); lower-middle class (households in which parents had stable but unionized blue-collar or lower-level white-collar jobs); middle class (usually two-income households in which parents had employment in professional careers that required post-secondary education, e.g., nursing, teaching, or skilled trades; included some small business owners); and upper-middle class (households based in more affluent neighborhoods in which parents were either owners of larger businesses or professionals in fields that required more advanced degrees, e.g., doctors or professors).

[3] In chapter 5, we discuss the constructed and problematic nature of "race," but we also point to some ways that the concept is deployed and experienced. It is for this reason that we list "race" here. Given our critique of the homogenizing nature of the "smart Asian" stereotype, we felt the need to contextualize our participants with Asian backgrounds beyond simply saying they were Asian, which is why we have distinguished between East, South, and Southeast Asian.

[4] At first, we did not systematically collect information about religion, but as it frequently came up in our interviews, we began to ask directly about participants' religious affiliations.

Notes

FOREWORD

1. Legendary Entertainment, "Legendary Acquires Amy Poehler's Smart Girls at the Party Network," Legendary Entertainment press release, October 13, 2014, http://corporate.legendary.com/amy-poehlers-smart-girls.

2. Chris Martins, "Zayn Malik's Own Direction," *Billboard* 128, no. 1 (2016). www.billboard.com/articles/news/cover-story/6835305/zayn-malik-solo-career-one-direction-new-music.

3. Michelle Fine, "Foreword," in *All about the Girl*, ed. Anita Harris (Routledge: New York, 2004), xiii.

4. Robin Ely, Pamela Stone, and Colleen Ammerman, "Rethink What You 'Know' about High-Achieving Women," *Harvard Business Review* 92, no. 12 (December 2014): 101–9.

5. Nalini Joshi, "The Future of Science: Women," address to the National Press Club of Australia, Canberra, Australia, March 30, 2016.

6. Danielle Paquette, "Why Young Women Leave Their Jobs," *Washington Post,* March 28, 2016.

7. Lauren Noël and Christine H. Arscott, *Millennial Women: What Executives Need to Know about Millennial Women* (Lexington, MA:

International Consortium for Executive Development Research, 2016), www.icedr.org/research/documents/15_millennial_women.pdf.

1. ARE GIRLS TAKING OVER THE WORLD?

Epigraph: Christina Hoff Sommers, "The War against Boys," *Atlantic,* May 2000, www.theatlantic.com/magazine/archive/2000/05/the-war-against-boys/304659.

1. All names of participants, local places, and other identifiers have been changed to maintain anonymity. We changed slightly personal details in cases where a participant's activities might reveal their identity. Most girls and boys we interviewed chose their own pseudonyms. A few names were changed to avoid repetition, but wherever possible, we elected to retain the names that participants picked for themselves, however awkward they may be. Readers may find these names—which include Smartypants, McLovin, Jenny-Po, Tony M., Tony B., and Batman—a little distracting, but rather than impose our own smooth reading, we were committed to giving our participants this small form of self-presentation.

2. See the appendix for details about the girls' class backgrounds and how we determined them.

3. In excerpts from interviews, we have used suspension points to indicate when a speaker paused or trailed off and bracketed ellipses to denote omitted material.

4. While the majority of interviews were conducted between 2008 and 2013, a few of our participants were interviewed for a third time in 2015 so that we could hear about their senior year experiences.

5. We understand that the categories "girls" and "boys" can never adequately represent the full experience of all girls or all boys and cannot do justice to the nuances, intersections, and myriad subjectivities that exist for young people in the world. As Sinikka Aapola, Marnina Gonick, and Anita Harris acknowledge, we "struggle with how to talk about girls' [and boys'] lives when doing so also creates the very exclusions we are attempting to redress" (*Young Femininities: Girlhood, Power, and Social Change* [New York: Palgrave, 2005], 3). We

thus wish to recognize both the impossibilities inherent in any book that claims to be about girls or boys and the necessity of continuing to write about their experiences in order to complicate overly simplistic stories that generally circulate. In so doing, it is our hope that girls and boys are talked about in interesting, varying, and contradictory ways that proliferate over time to challenge universalizing discourses.

6. Daniel J. Kindlon, *Alpha Girls: Understanding the New American Girl and How She is Changing the World* (Emmaus, PA: Rodale Books, 2006).

7. Sara Rimer, "For Girls, It's Be Yourself, and Be Perfect, Too," *New York Times,* April 1, 2007, www.nytimes.com/2007/04/01/education /01girls.html.

8. Susannah Meadows and Mary Carmichael, "Meet the GAMMA Girls," *Newsweek,* June 3, 2002, 44–51; Laura Sessions Stepp, "Alpha Girls in Middle School: Learning to Handle the ABCs of Power," *Washington Post,* February 23, 2002, C1.

9. Laksmi Chaundry, "The Supergirl Syndrome," *Nation,* May 1, 2007, www.thenation.com/article/supergirl-syndrome.

10. Thomas A. DiPrete and Claudia Buchmann, *The Rise of Women: The Growing Gender Gap in Education and What It Means for American Schools* (New York: Russell Sage Foundation, 2013); Kay Hymowitz, *Manning Up: How the Rise of Women Has Turned Men into Boys* (New York: Basic Books, 2012); Kindlon, *Alpha Girls.*

11. Michelle Conlin, "The New Gender Gap: From Kindergarten to Grad School, Boys Are Becoming the Second Sex," *BusinessWeek,* May 25, 2003, www.bloomberg.com/bw/stories/2003-05-25/the-new-gender-gap; Lorenzo Esters and Richard Whitmire, "Where the Boys Aren't: Obama Must Attack the Gender Gap in Schooling," *Daily News,* May 16, 2010, www.nydailynews.com/opinion/boys-aren-college-obama-attack-gender-gap-schooling-article-1.449738.

12. Alice-Azania Jarvis, "The New Girl Power: Why We're Living in a Young Woman's World," *Independent,* September 9, 2010, www .independent.co.uk/voices/commentators/the-new-girl-power-why-were-living-in-a-young-womans-world-2074042.html; BBC News, "Why Are Girls Higher Achievers?," September 23, 2003, http://news

.bbc.co.uk/2/hi/talking_point/3112536.stm; Carolyn Abraham, "Part 1: Failing Boys and the Powder Keg of Sexual Politics," *Globe and Mail,* October 16, 2010, www.theglobeandmail.com/news/national/time-to-lead/part-1-failing-boys-and-the-powder-keg-of-sexual-politics /article4081751; Tamar Lewin, "At Colleges, Women Are Leaving Men in the Dust," *New York Times,* July 9, 2006, www.nytimes.com /2006/07/09/education/09college.html.

13. Beyoncé Knowles, "Run the World (Girls)," digital download (New York City: Columbia Records, 2011).

14. Both Rimer and Chaundry complicate the story of the smart girl by discussing issues such as stress, anxiety, and sexism, though this complexity makes these articles exceptions to the norm. See Rimer, "For Girls, It's Be Yourself"; and Chaundry, "Supergirl Syndrome."

15. For example, see Debbie Epstein, Janette Elwood, Valerie Hey, and Janet Maw, *Failing Boys? Issues in Gender and Achievement* (Maidenhead, UK: Open University Press, 1998); Becky Francis, *Boys, Girls, and Achievement: Addressing the Classroom Issues* (New York: RoutledgeFalmer, 2000); Becky Francis, Barbara Read, and Christine Skelton, *The Identities and Practices of High Achieving Pupils: Negotiating Achievement and Peer Cultures* (London: Bloomsbury, 2012); Emma Renold, "'Square-Girls': Femininity and the Negotiation of Academic Success in the Primary School," *British Educational Research Journal* 27, no. 5 (2001): 577–88; Emma Renold and Alexandra Allan, "Bright and Beautiful: High Achieving Girls, Ambivalent Femininities, and the Feminization of Success in the Primary School," *Discourse: Studies in the Cultural Politics of Education* 27, no. 4 (2006): 457–73; Jessica Ringrose, "Successful Girls? Complicating Post-Feminist, Neoliberal Discourses of Educational Achievement and Gender Equality," *Gender and Education* 19, no. 4 (2007): 471–89; Jessica Ringrose, *Postfeminist Education? Girls and the Sexual Politics of Schooling* (London: Routledge, 2013); Valerie Walkerdine, Helen Lucey, and June Melody, *Growing Up Girl: Psychosocial Explorations of Gender and Class* (Basingstoke, UK: Palgrave, 2001).

16. We put "race" in quotation marks to signal that it is a constructed concept. It signifies the shifting, arbitrary, and false correlation between physical traits and personality traits, skills, intelligence, and superiority or inferiority. But while "race" is a myth that has supported racism

throughout history, we also acknowledge that it has unequal, material effects: it is felt as very real through lived experiences. It is a social construct, but one with historical weight and powerful consequences. See Cynthia Levine-Rasky, "Whiteness: Normalization and the Everyday Practice of Power," in *Power and Everyday Practices,* ed. Deborah Brock, Rebecca Raby, and Mark P. Thomas (Toronto: Nelson, 2012), 86–109; and Linda Tuhiwai Smith, *Decolonizing Methodologies: Research and Indigenous Peoples* (Dunedin, NZ: University of Otago Press, 1999).

17. We take a social constructionist approach to gender, where gender is understood as produced within historical, economic, political, material, social, and cultural contexts that shape femininity and masculinity, and subsequently becomes entrenched in particular societies as natural and normal. Theoretically, this way of thinking about gender draws on the work of Judith Butler, a feminist post-structural philosopher, whose theory of gender performativity has had remarkable traction in the social sciences and humanities. She posits that gender is a set of repeated acts that congeal over time to appear natural. She also posits that subversive citation, or the failure to repeat acts that give one the appearance of being feminine or masculine (and thus female or male), denaturalizes the link between gender and sex, revealing them to be artificially, rather than naturally, produced. See Judith Butler, *Gender Trouble: Feminism and the Subversion of Identity* (New York: Routledge, 1990); and Butler, *Bodies That Matter: On the Discursive Limits of "Sex"* (New York: Routledge, 1993).

18. We interviewed fifty-seven girls and a subset of seventeen boys. We discuss the details of our recruitment strategy and our decision to include boys at the end of this chapter.

19. In this book, we use the word "negotiate" to signal a contextualized form of agency. Agency is typically understood through a humanist lens, where the individual is placed at the center of all things and is capable of rational, autonomous choice (see Elizabeth Adams St. Pierre, "Poststructural Feminism in Education: An Overview," *International Journal of Qualitative Studies in Education* 13, no. 5 [2000]: 477–515). But this understanding of agency has undergone significant critique, including from post-structural feminists (see Judith Butler, *The Psychic Life of Power: Theories in Subjection* [Stanford:

Stanford University Press, 1997]; and Bronwyn Davies, "The Subject of Post-Structuralism: A Reply to Alison Jones" *Gender and Education* 9, no. 3 [1997]: 271–84) and new material feminists (see Karen Barad, *Meeting the Universe Halfway: Quantum Physics and the Entanglement of Matter and Meaning* [Durham: Duke University Press, 2007]; Bronwyn Davies, "Reading Anger in Early Childhood Intra-Actions: A Diffractive Analysis," *Qualitative Inquiry* 20, no. 6 [2014]: 734–41; and Gabrielle Ivinson and Emma Renold, "Valleys' Girls: Re-Theorising Bodies and Agency in a Semi-Rural Post-Industrial Locale," *Gender and Education* 25, no. 6 [2013]: 704–21). While a humanist understanding of agency views the individual as existing outside of history, culture, and society, a contextualized understanding of agency suggests that we are enmeshed in material and discursive contexts that shape how our lives unfold and how they are experienced. Karen Barad suggests that agency is the result of the ontological enmeshment of all things, where nothing precedes anything else but is, rather, co-contingent and co-constituting. Agency is thus conceived as the dynamism of everyday life. We have been influenced by Barad's work and the deep contextualization that it brings to a discussion of girls' negotiations of academic success. But while we attend to the material and discursive elements in which girls are enmeshed, we also respect girls' understanding of themselves as choice-making individuals and have thus retained some of their individualizing language in our analysis.

20. David Brooks, "Mind over Muscle," *New York Times,* October 16, 2005, www.nytimes.com/2005/10/16/opinion/mind-over-muscle.html.

21. See Pamela Bettis, Nicole C. Ferry, and Mary Roe, "Lord of the Guys: Alpha Girls and the Post-Feminist Landscape of American Education," *Gender Issues* 33, no. 2 (2016): 163–81; and Carolyn Jackson, Carrie Paechter, and Emma Renold, *Girls and Education 3–16: Continuing Concerns, New Agendas* (Buckingham: Open University Press, 2010).

22. For an overview of how the failing boys discourse emerged across these countries, see Ringrose, *Postfeminist Education?*

23. Abraham, "Part 1: Failing Boys"; Michael Gurian and Kathy Stevens, *The Minds of Boys: Saving Our Sons from Falling behind in School and in Life* (New York: Jossey-Bass, 2007); Christina Hoff Sommers,

The War against Boys: How Misguided Policies are Harming Our Young Men (New York: Simon and Schuster, 2013); Tamar Lewin, "How Boys Lost Out to Girl Power," *New York Times,* December 13, 1998, www .nytimes.com/1998/12/13/weekinreview/ideas-trends-how-boys-lost-out-to-girl-power.html; Richard Whitmire, *Why Boys Fail: Saving Our Sons from an Educational System That's Leaving Them Behind* (New York: AMACOM, 2011).

24. For an overview of how girls have been pitted against boys in education, see Epstein et al., *Failing Boys?*; Francis, *Boys, Girls, and Achievement;* and Wayne Martino, "Failing Boys!: Beyond Crisis, Moral Panic and Limiting Stereotypes," *Education Canada* 51, no. 4 (Fall 2011), www.cea-ace.ca/education-canada/article/failing-boys-beyond-crisis-moral-panic-and-limiting-stereotypes.

25. Numerous researchers have endeavored to prove or disprove the gender gap in education. Most statistical analyses suggest that girls do better than boys in literature and arts subsets (Dea Conrad-Curry, "A Four-Year Study of ACT Reading Results: Achievement Trends among Eleventh-Grade Boys and Girls in a Midwestern State," *Journal of Education* 191, no. 3 [2011]: 27–37), just as well or slightly less well than boys in mathematics and sciences (Daniel Voyer and Susan D. Voyer, "Gender Differences in Scholastic Achievement: A Meta-Analysis," *Psychological Bulletin* 140, no. 4 [2014]: 1174–204), and better overall on standardized tests and classroom grades (Emma Smith, "Underachievement, Failing Youth and Moral Panics," *Evaluation and Research in Education* 23, no. 1 [2010]: 37–49; Voyer and Voyer, "Gender Differences in Scholastic Achievement"). Interestingly, a highly publicized study from the American Psychological Association examined data from thirty countries between 1914 and 2011 and found that the gender gap is not a new phenomenon at all. Focusing on classroom marks, the data show that the "sudden" boy crisis in education is a fallacy, as girls have done better than boys across all subjects for nearly a century (see Voyer and Voyer, "Gender Differences in Scholastic Achievement"). While these statistics are both troubling and gripping, like other post-structural researchers of this topic (see Ringrose, *Postfeminist Education?*), we do not intend to enter into the debate over whether they prove or disprove the gender gap in

education, given the lack of differentiation and sociocultural context in statistical analyses of this kind. Rather, we are interested in how the use of such statistics has contributed to the smart girl stereotype, which not only positions girls as taking over the world but also positions them as beyond the need for help or resources in school.

26. Lori Day, "Why Boys Are Failing in an Educational System Stacked against Them," *Huffington Post Education,* August 27, 2011, www.huffingtonpost.com/lori-day/why-boys-are-failing-in-a_b_884262.html.

27. For reviews of the literature, as well as critiques, see Wayne Martino and Bob Meyenn, eds., *What about the Boys? Issues of Masculinity and Schooling* (Buckingham: Open University Press, 2001); Michael Kimmel, "'What about the Boys'? What Current Debates Tell Us—and Don't Tell Us—about Boys in School," in *Reconstructing Gender: A Multicultural Anthology,* ed. Estelle Disch (New York: McGraw Hill, 2009), 369–81; Epstein et al., *Failing Boys?;* Martino, "Boys!: Beyond the Crisis"; and Bob Lingard, "Contextualising and Utilising the 'What about the Boys?' Discourse in Education," *Change: Transformations in Education* 1, no. 2 (1998): 16–30.

28. Day, "Why Boys Are Failing"; Robert Smoi, "Why Our Schools Are Failing Boys," *CBC News Canada,* January 8, 2010, www.cbc.ca/news/canada/why-our-schools-are-failing-boys-1.952880; Christina Hoff Sommers, "The Boys at the Back," *New York Times,* February 2, 2013, http://opinionator.blogs.nytimes.com/2013/02/02/the-boys-at-the-back; Sommers, "How to Make School Better for Boys," *Atlantic,* September 13, 2013, www.theatlantic.com/education/archive/2013/09/how-to-make-school-better-for-boys/279635.

29. Conlin, "The New Gender Gap."

30. See Martino, "Failing Boys!"

31. Linda Nicholson, ed., *The Second Wave: A Reader in Feminist Theory* (New York: Routledge, 1999).

32. American Association of University Women, *The AAUW Report: How Schools Shortchange Girls; A Study of Major Findings on Girls and Education* (Washington, DC: AAUW Educational Foundation, 1999); Myra Sadker and David Miller Sadker, *Failing at Fairness: How America's Schools Cheat Girls* (New York: Scribner, 1994); David Miller

Sadker and Karen R. Zittleman, *Still Failing at Fairness: How Gender Bias Cheats Girls and Boys in School and What We Can Do about It* (New York: Scribner, 2009).

33. See Ringrose, "Successful Girls?"; Christine Skelton, "Gender and Achievement: Are Girls the 'Success Stories' of Restructured Education Systems?," *Educational Review* 62, no. 10 (2010): 131–42.

34. The imperative of tracking grades in the West began in response to the newly emerging neoliberal drive to stay competitive, "leave no child behind," and ensure that equity regulations were being followed. See Erica Burman, "Childhood, Neo-Liberalism and the Feminization of Education," *Gender and Education* 17, no. 4 (2005): 251–67; Bob Lingard, Wayne Martino, and Martin Mills, *Boys and Schooling: Beyond Structural Reform* (Hampshire, UK: Palgrave Macmillan, 2009); Wayne Martino and Deborah Berrill, "Boys, Schooling, and Masculinities: Interrogating the 'Right' Way to Educate Boys," *Educational Review* 55, no. 2 (2003): 99–117; and Ringrose, *Postfeminist Education?*

35. David Benatar, *The Second Sexism: Discrimination Against Men and Boys* (Hoboken, NJ: Wiley-Blackwell, 2012); Conlin, "The New Gender Gap"; Gurian and Stevens, *The Minds of Boys;* Hannah Rosin, *The End of Men: And the Rise of Women* (New York: Riverhead Books, 2012); Christina Hoff Sommers, *The War against Boys.*

36. Daniel J. Kindlon and Michael Thompson, *Raising Cain: Protecting the Emotional Life of Boys* (New York: Ballantine Books, 2000); Leonard Sax, *Why Gender Matters: What Parents and Teachers Need to Know about the Emerging Science of Sex Difference* (New York: Harmony, 2006); Sax, *Boys Adrift: The Five Factors Driving the Growing Epidemic of Unmotivated Boys and Underachieving Young Men* (New York: Basic Books, 2009); Sommers, *The War against Boys.*

37. DiPrete and Buchman, *The Rise of Women;* Rosin, *The End of Men.*

38. Lyndsay Layton, "National High School Graduation Rates at Historic High, but Disparities Still Exist," *Washington Post,* April 8, 2014, www.washingtonpost.com/local/education/high-school-graduation-rates-at-historic-high/2014/04/28/84eb0122-cee0–11e3–937f-d3026234b51c_story.html.

39. Abraham, "Part 1: Failing Boys."

40. See Sarah Jane Twomey, review of *The Rise of Women: The Growing Gender Gap in Education and What It Means for American Schools,* by Thomas A. DiPrete and Claudia Buchmann, *Teacher's College Record,* April 13, 2015, www.tcrecord.org/Content.asp?ContentID=17929.

41. Michael Gurian and Kathy Stevens, *Girls and Boys Learn Differently: A Guide For Teachers and Parents* (New York: Jossey-Bass, 2010); Sax, *Why Gender Matters;* Sax, *Boys Adrift.*

42. Hoff Sommers, *The War against Boys;* Gurian and Stevens, *The Minds of Boys;* Gurian and Stevens, *Girls and Boys Learn Differently;* Whitmire, *Why Boys Fail;* Esters and Whitmire, *Where the Boys Aren't;* Christina Hoff Sommers, "The Boys at the Back." For a critique of the idea that gender is hardwired, see Lise Eliot, *Pink Brain, Blue Brain: How Small Differences Grow into Troublesome Gaps—And What We Can Do about It* (Boston: Mariner Books, 2010).

43. Erika Christakis, "Do Teachers Really Discriminate against Boys?," *Time,* February 6, 2013, www.ideas.time.com/2013/02/06/do-teachers-really-discriminate-against-boys.

44. Kate Hammer, "Feminization of Education: One of Five Reasons Why Boys Are Failing," *Globe and Mail,* October 15, 2010, www.theglobeandmail.com/news/national/time-to-lead/feminization-of-education-one-of-five-reasons-why-boys-are-failing/article1215014.

45. See Martino, *Failing Boys!*

46. Rosin, *The End of Men.*

47. DiPrete and Buchman, *The Rise of Women.*

48. Benatar, *The Second Sexism.*

49. Sommers, *The War against Boys.*

50. See Jessica Taft, "Girl Power Politics: Pop-Culture Barriers and Organizational Resistance," in *All about the Girl: Culture, Power, and Identity,* ed. Anita Harris (New York, London: Routledge, 2004), 69–78.

51. The term "post-feminism" is used extensively in critical girlhood studies in analyses of sexualization debates. See Sue Jackson and Tiina M. Vares, "Media 'Sluts': 'Tween' Girls' Negotiations of Postfeminist Sexual Subjectivities in Popular Culture," in *New Femininities: Postfeminism, Neoliberalism and Subjectivity,* ed. Rosalind Gill and Christina Scharff (Basingstoke, UK: Palgrave, 2011), 134–46; and Emma Renold and Jessica Ringrose, "Schizoid Subjectivities?

Re-Theorizing Teen Girls' Sexual Cultures in an Era of 'Sexualization,'" *Journal of Sociology* 47, no. 4 (2011): 389–409.

The term is also used in gender and achievement debates. See Joanne Baker, "Great Expectations and Post-Feminist Accountability: Young Women Living Up to the 'Successful Girls' Discourse," *Gender and Education* 22, no. 1 (2010): 1–15; Shauna Pomerantz and Rebecca Raby, "'Oh, She's So Smart': Girls' Complex Engagements with Post-Feminist Narratives of Academic Success," *Gender and Education* 23, no. 5 (2011): 549–64; Shauna Pomerantz, Rebecca Raby, and Andrea Stefanik, "Girls Run the World? Caught between Sexism and Post-Feminism in the School," *Gender and Society* 27, no. 2 (2013): 185–207; Ringrose, *Successful Girls?*; Ringrose, *Postfeminist Education?*; Francis et al., *The Identities and Practices of High Achieving Pupils.*

Post-feminism has been discussed extensively through the lens of emergent femininities and feminisms in the twenty-first century. See Feona Attwood, "Through the Looking Glass? Sexual Agency and Subjectification in Cyberspace," in *New Femininities? Postfeminism, Neoliberalism and Identity,* ed. Rosalind Gill and Christina Scharff (Basingstoke, UK: Palgrave, 2011), 203–14; Shelley Budgeon, "The Contradictions of Successful Femininity: Third Wave Feminism, Postfeminism and 'New' Femininities," in *New Femininities: Postfeminism, Neoliberalism, and Subjectivity,* ed. Rosalind Gill and Christina Scharff (Basingstoke, UK: Palgrave, 2011), 279–92; and Dawn H. Currie, Deirdre M. Kelly, and Shauna Pomerantz, *"Girl Power": Girls Reinventing Girlhoods* (New York: Peter Lang, 2009).

The term has gained particular purchase in feminist media studies, where it has been taken up as a "sensibility" or a cultural mood. See Rosalind Gill, "Postfeminist Media Culture: Elements of a Sensibility," *European Journal of Cultural Studies* 10, no. 2 (2007): 147–66; Gill, "Empowerment/Sexism: Figuring Female Sexual Agency in Contemporary Advertising," *Feminism and Psychology* 18, no. 1 (2008): 35–60; Angela McRobbie, "Notes on Postfeminism and Popular Culture: Bridget Jones and the New Gender Regime," in *All about the Girl: Culture, Power, and Identity,* ed. Anita Harris (New York: Routledge, 2004), 3–14; McRobbie, "Young Women and Consumer Culture: An Intervention," *Cultural Studies* 22, no. 5 (2008): 531–50;

Alison Horbury, "Post-Feminist Impasses in Popular Heroine Television," *Continuum: Journal of Media and Cultural Studies* 28, no. 2 (2014): 213–25; and Yvonne Tasker and Dianne Negra, *Interrogating Postfeminism: Gender and the Politics of Popular Culture* (Durham: Duke University Press, 2007).

52. Conversely, up until the early 1990s, girls were cast as victims of culture due to a so-called lack of confidence that was said to emerge in the teen years. In 1990, Harvard researchers Carol Gilligan and her colleagues famously located preteen girls at the "crossroads" of childhood and adolescence, where they determined that girls enter into a period of great risk that coincides with an inevitable loss of voice and self (see Carol Gilligan, Nona Lyons, and Trudy Hanmer, eds., *Making Connections: The Relational Worlds of Adolescent Girls at Emma Willard* [Cambridge, MA: Harvard University Press, 1990]). Soon after, a cottage industry developed around self-esteem crises. Popular psychologists and journalists joined the conversation around girls, who they deemed to be "in trouble," "drowning," and "lost." In fact, in 1994, Mary Bray Pipher's book *Reviving Ophelia: Saving the Selves of Adolescent Girls* (New York: Putnam) generated so much concern for girls that it lingered on the *New York Times* bestseller list for three years. The book operated as a wake-up call to the plight of American girlhood, and Pipher saw the teen years as a veritable Bermuda Triangle. But by the turn of the twenty-first century, this victim narrative was somewhat replaced by the powerful and problematic notion that girls were past the need for feminist intervention, as it was deemed to be a time in history where feminism was no longer needed.

53. Kindlon, *Alpha Girls,* 30.

54. Ibid., xix.

55. For a trenchant critique of Kindlon's alpha girl thesis, see Bettis et al., *Lord of the Guys.*

56. Angela McRobbie suggests that the word "sexism" has disappeared from the conversation precisely when it is needed to interrogate "the new sexual contract" between young women and institutions such as government, education, and media. This unspoken contract offers girls and young women entrée into social, economic, and political life, but only if they adhere to the new

feminine subjectivities of neoliberalism. See McRobbie, "Top Girls? Young Women and the Post-Feminist Sexual Contract," *Cultural Studies* 21, no. 4 (2007): 720.

57. Currie et al., *Girl Power;* Susan Douglas, *The Rise of Enlightened Sexism: How Pop Culture Took Us from Girl Power to Girls Gone Wild* (New York: St. Martin's, 2010); Marnina Gonick, "Between 'Girl Power' and 'Reviving Ophelia': Constituting the Neoliberal Girl Subject," *NWSA Journal* 18, no. 2 (2006): 1–23; Taft, "Girl Power Politics."

58. For an overview and critique, see Currie et al., *Girl Power;* Joanne Baker, "Claiming Volition and Evading Victimhood: Post-Feminist Obligations for Young Women," *Feminism and Psychology* 20, no. 2 (2010): 186–204; Pomerantz and Raby, "Oh, She's So Smart"; Pomerantz et al., "Girls Run the World?"; Angela McRobbie, *The Aftermath of Feminism: Gender, Culture and Social Change* (London: SAGE, 2009).

59. While riot grrrl bands brought attention to the term "girl power" in the early 1990s, it first appeared in 1993 in the single "Formula One Racing Girls," by the Welsh indie band Helen Love. In 1995, riot grrrl band Bikini Kill released an album and a single called "Girl Power." See Currie et al., *Girl Power.*

60. Ednie D. Garrison, "U.S. Feminism—Grrrl Style!: Youth (Sub) Cultures and the Technologics of the Third Wave," *Feminist Studies* 26, no. 1 (2000): 141–70; Marnina Gonick, "Girl Power," in *Girl Culture: An Encyclopedia,* ed. Claudia A. Mitchel and Jacqueline Reid-Walsh (Westport, CA: Greenwood Press, 2008), 310–14; Mary Celeste Kearney, "The Missing Links: Riot Grrrl-Feminism-Lesbian Culture," in *Sexing the Groove: Popular Music and Gender,* ed. Sheila Whiteley (London: Routledge, 1997), 67–99; Marion Leonard, "'Rebel Girl, You Are the Queen of My World': Feminism, 'Subculture' and Grrrl Power," in *Sexing The Groove: Popular Music and Gender,* ed. Sheila Whitely (London: Routledge, 1997), 230–55.

61. Currie et al., *Girl Power;* Douglas, *The Rise of Enlightened Sexism;* Gonick, "Between 'Girl Power' and 'Reviving Ophelia'"; Taft, "Girl Power Politics."

62. Spice Girls, *Girl Power: The Official Book by the Spice Girls* (London: Andre Deutsch, 1997).

63. Leslie C. Bell, *Hard to Get: 20-Something Women and the Paradox of Sexual Freedom* (Berkeley: University of California Press, 2013); McRobbie, *The Aftermath of Feminism.*

64. *Oxford English Dictionary,* 2nd ed. (online version), s.v. "girl power."

65. Catalyst, "Women CEOs of the S&P 500," April 3, 2015, www.catalyst.org/knowledge/women-ceos-sp-500.

66. Ibid.

67. World Bank, "Proportion of Seats Held by Women in National Parliaments (%)," accessed May 3, 2015, http://data.worldbank.org/indicator/SG.GEN.PARL.ZS.

68. Catalyst, "Women in Law in Canada and the U.S.," March 3, 2015, www.catalyst.org/knowledge/women-law-canada-and-us.

69. Heather R. Huhman, "STEM Fields and the Gender Gap: Where Are the Women?," *Forbes,* June 20, 2012, www.forbes.com/sites/work-in-progress/2012/06/20/stem-fields-and-the-gender-gap-where-are-the-women.

70. Catherine Hill, *The Simple Truth about the Gender Pay Gap (Spring 2015)* (Washington, DC: AAUW, 2015), www.aauw.org/research/the-simple-truth-about-the-gender-pay-gap.

71. Francine D. Blau and Lawrence K. Kahn, "The Gender Pay Gap: Have Women Gone as Far as They Can?," *Academy of Management Perspectives* 21, no. 1 (2007): 7–23.

72. In Canada, the pay gap in relation to intersections of "race" and gender is similarly disheartening. In Ontario, for example, women of color make 53.4 cents for every dollar that white men make and 84.7 cents for every dollar that white women make. See Sheila Block, *Ontario's Growing Gap: The Role of Race and Gender,* (Ottawa: Canadian Centre for Policy Alternatives, June 2010), www.ywcacanada.ca/data/research_docs/00000140.pdf.

73. Rachel Wallace, "By the Numbers: A Look at the Gender Pay Gap," *AAUW Career and Workplace Blog,* September 18, 2014, www.aauw.org/2014/09/18/gender-pay-gap.

74. In Canada, the statistics are no rosier. Women make up 70 percent of the part-time workforce, are only 23 percent of graduates in engineering and 30 percent in mathematics and computer science, and

earn an average annual salary of Can$30,100, compared to Can$47,000 for men. See Cara Williams, *Economic Well-Being,* Statistics Canada, May 13, 2013, www.statcan.gc.ca/pub/89-503-x/2010001/article/11388-eng .htm.

75. Brooks, "Mind Over Muscle."

76. Anthony Giddens, *Modernity and Self Identity: Self and Society in the Late Modern Age* (Cambridge, UK: Polity Press, 1991).

77. Baker, "Claiming Volition."

78. Wendy Brown, "Neo-Liberalism and the End of Liberal Democracy," *Theory and Event* 7, no. 1 (2003): 1–19; Nikolas Rose, *Inventing Our Selves: Psychology, Power and Personhood* (Cambridge: Cambridge University Press, 1996).

79. Marianne Cooper, *Cut Adrift: Families in Insecure Times* (Berkeley: University of California Press, 2013).

80. Ibid.

81. McRobbie, *The Aftermath of Feminism;* Walkerdine et al., *Growing Up Girl.*

82. A number of studies show girls' disengagement with feminist politics. See, for example, Baker, "Claiming Volition"; Currie et al., *Girl Power;* McRobbie, *The Aftermath of Feminism;* Pomerantz and Raby, "Oh, She's So Smart"; Pomerantz et al., "Girls Run the World?"

83. Anita Harris, *Future Girl: Young Women in the Twenty-First Century* (New York: Routledge, 2004).

84. See Walkerdine et al., *Growing up Girl;* and Harris, *Future Girl.*

85. Globally, for example, such responsibilities include the "girl effect," or the idea that girls have more power than anyone to change the world by lifting their families and communities out of poverty. In this discourse, girls are sited as "the most powerful force for change on the planet." See *Girl Effect,* accessed May 4, 2015, www.girleffect .org; and Kathryn K. Moeller, "Proving 'the Girl Effect': Corporate Knowledge Production and Educational Intervention," *International Journal of Educational Development* 33, no. 6 (2013): 612–21.

86. We focus on inequalities that make it easier for some girls to succeed over others in chapters 2 and 5. See Harris, *Future Girl;* and Walkerdine et al., *Growing up Girl.*

87. We are grateful to the Social Sciences and Humanities Research Council of Canada for funding the last three years of this study.

88. Shauna and Rebecca, along with an undergraduate research assistant, Andrea Stefanik, conducted the interviews. In 2008, we also conduced a pilot study entitled, "Smart Girls: 'Race', Class, and Grades in the Global Era." Shauna and Rebecca, along with a graduate research assistant, Lindsay Cramp, conducted four group interviews, two with each set of girls. Candace, Hayden, and Magda comprised the first group, and Brooke, Jamila, and Laney comprised the second group. For a more detailed discussion of our pilot study, see Pomerantz and Raby, "Oh, She's So Smart."

89. We are grateful to Dawn Currie for her insights into our recruitment methods and sample.

90. All but seven participants partook in a follow-up interview, during which we asked them new questions, inquired about how their thinking might have changed since the first interview, and sought clarifications from the first interview.

91. All interviews were transcribed and thematically coded. Rebecca developed a codebook that included general and specific themes; Rebecca and Shauna coded the transcripts, using the codebook as a guide. After coding, Larissa Bablak, an undergraduate research assistant, inputted all transcripts and codes into Atlas TI, a qualitative data analysis software program. Rebecca and Shauna then analyzed the data by looking at common themes and differences across interviews.

92. In Canada, schools are governed provincially. In Ontario, there are elementary schools (grades kindergarten to five or kindergarten to eight), middle schools (grades six to eight), and high schools (grades nine to twelve) in both nondenominational and Catholic public systems, as well as myriad private schools. While we primarily drew our sample from high school students, we also talked to some middle school and upper elementary school students.

93. Cooper, *Cut Adrift*.

94. See Walkerdine et al., *Growing Up Girl*.

95. The geographic area where our study took place is dominated by people of British origin, followed by those of European descent, with a smaller population of visible minorities than in much of Ontario and a much smaller black community than directly to the south of the border. These demographics are reflected in our study sample.

96. See Francis et al., *The Identities and Practices of High Achieving Pupils;* Emma Renold and Alexandra Allan, "Bright and Beautiful: High Achieving Girls, Ambivalent Femininities, and the Feminization of Success in the Primary School," *Discourse: Studies in the Cultural Politics of Education* 27, no. 4 (2006): 457–73.

97. Louise Archer, Jennifer DeWitt, and Beatrice Willis, "Adolescent Boys' Science Aspirations: Masculinity, Capital, and Power," *Journal of Research in Science Teaching* 51, no. 1 (2014): 1–30; Francis et al., *The Identities and Practices of High Achieving Pupils;* Heather Mendrick and Becky Francis, "Boffin and Geek Identities: Abject or Privileged?" *Gender and Education* 24, no. 1 (2012): 15–24;

98. Julie Bettie, *Women without Class: Girls, Race, and Identity* (Berkeley: University of California Press, 2003); Harris, *Future Girl;* Angela McRobbie, *Feminism and Youth Culture,* 2nd ed. (Basingstoke, UK: Palgrave, 2000); Walkerdine et al., *Growing Up Girl.*

2. DRIVEN TO PERFECTION

Epigraph: Rimer, "For Girls, It's Be Yourself."

1. The term "ghetto" arose a number of times in our interviews as a pejorative, usually in reference to a few specific schools. Ghettoization, the growth of increasingly segregated areas of low-income and racial concentration, is not evident in Canada to nearly the degree that it is in the United States (R. Alan Walks and Larry S. Bourne, "Ghettos in Canada's Cities? Racial Segregation, Ethnic Enclaves and Poverty Concentration in Canadian Urban Areas," *Canadian Geographer* 50, no. 3 [2006]: 273–97), and generally not in Secord. The participants' comments seem to reflect a loose, popular, mainstream, and diluted use of the term (Loïc J. D. Wacquant, "Three Pernicious

Premises in the Study of the American Ghetto," *Journal of Urban and Regional Research* 21, no. 2 [1997]: 341–53) to informally reference poverty, although the racialized nature of the term was also invoked, as the school to be called "ghetto" most often, Central Secondary, was the most racial diverse.

2. We use the term "supergirl" to refer to girls who seem able to successfully and easily combine smartness, high extracurricular involvement (including in athletics), and popularity. That said, when we discuss specific girls in our study as supergirls, it is always with the recognition that these girls only approximate an impossible, imagined ideal and that this is a shifting, constructed, and unstable identity.

3. Another relevant term in relation to popular media representations is "post-nerd girl." While the popular girl has been conventionally portrayed in dominant media as attractive but not academically driven, female characters that have brains, conventional beauty, and popularity have now emerged. Like Gabriella in *High School Musical* or Rory in the *Gilmore Girls*, these post-nerds are the epitome of post-feminist popular culture. See Shauna Pomerantz and Rebecca Raby, "Reading Smart Girls: Post-Nerds in Post-Feminist Popular Culture," in *Girls, Texts, Cultures*, ed. Clare Bradford and Mavis Reimer (Waterloo, ON: Wilfred Laurier University Press, 2015), 287–312.

4. Kindlon, *Alpha Girls*, xv.

5. Chaudhry, Lakshmi, "The Supergirl Syndrome," *Nation*, May 14, 2007, www.thenation.com/article/supergirl-syndrome.

6. Conlin, "The New Gender Gap."

7. Rimer, "For Girls, It's Be Yourself."

8. Liz Funk defines "supergirl" slightly differently than we do. Her supergirls combine good grades, heterosexual dating, stereotypically good looks, a trendy fashion sense, and ambition in a frenzy of perfectionism and competition that often prevents them from being either popular or truly happy. See Liz Funk, *Supergirls Speak Out* (New York: Touchstone, 2009).

9. Ibid., 200.

10. See Christine Skelton, Becky Francis, and Barbara Read, "Brains before 'Beauty'? High Achieving Girls, School and Gender Identities," *Educational Studies* 36, no. 2 (2010): 185–94.

11. During our interviews, the girls tended to define popularity as being social, having many friends, and being well known, although as we discuss in the next chapter, these characteristics frequently linked popularity to fulfilling dominant gender expectations and compulsory heterosexuality.

12. Pierre Bourdieu defines cultural capital as the "dispositions of the mind and body [and the] educational qualifications" that are rewarded within a field. While researchers often focus on dominant institutions, such as school, a field can also be less structured. For example, a peer culture can be a field—one that can be both distinct from and entwined with school. See Pierre Bourdieu, "The Forms of Capital," in *The Sociology of Economic Life,* 2nd ed., edited by Mark Granovetter and Richard Swedberg (Cambridge, MA: Westview Press, 2001), 96–111; and Bourdieu and Jean-Claude Passeron, *Reproduction in Education, Society, and Culture,* trans. Richard Nice (London: SAGE, 1990).

13. Many school districts in Canada offer French immersion programming to support the two official languages: French and English.

14. Pomerantz and Raby, "Oh, She's So Smart."

15. Most of the boys we interviewed also had their eyes on professional jobs—for example, in teaching, medicine, aviation, computers, policing, and accountancy—although a few also mentioned trade jobs.

16. See Francis et al., *The Identities and Practices of High Achieving Pupils;* Harris, *Future Girl;* Walkerdine et al., *Growing Up Girl;* Pomerantz et al., "Girls Run the World?"; and Pomerantz and Raby "Oh She's So Smart."

17. Ulrich Beck, *Risk Society: Towards a New Modernity,* trans. Mark Ritter (London: SAGE, 1992); Andy Furlong and Fred Cartmel, *Young People and Social Change: Individualization and Risk in Late Modernity* (Buckingham: Open University Press, 1997); Nick Lee, *Childhood and Society: Growing Up in an Age of Uncertainty* (Buckingham: Open University Press, 2005).

18. Cooper, *Cut Adrift.*

19. Like many other areas in North America, Central Canada has seen a serious loss in stable manufacturing jobs. Since the beginning of

the new century, there has been a loss of three hundred thousand manufacturing jobs in Ontario, and the sector is reported to have shrunk by almost 30 percent, most of which is due to plants closing or relocating outside of the province (Jeff Rubin, "The Future Looks Bleak for Ontario's Manufacturing Sector," *Globe and Mail,* December 30, 2013, www.theglobeandmail.com/report-on-business/economy/the-future-looks-bleak-for-ontarios-manufacturing-sector/article16132219). Consequently, steady jobs have taken a beating. They are generally replaced by more flexible, less secure, and less well-paid work in service industries (Kaylie Tiessen, *Seismic Shift: Ontario's Changing Labour Market* [Toronto: Canadian Centre for Policy Alternatives, 2014], www .policyalternatives.ca/publications/reports/seismic-shift). Secord and the surrounding area have been hit particularly hard and have seen a decline in income and employment, particularly in stable, full-time, and unionized jobs.

20. Beck, *Risk Society;* Furlong and Cartmel, *Young People and Social Change;* Walkerdine et al., *Growing Up Girl;* Cooper, *Cut Adrift.*

21. One of the most frequently cited scholars on this rising precarity is Ulrich Beck, who argues that modern societies have eroded more predictable identity pathways, contributing to individual reflexivity about our life trajectories as we negotiate increased risk. This critique of class as an ongoing force in modern society has received significant challenges, however (see Furlong and Cartmel, *Young People and Social Change*). These critiques have led to a recent debate within youth studies between those arguing that Beck's work has been used by researchers such as Furlong and Cartmel as a kind of straw man to argue for the ongoing salience of structural inequalities (Dan Woodman, "The Mysterious Case of the Pervasive Choice Biography: Ulrich Beck, Structure/Agency, and the Middling State of Theory in the Sociology of Youth" *Journal of Youth Studies* 12, no. 3 [2009]: 243–56) and those insisting that Beck's focus on "choice biographies" neglects such structural inequalities (Steven Roberts, "Misrepresenting 'Choice Biographies'? A Reply to Woodman," *Journal of Youth Studies* 13, no. 1 [2010]: 137–49). Others argue for a middle ground, embracing Beck's emphasis on individualization and

reflexivity in the rise of risk while simultaneously recognizing that such reflexivity and risk is significantly shaped by structural advantages and disadvantages (Steven Threadgold, "Should I Pitch My Tent in the Middle Ground? On 'Middling Tendency,' Beck and Inequality in Youth Sociology," *Journal of Youth Studies* 14, no. 4 [2011]: 381–93; David Farrugia, "Young People and Structural Inequality: Beyond the Middle Ground," *Journal of Youth Studies* 16, no. 5 [2013]: 670–93).

22. Cooper, *Cut Adrift*.

23. Furlong and Cartmel (*Young People and Social Change*) specifically raise concerns about what these deep social changes mean for youth as they enter the increasingly competitive world of education and work. Young people, they argue, are growing up in a world where the language of individual choice, self-invention, and responsibility is ubiquitous, but so are the structural inequalities that seriously affect that choice and responsibility. Girlhood studies scholars specifically link this conversation to the rise of the supergirl. See Jessica Ringrose and Valerie Walkerdine, "What Does It Mean to Be a Girl in the Twenty-First Century? Exploring Some Contemporary Dilemmas of Femininity and Girlhood in the West," *Girl Culture: An Encyclopedia*, vol. 1, ed. Claudia A. Mitchell and Jacqueline Reid-Walsh (Westport, CT: Greenwood Press, 2007), 6–16.

24. Harris, *Future Girl*, 37.

25. See also Ringrose and Walkerdine, "What Does It Mean to be a Girl." Ringrose and Walkerdine argue that the idealized neoliberal subject is embodied in middle-class femininities.

26. Harris, *Future Girl*, 44.

27. Kindlon, *Alpha Girls*.

28. "Soft skills" are seen as the social skills needed to smoothly manage customer relations and therefore are increasingly required for employment within deindustrialized economies that focus on the service industry. See Yasemin Besen-Cassino, *Consuming Work: Youth Labor in America* (Philadelphia: Temple University Press, 2014).

29. Ringrose and Walkerdine, "What Does It Mean to Be a Girl?"

30. Rosin, *The End of Men*.

31. Ringrose and Walkerdine, "What Does It Mean to Be a Girl?"

32. Walkerdine et al., *Growing Up Girl;* Furlong and Cartmel, *Young People and Social Change;* Harris, *Future Girl.*

33. Despite the range of definitions of "smartness" discussed in the interviews, both we and our participants frequently came back to grades, illustrating a form of intra-activity between the historical sedimentation of schools' evaluation processes, the production of smart student subjectivities through grades, the materiality of formal evaluation (tests, essays, the red pen, grades, and report cards), and the materiality of study (usually sitting still at a desk). See Barad, *Meeting the Universe Halfway.*

34. Howard Gardener, *Frames of Mind: The Theory of Multiple Intelligences* (New York: Basic Books, 1983).

35. Beth Hatt ("Street Smarts vs. Book Smarts: The Figured World of Smartness in the Lives of Marginalized, Urban Youth," *Urban Review* 39, no. 2 [2007]: 145–66) provides a contrast: the disenfranchised urban youth she studied valued "street smarts," but for these young people, street smarts were about making ends meet, avoiding bankruptcy, keeping a home going, getting out of dangerous situations, and knowing one's rights with the police.

36. Jordan was one of the exceptions. She was growing up in what some might consider a rougher part of town with her lower-middle-class family. Jordan's definition of "smartness" included "knowing when you are placed in a bad situation, how to get out, or how to not put yourself in a bad situation." For a few others, such as McLovin and Caramel, street smarts included successfully negotiating a particular geographic space that they considered dangerous.

37. Beth Hatt ("Smartness as a Cultural Practice in Schools," *American Educational Research Journal* 49, no. 3 [2012]: 438–60) illustrates how smartness and goodness can be conflated by focusing on the creation of smartness among kindergarten children in a southern American classroom. For Hatt, the construction of smartness is a "cultural practice of social control" (439) enacted through the repeated connection between smartness and obedience. Teachers evaluated students on their compliance, framed this compliance as being smart, and then gave privileges to those students deemed

"smart." The children thus learned that being smart is about maintaining a docile body and that docility and smartness are aligned with social status. Hatt also found that this process favored certain children over others, as some children had a greater "feel for the game" and as teachers were more likely to notice certain children breaking rules (notably black, working-class boys) than others (such as white, middle-class boys). See also Pierre Bourdieu, *The Logic of Practice* (Cambridge, UK: Polity Press, 1990).

38. See Michael Apple, *Education and Power,* 2nd ed. (New York: Routledge, 1995); Louise Archer, Sumi Hollingworth, and Anna Halsall, "'University's Not for Me—I'm a Nike Person': Urban, Working-Class Young People's Negotiations of 'Style,' Identity, and Educational Engagement," *Sociology* 41, no. 2 (2005): 219–37; Penelope Eckert, *Jocks and Burnouts: Social Categories and Identity in High School* (New York: Teachers College Press, 1989); and Rebecca Raby, *School Rules: Obedience, Discipline and Elusive Democracy* (Toronto: University of Toronto Press, 2012).

39. Michael Busseri, Linda Rose-Krasnor, Teena Willoughby, and Heather Chalmers, "A Longitudinal Examination of Breadth and Intensity of Youth Activity Involvement and Successful Development," *Developmental Psychology* 42, no. 6 (2006): 1313–26; Jennifer A. Fredericks, "Extracurricular Participation and Academic Outcomes: Testing the Over-Scheduling Hypothesis," *Journal of Youth and Adolescence* 41 (2012): 295–306; Joseph L. Mahoney, Angel L. Harris and Jacqelynne S. Eccles, "Organized Activity Participation, Positive Youth Development, and the Over-Scheduling Hypothesis," *Social Policy Report* 20, no. 4 (2006): 1–32.

40. This intense focus on extracurricular involvement raises concern that young women are so obsessed with striving to be perfect that there is no time or space for engagement with feminism. They are focused instead on individualized solutions. See McRobbie, "Top Girls?"

41. Becky Francis, Christine Skelton and Barbara Read, "The Simultaneous Production of Educational Achievement and Popularity: How Do Some Pupils Accomplish It?," *British Educational Research Journal* 36, no. 2 (2010): 317–40.

42. Becky Francis, Christine Skelton, and Barbara Read link this pattern to Angela McRobbie's work on the "post-feminist masquerade" (*The Aftermath of Feminism*), in which young women need to combine a certain degree of hyper-femininity with their educational or work successes in order to soften the possible threat of their accomplishments. We return to this idea in the next chapter. See Francis et al., "The Simultaneous Production."

43. Kindlon, *Alpha Girl*.

44. In this way, these girls fit well with the idea of supergirls described by Jessica Ringrose and Valerie Walkerdine, who see these high achieving girls smoothly negotiating masculine and feminine traits. They argue, however, that this contradiction is partially reconciled through the rhetoric of mean girls, through which girls are seen as both aggressive and also hiding that aggression behind a veneer of niceness. See Ringrose and Walkerdine, "What Does It Mean to Be a Girl?" Funk similarly suggests that, due to their competitiveness, supergirls are in fact mean girls. See Funk, *Supergirls Speak Out*. Meanness is not a focus that we found in our own research, perhaps because a lot of the supergirls we interviewed played down competitiveness and focused on being genuinely nice.

45. Funk, *Supergirls Speak Out;* Courtenay Martin, *Perfect Girls, Starving Daughters* (New York: Berkley Books, 2007); Chaudhry, "The Supergirl Syndrome."

46. Francis et al., "The Simultaneous Production," 336.

47. Rebecca Raby and Shauna Pomerantz, "Landscapes of Academic Success: Girls, Location, and the Importance of School Culture," in *Girlhood Studies and the Politics of Place: Contemporary Paradigms for Research,* ed. Claudia A. Mitchell and Carrie Rentschler (New York: Berghahn Books, 2016), 68–86.

48. See also Skelton et al., "Brains before 'Beauty.'"

49. We take up the common distinction between being smart and being conventionally attractive and popular in chapter 3.

50. Kindlon, *Alpha Girls;* Walkerdine et al., *Growing Up Girl.*

51. Bourdieu and Passeron, *Reproduction in Education;* Annette Lareau, *Unequal Childhoods: Class, Race, and Family Life* (Berkeley: University of California Press, 2003).

52. Kindlon also observes alpha girls who have come from families with fewer resources. See Kindlon, *Alpha Girls*.

53. Harris, *Future Girl*; Walkerdine et al., *Growing Up Girl*.

54. Their stories are reminiscent of those told in Courtenay Martin's book, *Perfect Girls*, which tells of a number of successful, high-achieving girls who feel they must do everything both perfectly and effortlessly and yet also struggle privately with personal issues around anxiety and not feeling good enough, especially about their weight. See also Rimer, "For Girls, It's Be Yourself"; Funk, *Supergirls Speak Out*.

55. In Canada, teenage girls are more likely than teenage boys to experience mood disorders, anxiety disorders, eating disorders, and a lack of self-confidence, and they are also more likely to be hospitalized for self-harm. Boys, however, are more likely to commit suicide. See Government of Canada, *Chief Public Health Officer's Report on the State of Public Health in Canada* (Public Health Agency of Canada, 2011), www.phac-aspc.gc.ca/cphorsphc-respcacsp/2011/cphorsphc-respcacsp-06-eng.php.

56. Walkerdine et al., *Growing Up Girl*.

57. Ibid., 186.

3. FITTING IN OR FABULOUSLY SMART?

Epigraph: Anne Beatts, "Pilot," *Square Pegs*, directed by Kim Friedman (Sony Pictures Home Entertainment, 2008), DVD.

1. As we discuss in other chapters, many girls had a much more positive experience of Blue Ridge and saw it as a haven for smart girls.

2. The actions of teachers and administrators are important as well and are also embedded in ideas about appropriate and dominant masculinity and femininity, which we touch on in chapter 4. In this chapter, however, we focus our attention on peer relationships.

3. See also Francis et al., *The Identities and Practices of High Achieving Pupils*; Francis et al., "The Simultaneous Production of Educational Achievement"; Valerie Hey, *The Company She Keeps: An Ethnography of Girls' Friendships* (Buckingham: Open University Press, 1997); Renold

and Allan, "Bright and Beautiful"; Skelton et al., "Brains before 'Beauty'?"; and Walkerdine et al., *Growing Up Girl.*

4. See Sandra B. Conaway, "Girls Who (Don't) Wear Glasses: The Performativity of Smart Girls on Teen Television" (PhD diss., Bowling Green State University, 2007), https://etd.ohiolink.edu/ap/10?0::NO:10:P10_ACCESSION_NUM:bgsu1182800368; Sherrie A. Inness, *Geek Chic: Smart Women in Popular Culture* (New York: Palgrave Macmillan, 2007); Pomerantz and Raby, "Reading Smart Girls."

5. Examples of this kind of smart girl include Jan from *The Brady Bunch* in the 1970s, Carol from *Growing Pains* in the 1980s, Andrea from *Beverly Hills, 90210* and Angela from *My So-Called Life* in the 1990s, and Willow from *Buffy the Vampire Slayer* and Lindsay from *Freaks and Geeks* in the late 1990s and early 2000s.

6. See Pomerantz and Raby, "Reading Smart Girls."

7. Ibid.

8. Francis et al., "The Simultaneous Production of Educational Achievement."

9. Dawn H. Currie, Deirdre M. Kelly, and Shauna Pomerantz, "'The Geeks Shall Inherit the Earth': Girls' Agency, Subjectivity and Empowerment," *Journal of Youth Studies* 9, no. 4 (2006): 419–36; Currie et al., *"Girl Power"*; Francis et al., *The Identities and Practices of High Achieving Pupils*; Francis et al., "The Simultaneous Production of Educational Achievement"; Renold and Allan, "Bright and Beautiful"; Skelton et al., "Brains before 'Beauty'?"; Walkerdine et al., *Growing Up Girl.*

10. Terms like "geek" and "nerd" came up in the interviews, but in very mixed ways. Some participants noted that being seen as a geek or a nerd was linked to being smart and antisocial and that this was negative. Others suggested that these terms were not as much about being smart as they were about being narrowly obsessed with a specific, often technical activity or genre (for example, science fiction or manga). Still others spoke positively about these terms, suggesting they had been reclaimed and made acceptable through shows like *Big Bang Theory;* consequently, in the spirit of "geek chic," some were proud to call themselves geeks.

11. Mendrick and Francis, "Boffin and Geek Identities."

12. Raewyn Connell calls these culturally valorized forms of gender "hegemonic masculinity" and "emphasized femininity." Hegemonic masculinity is predicated on power, aggression, and physical strength, which Connell explains is the most culturally rewarded kind of masculinity in Western culture. Its corollary is emphasized femininity, the most culturally rewarded kind of femininity, which in the West is predicated on sexualized beauty, thinness, and passivity to men. Connell argues that, while there can be a "hegemonic" form of masculinity, no form of femininity usurps male power, and, therefore, femininity can never be considered hegemonic. See R. W. Connell, *Gender and Power: Society, the Person and Sexual Politics* (Stanford, CA: Stanford University Press, 1987).

13. American sociologist Mimi Schippers ("Recovering the Feminine Other: Masculinity, Femininity and Gender Hegemony," *Theoretical Sociology* 36 [2007]: 85–102) builds on Connell's work to suggest that hegemonic forms of masculinity and femininity support a hierarchical dynamic between men and women. In other words, masculinity is not viewed as more central than femininity but rather is entwined with femininity to bolster a "heterosexual matrix"—a norm of unequal power relations between men and women based on an assumed "fit" between dominant masculinity and supportive femininity (Butler, *Gender Trouble*).

14. Relevant context includes the unique dynamics of local places; broader historical changes, including the rise of post-feminism; everyday beliefs about gender and smartness; young people's bodies and the work young people do to shape and present them; family, social, and financial resources; and material practices, including those of specific schools and teachers, as they measure and reward certain actions over others.

15. Some girls and boys described what might be considered a male teacher's pet in their school, but in these instances, the boy's behavior was dismissed as insincere, and the boy was then reframed as a class clown.

16. Teacher's pets might thus be considered part of what Mimi Schippers calls a "pariah femininity." Schippers suggests that pariah

femininity is evident when certain girls or women are socially problematized and rejected for acting in masculine ways that might challenge the hierarchical and complimentary relationship between men and women. Dismissing and rejecting pariah femininities then contains their threat to dominant gender norms. Schippers ("Recovering the Feminine Other") provides examples of the "slut," the "bitch," and the "witch" as forms of pariah femininity. From the examples we give in the book, the teacher's pet can be seen as fitting into this category, too, in that attributes that might be valued in a boy are condemned in a girl. The brazen smart girl who speaks out, takes up space, and seems to curry favor is rejected and dismissed, which neutralizes her power to jeopardize dominant gender norms.

17. This pattern has been well described elsewhere. See Francis et al., "The Simultaneous Production of Educational Achievement"; and Renold and Allan, "Bright and Beautiful." For a more psychological treatment of girls' looks and popularity, see Patricia Adler and Peter Adler, *Peer Power: Preadolescent Culture and Identity* (New Brunswick, NJ: Rutgers University Press, 1998).

18. Boys were less likely to talk about their looks directly, although a few boys described instances that suggested that certain styles were best avoided if one did not want to look nerdy. Noah talked about how there was a typical "nerd look" to avoid that involved wearing glasses and being scrawny (a typically less masculine, unathletic look), and Paul suggested one of the reasons "nerds" were not cool was because they "don't have the money for the right clothes." This interesting thread was echoed by Rory, a female participant, who said, "If you are a smart boy, you are a nerd unless you are rich and wear Hollister and Abercrombie or [have a] super good look." We address these class-based intersections in chapter 5.

19. In his second interview, however, Louis suggested that, now that he was in high school, he was feeling that these appearance pressures were becoming more equal between girls and boys.

20. McRobbie, *The Aftermath of Feminism*.

21. Lyn Mikel Brown, *Raising Their Voices: The Politics of Girls' Anger* (Cambridge, MA: Harvard University Press, 1988); Edward W. Morris, "'Tuck In That Shirt!' Race, Class, Gender and Discipline in

an Urban School," *Sociological Perspectives* 48, no. 1 (2005): 25–48; Valerie Walkerdine, *Schoolgirl Fictions* (London: Verso, 1990).

22. Rebecca Raby and Shauna Pomerantz, "Playing It Down or Playing It Up: The Pleasures and Hazards of Doing 'Smart Girl' in High School," *British Journal of Sociology of Education* 36, no. 4 (2015): 507–25.

23. For a description of "cultural capital," see chapter 2, note 12.

24. For example, see Abraham, "Part 1: Failing Boys"; Gurian and Stevens, *The Minds of Boys*; Sommers, *The War against Boys*; and Whitmire, *Why Boys Fail*.

25. For instance, in 2009, Ontario's Ministry of Education named boys as a disadvantaged group alongside children who are new immigrants, indigenous children, low-income children, and children with special needs. This designation has influenced programs such as Ontario's What, Me Read?, which is organized around the idea that boys must be lured to reading through short, action-based stories. Wayne Martino and Gol Rezai Rashti ("Neoliberal Accountability and the Politics of Boys' Underachievement: Steering Policy by Numbers in the Ontario Context," *International Journal of Inclusive Education* 16, no. 4 [2012]: 423–40) are critical of this program, arguing that it treats all boys as if they have the same interests, thus reproducing the very form of hegemonic masculinity that stereotypes boys as uninterested in reading in the first place. See also Ringrose, *Postfeminist Education?*; and Skelton, "Gender and Achievement."

26. See, for example, Martino, "Failing Boys!"; Kimmel, "What about the Boys?"; Francis, "Boffin and Geek Identities"; and Francis et al., "The Simultaneous Production of Educational Achievement."

27. Martino, "Failing Boys!"

28. This clash between classroom expectations and masculinity has been emphasized by scholars who argue that boys have innate characteristics that are being shortchanged in the classroom (see, for example, Gurian and Stevens, "The Minds of Boys"; and Sommers, "The War against Boys"), as well as more critical, constructionist scholars studying hegemonic masculinity (see, for example, Kimmel, "What about the Boys?"; Martino, "Failing Boys!"; and Emma Renold, "Learning the 'Hard' Way: Boys, Hegemonic Masculinity and the

Negotiation of Learner Identities in the Primary School," *British Journal of Sociology of Education* 22 no. 3 [2001]: 369–85).

29. Francis et al. ("The Simultaneous Production of Educational Achievement," 187) argue that successful academic achievement requires "hard-nosed determination, singularity and concern with mental/intellectual (rather than social) pursuits."

30. For similar findings in a British context, see Stephen Frosh, Ann Phoenix, and Rob Pattman, *Young Masculinities: Understanding Boys in Contemporary Society* (Basingstoke, UK: Palgrave, 2001).

31. See Ibid.; and also the discussion of "real Englishmen" in Máirtín Mac an Ghaill, *The Making of Men: Masculinities, Sexualities and Schooling* (Buckingham: Open University Press, 1994).

32. Our findings on the significance of the terms "geek" and "nerd" are less stark than those of other studies conducted in Britain and the United States on boys and academics. See Adler and Adler, *Peer Power;* Mendrick and Francis, "Boffin and Geek Identities"; and Renold "Learning the 'Hard' Way."

33. Other research studies have similarly suggested that trying hard in school is problematic, although these studies found that studiousness was associated with being "wimpy" or effeminate. See Mac an Ghaill, *The Making of Men;* Renold, "Learning the 'Hard' Way"; and Paul Willis *Learning to Labour: How Working Class Kids Get Working Class Jobs* (Farnborough, UK: Saxon House, 1977).

34. It is also important to note that, as with the girls, the boys found that some school contexts and peer groups made it more or less comfortable for them to be focused on their schooling—a point we return to in chapter 6.

35. See, for example, Frosh et al., *Young Masculinities;* Andrew Parker, "The Construction of Masculinity within Boys' Physical Education" *Gender and Education* 8, no. 2 (1996), 141–58; C.J. Pascoe, *Dude You're a Fag: Masculinity and Sexuality in High School* (Berkeley: University of California Press, 2006); and Jon Swain, "The Role of Sport in the Construction of Masculinities in an English Independent Junior School," *Sport, Education and Society* 11, no. 4 (2006): 317–35. However, across these examples, authors also point to boys who complicate, challenge, or circumvent this prioritizing of sport as central to masculinity.

36. In a way that was reminiscent of the supergirl imperative, athletics were also important to girls' social success and could thus be a counterweight to girls' smartness in some contexts. Some of the girls argued that, in their schools, popular girls were frequently athletic. Involvement in sports was seen to provide opportunities to be skilled, social, and maintain a good figure. Overall, there was some overlap with boys in this sense, as athletics was often a ticket to social success for girls, but it was not as central as it was for boys.

37. Francis et al., "The Simultaneous Production of Educational Achievement"; Renold, "Learning the 'Hard' Way"; Christine Skelton and Becky Francis, "Successful Boys and Literacy," *Curriculum Inquiry* 41, no. 4 (2011): 456–78; according to Frosh et al. (*Young Masculinities*), this trade-off can be easier to attain in private schools or schools that prioritize academics.

38. Brothers Sam and Ben spoke most directly about a dichotomy between athletics and smartness, or as they explained it, between "jocks," who prioritize sports over all else, including grades, and "nerds," who focus on academics. They talked about their lack of success in trying to fit in with the jocks, which they explained was due to both showing their smartness and being quite focused on getting good grades.

39. For example, see note 35.

40. Recognizing the breadth of skills that can be valued in boys, Skelton and Francis ("The 'Renaissance Child': High Achievement and Gender in Late Modernity," *International Journal of Inclusive Education* 16, no. 4 [2012]: 441–59) suggest that being studious and being popular can fit well together for some boys, specifically if they are well-rounded boys who reflect what the scholars call "renaissance masculinity," evoking a time when boys were trained in humanist subjects, like philosophy, as well as athletics and the sciences. Skelton and Francis build on the concept of the "renaissance child" introduced by Carol Vincent and Stephen Ball (*Childcare, Choice and Class Practices* [London: Routledge, 2006]), who are interested in how middle-class parents have become invested in endowing their children with multiple accomplishments in order to compete in the new economy. Skelton and Francis ("Successful Boys and Literacy," 471) suggest that, today, neoliberal

demands for a flexible, multitalented workforce reward a modern "renaissance man"—someone who can be smart and athletic, rational and expressive, and masculine and feminine, a "good all-rounder." At first, renaissance masculinity might evoke the privileged supergirl from chapter 2, but in contrast to the girls aspiring to be supergirls, the well-rounded boys we interviewed did not seem over-the-top in their involvements and came across as fairly relaxed rather than driven to perfection.

41. For a detailed discussion of the ways humor is used to consolidate heterosexual masculinity, see Mary Jane Kehily and Anoop Nayak, "'Lads and Laughter': Humour and the Production of Heterosexual Hierarchies," *Gender and Education* 9, no. 1 (1997): 69–88. See also Frosh et al., *Young Masculinities;* and Renold, "Learning the 'Hard' Way."

42. Other researchers have described how boys link popularity to pushing against adult authority in the school. As Frosh et al. (*Young Masculinities,* 200) describe, "popular boys were generally expected to 'backchat' the teachers."

43. For further discussion of boys' disruption of class, see Molly Warrington and Michael Younger, "The Other Side of the Gender Gap," *Gender and Education* 12, no. 4 (2000): 493–508.

4. SEXISM AND THE SMART GIRL

Epigraph: Judith Williamson, quoted in Rosalind Gill and Christina Scharff, *New Femininities? Postfeminism, Neoliberalism and Identity* (Basingstoke, UK: Palgrave, 2011), 1.

1. *Women against Feminism,* accessed August 20, 2015, www.women againstfeminism.tumblr.com.

2. For a relevant critique, see Michelle Smith, "Actually, Women, You Do Need Feminism," *The Conversation,* April 17, 2014, www .theconversation.com/actually-women-you-do-need-feminism-30415.

3. Baker ("Claiming Volition," 190) found that the girls in her study went "to great lengths to avoid being regarded as a victim" and, therefore, drew heavily on post-feminist understandings of empowerment to define their lives. Baker subsequently notes that the young

women were not keen to be regarded as victims because it was negatively associated with "self-pity, insufficient personal drive and a lack of personal responsibility for one's own life." See also Pomerantz et al., "Girls Run the World?"; and McRobbie, *The Aftermath of Feminism.*

4. As Baker notes ("Claiming Volition," 186), obscuring sexism vis-à-vis post-feminism sets in motion innumerable "punitive social and psychological consequences" for girls, including the idea that any dependence (whether financial, social, or emotional) indicates individual weakness." See also Currie et al., *Girl Power;* McRobbie, *The Aftermath of Feminism;* Pomerantz et al., "Girls Run the World?"; and Walkerdine et al., *Growing Up Girl.*

5. Erica Burman ("Childhood, Neo-Liberalism and the Feminization of Education") suggests that girls associate dependence with failure, which then generates powerful psychological implications, including disappointment, bitterness, and frustration.

6. As Taft ("Girl Power Politics," 73) also notes, claims of equality "not only make gender oppression invisible but also hide the social forces of racism, classism, and homophobia."

7. Deirdre M. Kelly and Shauna Pomerantz, "Mean, Wild, and Alienated: Girls and the State of Feminism in Popular Culture," *Girlhood Studies: An Interdisciplinary Journal* 2, no. 1 (2009): 1–17; Pomerantz et al., "Girls Run the World?" For examples of girls identifying sexism in their own lives, see Everyday Sexism Project, accessed August 31, 2015, www.everydaysexism.com.

8. See for example, Elizabeth Church, "SlutWalk Sparks Worldwide Protest Movement," *Globe and Mail,* May 10, 2011, www.theglobeandmail .com/news/toronto/slutwalk-sparks-worldwide-protest-movement /article583076.

9. See, for example, Shauna Pomerantz and Rebecca Raby, "Taking on School Dress Codes: Teen Rebels with a Cause," *Globe and Mail,* June 1, 2015, www.theglobeandmail.com/globe-debate/taking-on-school-dress-codesteen-rebels-with-a-cause/article24704035.

10. See, for example, Christine Haughney, "Teenage Girls Lobby Teen Vogue Magazine over Depiction of Women," *New York Times,* July 11, 2012, http://mediadecoder.blogs.nytimes.com/2012/07/11/teenage-girls-lobby-teen-vogue-magazine-over-depiction-of-women.

11. See, for example, Ruby Hamad, "Five Times the Women against Feminism Tumblr Proved Women Really Need Feminism," *Daily Life,* July 17, 2014, www.dailylife.com.au/news-and-views/dl-opinion/five-times-the-women-against-feminism-tumblr-proved-women-really-need-feminism-20140717–3c2so.html.

12. See, for example, "Celebs Who've Spoken Out against Showbiz Sexism," *Daily Life,* accessed July 29, 2015, www.dailylife.com.au/photogallery/news-and-views/dl-culture/celebs-whove-spoken-out-against-showbiz-sexism-20150521-gh6sgs.html.

13. Malala Yousafzai and Christina Lamb, *I Am Malala: The Girl Who Stood Up for Education and Was Shot by the Taliban* (New York: Little, Brown, 2013).

14. Everyday Sexism Project.

15. Lizzie Croker, "The Feminists of Pussy Riot and Femen Who Stood Up to Putin," *Daily Beast,* March 10, 2014, www.thedailybeast.com/articles/2014/03/10/the-feminists-of-pussy-riot-and-femen-who-stood-up-to-putin.html.

16. See, for example, Ariel Levy, *Female Chauvinist Pigs: Women and the Rise of Raunch Culture* (New York: Free Press, 2005).

17. Rosalind Gill ("Sexism Reloaded, or, It's Time to Get Angry Again," *Feminist Media Studies* 11, no. 1 [2011]: 62) suggests that sexism has now become a subtle rather than obvious endorsement of men over women. She argues that we are in an era of "new sexism," which is about "unspeakable inequalities" that go "largely unnoticed and unspoken about by even those most adversely affected by them."

18. If a girl did not know what sexism meant, we offered the following very general definition to prompt further discussion: "It's when boys and men are treated better than girls and women." While we understand that boys and men can also experience sexism, sexism toward girls and women is normalized and institutionalized in Western culture through the intersecting oppressions of gender, "race," class, and sexuality. Gill ("Sexism Reloaded") names postfeminism *as* sexism because it operates outside of, and consequently undermines, the routine methods for identifying gender oppression, such as issues highlighted in gender equity programs and antidiscrimination laws.

19. These "other" women are often pictured as Third World and Muslim women in need of rescue. See Gill, "Sexism Reloaded"; Chandra Mohanty, "Under Western Eyes: Feminist Scholarship and Colonial Discourses," *Feminist Review* 30, no. 10 (1988): 51–79; and Christina Scharff, *Repudiating Feminism: Young Women in a Neoliberal World* (Aldershot, UK: Ashgate, 2011).

20. Gill, "Sexism Reloaded."

21. For an analysis of the phrase "just joking around" in relation to racism in school, see Rebecca Raby, "'There's No Racism at My School, It's Just Joking Around': Ramifications for Anti-Racist Education," *Race, Ethnicity and Education* 7 no. 4 (2004): 367–83; and Larissa Bablack, Rebecca Raby, and Shauna Pomerantz, "'I Don't Want to Stereotype, but It's True': Maintaining Whiteness at the Centre through the 'Smart Asian' Stereotype in High School," *Whiteness and Education* 1, no. 1 (2016): 54–68.

22. Interestingly, a number of other girls said boys joked with them about making sandwiches. It was a common refrain in our interviews.

23. A Reach competition is an extracurricular school activity where teams compete against each other and gain points based on their ability to answer questions in various academic categories. Reach is short for Reach for the Top.

24. However, in the United States, Title IX, when followed, offers protection against such discrimination.

25. Pomerantz et al., "Girls Run the World?"

26. Archetypal feminists are generally depicted as "man-hating, dungaree-wearing, hairy armpitted, butch dykes and 'Plain Janes' angry at the world because they can't get a man" (Camille Nurka, "Postfeminist Autopsies," *Australian Feminist Studies* 17, no. 38 [2002]: 185). See also Shelley Budgeon, "Emergent Feminist (?) Identities: Young Women and the Practice of Micropolitics," *European Journal of Women's Studies* 8, no. 1 (2001): 7–28; Currie et al., *Girl Power*; and Danielle M. Giffort, "Feminist Dilemmas and Implicit Feminism at Girls' Rock Camp," *Gender and Society* 25, no. 5 (2001): 569–88.

27. Lyn Mikel Brown, *Raising Their Voices: The Politics of Girls' Anger* (Cambridge, MA: Harvard University Press, 1998); Carol Gilligan,

et al., *Making Connections;* Valerie Hey, *The Company She Keeps: An Ethnography of Girls' Friendship* (Buckingham, UK: Open University Press, 1997); Peggy Orenstein and American Association of University Women, *Schoolgirls: Young Women, Self-Esteem, and the Confidence Gap* (New York: Doubleday, 1994).

28. Walkerdine et al., *Growing Up Girl.*

29. See Currie et al., "Girl Power"; Currie et al., "The Geeks Shall Inherit the Earth"; Dawn H. Currie, Deirdre M. Kelly, and Shauna Pomerantz, "The Power to Squash People: Understanding Girls' Relational Aggression," *British Journal of Sociology of Education* 28, no. 1 (2007), 23–37; and Pascoe, *Dude, You're a Fag.*

30. McLovin's candid understanding of sexual power reflects McRobbie's ("Top Girls?," 725) critique of the post-feminist masquerade, described in chapter 3, where young women connect power to the "spectacle of excessive femininity" and, especially, sexual desirability. McRobbie ("Young Women and Consumer Culture," 539) thus suggests that this kind of power is actually "a tidal wave of invidious insurgent patriarchalism which is hidden beneath the celebrations of female freedom." While this reading of girls' cultural practices tends to see post-feminism as a totalizing force that co-ops girls entirely, McRobbie's point is certainly a relevant one in relation to post-feminism's ability to obscure sexism vis-à-vis the belief in personal empowerment.

31. See McRobbie, "Notes on Postfeminism and Popular Culture"; and McRobbie, *The Aftermath of Feminism.*

32. See Harris, *Future Girl.*

33. American Association of University Women, *How Schools Shortchange Girls;* Sadker and Sadker, *Failing at Fairness.*

34. Mike O'Donnell and Sue Sharpe, *Uncertain Masculinities: Youth, Uncertainty and Class in Contemporary Britain* (London: Routledge, 2000).

35. Harris, *Future Girl.*

36. Gill, "Sexism Reloaded."

37. See Barbara R. Bergmann, "Sex Segregation in the Blue-Collar Occupations: Women's Choices or Unremedied Discrimination? Comment on England," *Gender and Society* 25, no. 1 (2011): 88–93.

5. A DEEPER LOOK AT CLASS AND "RACE"

Epigraph: Carolyn Chen, "Asians: Too Smart for Their Own Good?," *New York Times,* December 19, 2012, www.nytimes.com/2012/12/20/opinion/asians-too-smart-for-their-own-good.html.

1. For just a few examples, see Bettie, *Women without Class;* Kimberle Crenshaw, "Mapping the Margins: Intersectionality, Identity Politics, and Violence against Women of Color," *Standford Law Review* 43, no. 6 (1991): 1241–99; Ann Arnett Ferguson, *Bad Boys: Public Schools and the Making of Black Masculinity* (Ann Arbor: University of Michigan Press, 2000); Pascoe, *Dude, You're a Fag;* Stephanie A. Shields, "Gender: An Intersectionality Perspective," *Sex Roles* 59, no. 5 (2008): 301–11.

2. Shawn Arango Ricks, "Falling through the Cracks: Black Girls and Education," *Interdisciplinary Journal of Teaching and Learning* 4, no. 1 (2014): 10–21; Ralina L. Joseph, "'Tyra Banks Is Fat': Reading (Post-)Racism and (Post-)Feminism in the New Millenium," *Critical Studies in Media Communication* 26, no. 3 (2009): 237–54.

3. For example, see Furlong and Cartmel, *Young People and Social Change.*

4. Income includes benefits, and wealth includes investments, properties, and debt.

5. Reflecting Bettie's (*Women without Class*) position, we consider economic-related categories, including relations to the means of production, income, wealth, skill, education, and status, to be important parts of class. But like Bettie, we also consider class to be performative (see also Walkerdine et al., *Growing Up Girl*). There is concreteness to class in terms of material relations, the routines of daily life, and shared histories in the body—or a lifelong durable inculcation of habitus (Bourdieu and Passeron, *Reproduction in Education*)—but sometimes, class positions can be embraced or eschewed and made more or less visible. Class can be given significance not only through what kind of work someone does but also through shifting processes of consumption, self-presentation, relationship building, personal goals, and life experiences (see Bettie, *Women without Class;* and Walkerdine et al., *Growing Up Girl*).

6. Raby and Pomerantz, "Landscapes of Academic Success."

7. This may, in part, be why so many students from Blue Ridge signed up for our study, as their sense of themselves as being smart was linked to *being* Blue Ridge students.

8. See Eckert, *Jock and Burnouts;* and Shauna Pomerantz, *Girls, Style, and School Identities: Dressing the Part* (New York: Palgrave, 2008).

9. For an excellent sociological analysis of the role of consumption in children's peer cultures, see Alison Pugh, *Longing and Belonging: Parents, Children, and Consumer Culture* (Berkeley: University of California Press, 2009). Not only does Pugh illustrate how purchasing practices play a central role in children's cultures, she also points to parental purchases that are about bolstering their children's belonging and peer status. She raises concerns about the young people who cannot, or will not, participate and also about the centrality of consumption in these processes.

10. Amira Proweller, who studied an elite private girls' school, argues that brand names were used within the peer culture to sort the girls by class, although this sorting was also used to critique upper-middle-class girls' privilege and how they used it to exclude others (see Proweller, *Constructing Female Identities: Meaning Making in an Upper Middle Class Youth Culture* [New York: State University of New York Press, 1998]).

11. Pamela Davis-Kean, "The Influence of Parent Education and Family Income on Child Achievement: The Indirect Role of Parental Expectations and the Home Environment," *Journal of Family Psychology* 19, no. 2 (2005): 294–304.

12. Classic critical theory on the inequities of education systems includes Samuel Bowles and Herbert Gintis, *Schooling in Capitalist America: Educational Reform and the Contradictions of Economic Life* (New York: Basic Books, 1977); Peter McLaren, *Life in Schools: An Introduction to Critical Pedagogy and the Foundations of Education,* 6th ed. (Boulder, CO: Paradigm Publishers, 2014); and Willis, *Learning to Labour.* Feminist research on the topic includes Julie Bettie, *Women without Class;* Angela McRobbie and Jenny Garber, "Girls and Subcultures" in *The Subcultures Reader,* 2nd ed., ed. Ken Gelder (London: Routledge, 1997), 112–20; Walkerdine et al. *Growing Up Girl;* and Lois Weis, *Working*

Class without Work: High School Students in a De-Industrializing Economy
(New York: Routledge, 1990).

13. Much like Flowerpower's observations at the beginning of this
chapter, Rory's position differed from these interpretations, and she
had rare insight into some of the ways privilege might work. She did
not focus on presumed family culture, but instead noted certain
advantages that privilege might bring, such as time and social
connections to the school (see Bourdieu, "The Forms of Capital"; and
Lareau, *Unequal Childhoods*). She talked about how children from
richer families sometimes have an advantage because their parents
are more involved in their schooling: "Their parents know all the
teachers, so if they get a bad grade and their parents ask for a retest,
it's like, 'Oh, yeah, sure!'" She did not feel that such privileges would
extend to her own family: "If my mom called in, they would be like,
'Sorry, that's not allowed.' They give favors."

14. For a more traditionally Marxist analysis of how schools
reproduce the class inequalities embedded in capitalism, see Bowles
and Gintis, *Schooling in Capitalist America*.

15. Bourdieu and Passeron, *Reproduction in Education*.

16. Rather than problematizing the young person's family or
culture, the focus on cultural capital suggests that the dominant
culture of the school is too narrow to meet the diverse backgrounds
of all students. See Lareau, *Unequal Childhoods*.

17. As Louise Archer, Sumi Hollingsworth, and Anna Halsall
("University's Not for Me—I'm a Nike Person": Urban, Working-Class
Young People's Negotiations of 'Style,' Identity, and Educational
Engagement," *Sociology* 41, no. 2 [2005], 220) put it, "More powerful
groups, like the middle classes, tend to enjoy a greater synergy between
their own life-worlds and those of dominant societal institutions and
structures, and hence benefit from a privileged ability to know,
understand and play the 'game.'" See also Lareau, *Unequal Childhoods*.

18. Raby, *School Rules*.

19. "Asian" is a contextual, homogenizing, and racialized term that
is used to refer to people across diverse cultures and countries
(Stacey J. Lee, "Additional Complexities: Social Class, Ethnicity,
Generation, and Gender in Asian American Student Experiences,"

Race, Ethnicity and Education 9, no. 1 [2006]: 17–28). Participants in our study frequently used the term "Asian," but they also identified themselves or other students as being from specific countries, such as Korea or China. We use the term "Asian" here as a problematically generalized, overarching category in order to focus on its effects. We have also opted to identify certain respondents as having East Asian, South Asian, or Southeast Asian heritage to indicate certain participants' positionality in this conversation and to gesture towards diversity within the term "Asian" but also to flag that "race" is not about a specific country or culture but rather about problematic meaning that is imputed to physical appearance. While we understand that people from South Asia, Southeast Asia, and East Asia are subject to different stereotypes, participants in our study invoked the "smart Asian" stereotype across these categories.

20. Flowerpower said that she was uncomfortable with her own ethnicity, a term that is used to refer to a group of people who feel united by a sense of shared history, language, and cultural practices (Stephen Cornell and Douglas Harmann, *Ethnicity and Race: Making Identities in a Changing World,* 2nd ed. [Thousand Oaks: Pine Forge, 2007]). In this chapter, we have opted to focus primarily on the concept of "race," however, as "ethnic distinctions within racial categories have tended to be overshadowed by the racial designations [usually asserted by others from outside the group]" (27). In our research, this observation has certainly been the case, as illustrated by the "smart Asian" stereotype, a form of categorizing that overshadows specific references to ethnicity and contributes to a shared experience among young people perceived to be Asian (see also Bettie, *Women without Class*).

21. Mythili Rajiva ("Brown Girls, White Worlds: Adolescence and the Making of Racialized Selves," *Canadian Review and Anthropology* 43, no. 2 [2006]: 165–83) explains how second generation South Asian girls in Canada generally feel a sense of belonging but then experience a "boundary moment" through which they become Othered as outside of dominant white culture.

22. See Enora R. Brown, "Freedom for Some, Discipline for 'Others,'" in *Education as Enforcement: The Militarization and Corporatiza-*

tion of Schools, ed. Kenneth J. Saltman and David A. Gabbard (New York: Routledge, 2003), 130–64; Ferguson, *Bad Boys;* Aaron Kupchik and Nicholas Ellis, "School Discipline and Security: Fair for All Students?," *Youth and Society* 39, no. 4 (2008): 549–74; Russell J. Skiba and M. Karega Rausch, "Zero Tolerance, Suspension, and Expulsion: Questions of Equity and Effectiveness," in *Handbook of Classroom Management: Research, Practice and Contemporary Issues,* ed. Carolyn M. Evertson and Carol S. Weinstein (Mahway, NJ: Lawrence Erlbaum Associates, 2006), 1063–92; Richard R. Verdugo, "Race-Ethnicity, Social Class, and Zero Tolerance Policies: The Cultural and Structural Wars," *Education and Urban Society* 35, no. 1 (2002): 50–75; and John M. Wallace, Sara Goodkind, Cynthia M. Wallace, and Jerald G. Bachman, "Racial, Ethnic and Gender Differences in School Discipline among U.S. High School Students: 1991–2005," *Negro Educational Review* 59, nos. 1–2 (2008): 47–62. For a rich, ethnographic examination of intersectionality and the unequal application of discipline across gender and "race," see Morris, "'Tuck In That Shirt!.'" For a focus on Canada, see Carl James, "Students 'at Risk': Stereotypes and the Schooling of Black Boys," *Urban Education* 47, no. 2 (2012): 464–94.

23. Celia B. Fisher, Scyatta A. Wallace, and Rose E. Fenton, "Discrimination Distress during Adolescence," *Journal of Youth and Adolescence* 29, no. 6 (2000): 679–95; Sandra Graham, April Z. Taylor, and Alice Y. Ho, "Race and Ethnicity in Peer Relations Research," in *Handbook of Peer Interactions, Relationships and Groups,* ed. Kenneth H. Rubin, William M. Bukowski, and Brett Laursen (New York: Guilford, 2009), 394–413; Susan Rosenbloom and Niobe Way, "Experiences of Discrimination among African American, Asian American, and Latino Adolescents in an Urban High School," *Youth and Society* 35, no. 4 (2004): 420–51.

24. Whiteness can be understood as a constructed, shifting, relational, and privileged boundary that positions people who either are not visibly "raced" or are perceived to be white. Whiteness is commonly the unspoken or "un/marked" norm (Richard Dyer, "The Matter of Whiteness," in *Theories of Race and Racism: A Reader,* ed. Les Back and John Solomos [London: Routledge, 2000], 539–48), problematically and favorably produced in contrast to "nonwhiteness" (Karen Deliovsky,

White Femininity: Race, Gender, and Power [Nova Scotia: Fernwood, 2010], 26). As Frances Henry and Carol Tator describe, "White culture, norms, and values […] become normative natural. They become the standard against which all other cultures, groups, and individuals are measured and usually found to be inferior" (*The Colour of Democracy: Racism in Canadian Society,* 3rd ed. [Toronto: Nelson, 2006]). As such, while intersected by other inequalities, whiteness "refers to a position of structural advantage and social dominance facilitating the practice of power over subdominant groups" (Levine-Rasky, "Whiteness," 86).

25. We are grateful to Larissa Bablak for her keen analytical insights into this topic. The article we coauthored with her deeply informed this section. See Bablak et al., "'I Don't Want to Stereotype.'"

26. Catherine Costigan, Tina F. Su, and Josephine M. Hua, "Ethnic Identity among Chinese Canadian Youth: A Review of the Canadian Literature," *Canadian Psychology* 50, no. 4 (2009): 261–72; Dan Cui and Jennifer Kelly, "'Too Asian?' or the Invisible Citizen on the Other Side of the Nation?," *Journal of International Migration and Integration* 14, no. 1 (2013): 157–74; Stacey J. Lee, *Unraveling the "Model Minority" Stereotype: Listening to Asian American Youth* (New York: Teachers College Press, 2009); Stacey J. Lee, *Up against Whiteness: Race, School, and Immigrant Youth* (New York: Teacher's College Press, 2005); Julie Matthews, "Racialised Schooling, 'Ethnic Success' and Asian-Australian Students," *British Journal of Sociology and Education* 23, no. 2 (2002): 193–207; Qin Zhang, "Asian Americans beyond the Model Minority Stereotype: The Nerdy and the Leftout," *Journal of International and Intercultural Communication* 3, no. 1 (2010): 20–37.

27. Cui and Kelly, "Too Asian?"; S. Lee, *Unraveling;* S. Lee, *Up against Whiteness;* Raby, "'There's No Racism at My School"; Jean Yonemura Wing, "Beyond Black and White: The Model Minority Myth and the Invisibility of Asian American Students," *Urban Review* 39, no. 4 (2007): 455–87; Zhang, "Asian Americans."

28. Daniel A. Yon, *Elusive Cultures: Schooling, Race and Identity in Global Times* (New York: State University of New York Press, 2000).

29. Cui and Kelly, "Too Asian?"; Lee, *Up against Whiteness;* Lee, *Unraveling the Model Minority;* Matthews, "Racialised Schooling"; Wing, "Beyond Black and White"; Zhang, "Asian Americans."

30. Gilberto Q. Conchas and Christina C. Pérez, "Surfing the 'Model Minority' Wave of Success: How the School Context Shapes Distinct Experiences among Vietnamese Youth," *New Directions for Youth Development* 2003, no. 100 (2003): 41–56; S. Lee, *Unraveling.*

31. Chen, "Asians: Too Smart"; Conchas and Pérez, "Surfing the 'Model Minority.'" See also Kim Zarzour, "Asian Students Are Feeling Stressed, Survey Shows," Yorkregion.com, July 12, 2013, www .yorkregion.com/news-story/3890884-asian-students-are-feeling-stressed-survey-shows; and Daniel A. Yon, "Urban Portraits of Identity: On the Problem of Knowing Culture and Identity in Intercultural Studies," *Journal of Intercultural Studies* 21, no. 2 (2000): 143–57.

32. Frances Henry, Carol Tator, Winston Mattis, and Tim Rees, "The Ideology of Racism," in *The Politics of Race in Canada: Readings in Historical Perspectives, Contemporary Realities, and Future Possibilities,* ed. Maria Wallis and Augie Fleras (Don Mills, ON: Oxford University Press, 2009), 108–18.

33. The related concept of "new racisms" attempts to broaden our understandings of racism, recognizing that people can "maintain two apparently conflicting sets of values"—a liberal openness to diversity and equality alongside "negative feelings about people of colour ... that result in differential treatment of them, or discrimination against them" (Henry et al., "Ideology of Racism," 108).

34. A similar comment was made by Caramel, who said she noticed "that more English people are slack about grades. People who came here from anywhere are all grade imperative." This problematically suggests that people who are from "here" are English and people from elsewhere are not. Stacey Lee ("Additional Complexities," 21) discusses this as a problem of being seen as "perpetual foreigners." See also page 147.

35. For example, when Shauna asked if there was any racism at Blue Ridge, Jenny-Po said, "There isn't much of it, there aren't many kids to be targeted. [Where I used to live,] there are a lot more kids,

and it's way more multicultural." In another example, Andrea asked Darlene and Maggie if Blue Ridge had a mix of ethnicities, and Darlene said that it didn't in comparison to the school she previously went to in another city: "I would say there is a bigger Asian population in [this other city], whereas now there's like five Asians at our school. Maybe that's an exaggeration, but there's not as many as before."

36. Raby, "There's No Racism."

37. S. Lee, "Additional Complexities."

38. As a case in point, Stacey Lee ("Additional Complexities") notes that, in the United States, Asian Americans are more likely to have higher *and* lower income than white people.

39. Ricks (*Falling through the Cracks*) points particularly to the dearth of research on black girls and academic success in the United States. The same can certainly be said for Canada.

6. COOL TO BE SMART

Epigraph: Pink, "Stupid Girls," digital download (Atlanta: LaFace Records, 2006).

1. Hollister is an American "lifestyle" brand owned by Abercrombie and Fitch. Its SoCal designs are targeted at teens and young adults. At the time of our interview, Hollister was very trendy. Lil' Wayne is an American rapper from New Orleans, who, at the time of our interview, had a number one hit on the Billboard charts.

2. See, for example, Bettie, *Women without Class;* Currie et al., *Girl Power;* Marnina Gonick, *Between Femininities: Ambivalence, Identity, and the Education of Girls* (New York: State University of New York Press, 2003); Yasmin Jiwani, Candis Steenbergen, and Claudia Mitchell, *Girlhood: Redefining the Limits* (Montreal: Black Rose, 2006); Lauraine Leblanc, *Pretty in Punk: Girls' Gender Resistance in a Boys' Subculture* (New Brunswick, NJ: Rutgers University Press, 1999); Angela McRobbie, *Feminism and Youth Culture;* Pomerantz, *Girls, Style, and School Identities;* Rebecca Raby, "Talking (behind Your) Back: Young Women and Resistance," in *Girlhood: Redefining the Limits,* ed. Yasmin Jiwani, Candis Steenbergen, and Claudia Mitchell (Montreal: Black Rose, 2006), 138–54; and Emma Renold and Jessica Ringrose, "Regulation and Rupture: Mapping

Tween and Teenage Resistances to the Heterosexual Matrix," *Feminist Theory* 9, no. 3 (2008); Ringrose, *Postfeminist Education?*

3. Butler (*Gender Trouble* and *Bodies That Matter*) names these gender constructs, along with the associated relationship between dominant gender dynamics, as part of the heterosexual matrix, where heterosexuality is assumed and also naturalized, normalized, and enforced through cultural norms and values. For more information, see chapter 3, note 13.

4. Rebecca Raby ("Talking [behind Your] Back"; "What Is Resistance?," *Journal of Youth Studies* 8, no. 2 [2005]: 151–71) offers a detailed look at the various ways that resistance has been explored in the social sciences from modernist and postmodernist perspectives. While modernist perspectives focus on organized resistance, oppositional deviance, and appropriation models, postmodernist perspectives focus on linguistic and discursive practices, multiplicities, and ambivalent possibilities. In keeping with a postmodern perspective, our use of the term "microresistance" draws on the work of French philosophers Giles Deleuze and Félix Guattari (*A Thousand Plateaus: Capitalism and Schizophrenia* [Minneapolis: University of Minnesota Press, 1987], 217), whose concept of micropolitics explores the nonintentional possibilities that exist among colliding forces, such as people, things, environments, and technologies. Micropolitics "implies hit-and-miss changes in rhythm and mode rather than any omnipotence; and something always escapes."

5. Renold and Ringrose, "Regulation and Rupture." See also Raby, "Talking (behind Your) Back," which argues that girls' resistance, in particular, tends to go unnoticed when we focus only on organized, oppositional forms of resistance.

6. Renold and Ringrose, "Regulation and Rupture," 313.

7. Renold and Ringrose ("Regulation and Rupture") draw on the Deleuzo-Guattarian notions of deterritorializaiton (ruptures) and reterritoralization (recuperations) to explore this process. See Deleuze and Guattari, *Thousand Plateaus.*

8. Ringrose, *Postfeminsit Education?,* 147. See also Shauna Pomerantz, "Spaces of Possibility: Mapping the Molecular in the Lives of Girls," *Girlhood Studies: An International Journal* 8, no. 2 (2015): 157–61.

9. Deleuze and Guattari (*Thousand Plateaus*) call these more sustained escapes "lines of flight."

10. "Jersey Shore Wiki," Wikia, accessed December 8, 2015, www.jerseyshore.wikia.com/wiki/Nicole_Polizzi.

11. Ibid.

12. Renold and Ringrose ("Regulation and Rupture," 332) analyze a similar situation where girls in their study "resisted hyper-feminine, heterosexualized embodiments, but these seemed to work to reclassify Other girls. Not surprisingly, resistance to hypersexual embodiment often resulted in a renewed class binary through the abject category of slut."

13. For example, see American Association of University Women, *How School Shortchange Girls;* Gilligan et al., *Making Connections;* Mikel Brown, *Raising Their Voices;* Raby, "'Tank Tops are OK but I Don't Want to See Her Thong': Girls' Engagements with Secondary School Dress Codes," *Youth and Society* 41, no. 3 (2010): 333–56; and Emma Renold, *Girls, Boys, and Junior Sexualities: Exploring Children's Gender and Sexual Relations in the Primary School* (London: Routledge, 2005).

14. As important as school culture is to the stories of girls who found being smart less socially challenging, it is equally important to acknowledge that school culture is always in flux; it changes with demographics and is influenced by historical moments and shifting social circumstances. In saying that school culture is never static, we draw attention to the fact that schools are created by the contextualized stories that girls (and others) tell about what their school is like. Deborah Britzman ("The Question of Belief: Writing Poststructural Ethnography," in *Working the Ruins: Feminist Poststructural Theory and Methods in Education,* ed. Elizabeth A. St. Pierre and Wanda S. Pillow [New York: Routledge, 2000], 32) notes that every telling of a school "is constrained, partial, and determined by the discourses and histories that prefigure, even as they might promise, representation."

15. Yon (*Elusive Culture,* 33) notes a similar camaraderie in his ethnography of an inner-city Toronto high school: "negative associations produce a sense of cohesiveness, mutual dependence, and community because of a 'pervasive' feeling of being threatened."

16. Given the shifting nature of school culture, it was certainly possible for different girls to have very different experiences of the same school. For Candace, Central was a nightmare. Deemed a "show-off" due to her high grades, she bluntly stated that "everyone there is focused on the worst, and nobody gives a shit about the best." In fact, Candace switched out of Central between her two group interviews because she felt "hated on" for being smart there. But for others, Central still emerged as a place where, as Margot put it, "being yourself" was possible.

17. Jenny-Po was interviewed alone, whereas Sara and Basil were interviewed together and Jacqueline and Cindy were interviewed together.

18. Huhman, "STEM Fields and the Gender Gap."

19. Some feminist and educational researchers have long argued that girls do better in a single-gender environment and that both girls and boys are less likely to pursue gender-nonconforming subjects (i.e., girls pursuing mathematics and sciences [especially physics] and boys pursuing arts and humanities [especially languages]) in coeducational schools. The pressure to conform to popular masculinity and popular femininity is argued to be too great in mixed gender environments. See American Association of University Women, *Separated by Sex: A Critical Look at Single-Sex Education for Girls* (Washington, DC: AAUW Educational Foundation, 1998). Yet others have problematized single-sex schooling as a form of enhancing (not diminishing) separate and essentialized gender roles. For an overview of these debates, see Diana Leonard, "Single-Sex Schooling," in The SAGE Handbook of Gender and Education, ed. Christine Skelton, Becky Francis, and Lisa Smulyan (London: SAGE, 2006), 190–204.

20. Pascoe (*Dude, You're a Fag*) notes that drama was one of the safe spaces for boys who challenged popular masculinity because of the expectation of creativity, risk-taking, and general nonconformity.

21. Emma Renold, "'Other' Boys: Negotiating Non-Hegemonic Masculinities in the Primary School," *Gender and Education* 16, no. 2 (2004): 247–65. Numerous other feminist researchers have supported Renold's supposition, urging for less dichotomized gender constructions

in order to create a culture where girls can thrive without fear of ridicule or pressure to conform to a particular way of "doing girl." See also Francis et al., *Identities and Practices of High Achieving Pupils.*

22. Gonick (*Between Femininities*) argues that ambivalence *is* the central experience of girlhood.

23. For example, see bell hooks, *Feminism Is for Everybody: Passionate Politics* (Boston: South End, 2010); Jill Blackmore, Jane Kenway, Leonnie Rennie, and Sue Willis, *Answering Back: Girls, Boys, and Feminism in Schools* (London: Routledge, 1998); and Ringrose, *Postfeminist Education?*

Bibliography

Abraham, Carolyn. "Part 1: Failing Boys and the Powder Keg of Sexual Politics." *Globe and Mail,* October 16, 2010. www.theglobeandmail.com /news/national/time-to-lead/part-1-failing-boys-and-the-powder-keg-of-sexual-politics/article4081751.

Adler, Patricia, and Peter Adler. *Peer Power: Preadolescent Culture and Identity.* New Brunswick, NJ: Rutgers University Press, 1998.

American Association of University Women. *The AAUW Report: How Schools Shortchange Girls; A Study of Major Findings on Girls and Education.* Washington, DC: AAUW Educational Foundation, 1999.

———. *Separated by Sex: A Critical Look at Single-Sex Education for Girls.* Washington, DC: AAUW Educational Foundation, 1998.

Apple, Michael. *Education and Power.* 2nd ed. New York: Routledge 1995.

Archer, Louise, Jennifer DeWitt, and Beatrice Willis. "Adolescent Boys' Science Aspirations: Masculinity, Capital, and Power." *Journal of Research in Science Teaching* 51, no. 1 (2014): 1–30.

Archer, Louise, Sumi Hollingworth, and Anna Halsall. "'University's Not for Me—I'm a Nike Person': Urban, Working-Class Young People's Negotiations of 'Style,' Identity, and Educational Engagement." *Sociology* 41, no. 2 (2005): 219–37.

Attwood, Feona. "Through the Looking Glass? Sexual Agency and Subjectification in Cyberspace." In *New Femininities? Postfeminism, Neoliberalism and*

Identity, edited by Rosalind Gill and Christina Scharff, 203–14. Basingstoke, UK: Palgrave, 2011.

Bablak, Larissa, Rebecca Raby, and Shauna Pomerantz. "'I Don't Want to Stereotype, but It's True': Maintaining Whiteness at the Centre through the 'Smart Asian' Stereotype in High School." *Whiteness and Education* 1, no. 1 (2016): 54–68.

Baker, Joanne. "Claiming Volition and Evading Victimhood: Post-Feminist Obligations for Young Women." *Feminism and Psychology* 20, no. 2 (2010): 186–204.

———. "Great Expectations and Post-Feminist Accountability: Young Women Living Up to the 'Successful Girls' Discourse." *Gender and Education* 22, no. 1 (2010): 1–15.

Barad, Karen. *Meeting the Universe Halfway: Quantum Physics and the Entanglement of Matter and Meaning*. Durham: Duke University Press, 2007.

———. "Posthumanist Performativity: Toward an Understanding of How Matter Comes to Matter." In *Material Feminisms*, edited by Stacy Alaimo and Susan Heckman, 120–56. Bloomingon: Indiana University Press, 2008.

BBC News. "Why Are Girls Higher Achievers?" September 23, 2003. http://news.bbc.co.uk/2/hi/talking_point/3112536.stm.

Beatts, Anne. "Pilot." *Square Pegs*, DVD. Directed by Kim Friedman. Sony Pictures Home Entertainment, 2008.

Beck, Ulrich. *Risk Society: Towards a New Modernity*. Translated by Mark Ritter. London: SAGE, 1992.

Bell, Leslie C. *Hard to Get: 20-Something Women and the Paradox of Sexual Freedom*. Berkeley: University of California Press, 2013.

Benatar, David. *The Second Sexism: Discrimination against Men and Boys*. Hoboken, NJ: Wiley-Blackwell, 2012.

Bergmann, Barbara R. "Sex Segregation in the Blue-Collar Occupations: Women's Choices or Unremedied Discrimination? Comment on England." *Gender and Society* 25, no. 1 (2011): 88–93.

Besen-Cassino, Yasemin. *Consuming Work: Youth Labor in America*. Philadelphia: Temple University Press, 2014.

Bettie, Julie. *Women without Class: Girls, Race, and Identity*. Berkeley: University of California Press, 2003.

Bettis, Pamela, Nicole C. Ferry, and Mary Roe. "Lord of the Guys: Alpha Girls and the Post-Feminist Landscape of American Education." *Gender Issues* 33, no. 2 (2016): 163–81.

Blackmore, Jill, Jane Kenway, Leonnie Rennie, and Sue Willis. *Answering Back: Girls, Boys, and Feminism in Schools.* London: Routledge, 1998.

Blau, Francine D., and Lawrence K. Kahn. "The Gender Pay Gap: Have Women Gone as Far as They Can?" *Academy of Management Perspectives* 21, no. 1 (2007): 7–23.

Block, Sheila. *Ontario's Growing Gap: The Role of Race and Gender.* Ottawa: Canadian Centre for Policy Alternatives, June 2010. www.ywcacanada .ca/data/research_docs/00000140.pdf.

Bourdieu, Pierre. "The Forms of Capital." In *The Sociology of Economic Life,* 2nd ed., edited by Mark Granovetter and Richard Swedberg, 96–111. Bolder, CO: Westview Press, 2001.

———. *The Logic of Practice.* Cambridge, UK: Polity Press, 1990.

Bourdieu, Pierre, and Jean-Claude Passeron. *Reproduction in Education, Society, and Culture.* Translated by Richard Nice. London: SAGE, 1990.

Bowles, Samuel, and Herbert Gintis. *Schooling in Capitalist America: Educational Reform and the Contradictions of Economic Life.* New York: Basic Books, 1977.

Britzman, Deborah P. "The Question of Belief: Writing Poststructural Ethnography." In *Working the Ruins: Feminist Poststructural Theory and Methods in Education,* edited by Elizabeth A. St. Pierre and Wanda S. Pillow, 27–40. New York: Routledge, 2000.

Brooks, David. "Mind over Muscle." *New York Times,* October 16, 2005. www.nytimes.com/2005/10/16/opinion/mind-over-muscle.html.

Brown, Enora R. "Freedom for Some, Discipline for 'Others.'" In *Education as Enforcement: The Militarization and Corporatization of Schools,* edited by Kenneth J. Saltman and David A. Gabbard, 130–64. New York: Routledge, 2003.

Brown, Lyn Mikel. *Raising Their Voices: The Politics of Girls' Anger.* Cambridge, MA: Harvard University Press, 1988.

Brown, Wendy. "Neo-Liberalism and the End of Liberal Democracy." *Theory and Event* 7, no. 1 (2003): 1–19.

Budgeon, Shelley. "The Contradictions of Successful Femininity: Third Wave Feminism, Postfeminism and 'New' Femininities." In *New*

Femininities: Postfeminism, Neoliberalism, and Subjectivity, edited by Rosalind Gill and Christina Scharff, 279–92. Basingstoke, UK: Palgrave, 2011.

———. "Emergent Feminist (?) Identities: Young Women and the Practice of Micropolitics." *European Journal of Women's Studies* 8, no. 1 (2001): 7–28.

Burman, Erica. "Childhood, Neo-Liberalism and the Feminization of Education." *Gender and Education* 17, no. 4 (2005): 251–67.

Busseri, Michael, Linda Rose-Krasnor, Teena Willoughby, and Heather Chalmers. "A Longitudinal Examination of Breadth and Intensity of Youth Activity Involvement and Successful Development." *Developmental Psychology* 42, no. 6 (2006): 1313–26.

Butler, Judith. *Bodies That Matter: On the Discursive Limits of "Sex."* New York: Routledge, 1993.

———. *Gender Trouble: Feminism and the Subversion of Identity.* New York: Routledge, 1990.

———. *The Psychic Life of Power: Theories in Subjection.* Stanford: Stanford University Press, 1997.

Catalyst. "Women CEOs of the S&P 500." April 3, 2015. www.catalyst.org /knowledge/women-ceos-sp-500.

———. "Women in Law in Canada and the U.S." March 3, 2015. www .catalyst.org/knowledge/women-law-canada-and-us.

Chaudhry, Lakshmi. "The Supergirl Syndrome." *Nation,* May 14, 2007. www .thenation.com/article/supergirl-syndrome.

Chen, Carolyn. "Asians: Too Smart for Their Own Good?" *New York Times,* December 19, 2012. www.nytimes.com/2012/12/20/opinion/asians-too-smart-for-their-own-good.html.

Christakis, Erika. "Do Teachers Really Discriminate against Boys?" *Time,* February 6, 2013. www.ideas.time.com/2013/02/06/do-teachers-really-discriminate-against-boys.

Church, Elizabeth. "SlutWalk Sparks Worldwide Protest Movement." *Globe and Mail,* May 10, 2011. www.theglobeandmail.com/news/toronto/slutwalk-sparks-worldwide-protest-movement/article583076.

Conaway, Sandra B. "Girls Who (Don't) Wear Glasses: The Performativity of Smart Girls on Teen Television." PhD diss., Bowling Green State University, 2007. https://etd.ohiolink.edu/ap/10?0::NO:10:P10_ACCESSION_NUM:bgsu1182800368.

Conchas, Gilberto Q., and Christina C. Pérez. "Surfing the 'Model Minority' Wave of Success: How the School Context Shapes Distinct Experiences among Vietnamese Youth." *New Directions for Youth Development* 2003, no. 100 (2003): 41–56.

Conlin, Michelle. "The New Gender Gap: From Kindergarten to Grad School, Boys Are Becoming the Second Sex." *BusinessWeek*, May 25, 2003. www.bloomberg.com/bw/stories/2003-05-25/the-new-gender-gap.

Connell, R.W. *Gender and Power: Society, the Person and Sexual Politics*. Stanford, CA: Stanford University Press, 1987.

Conrad-Curry, Dea. "A Four-Year Study of ACT Reading Results: Achievement Trends among Eleventh-Grade Boys and Girls in a Midwestern State." *Journal of Education* 191, no. 3 (2011): 27–37.

Cooper, Marianne. *Cut Adrift: Families in Insecure Times*. Berkeley: University of California Press, 2013.

Cornell, Stephen, and Douglas Harmann. *Ethnicity and Race: Making Identities in a Changing World*. 2nd ed. Thousand Oaks: Pine Forge, 2007.

Costigan, Catherine, Tina F. Su, and Josephine M. Hua. "Ethnic Identity among Chinese Canadian Youth: A Review of the Canadian Literature." *Canadian Psychology* 50, no. 4 (2009): 261–72.

Crenshaw, Kimberle. "Mapping the Margins: Intersectionality, Identity Politics, and Violence against Women of Color." *Standford Law Review* 43, no. 6 (1991): 1241–99.

Croker, Lizzie. "The Feminists of Pussy Riot and Femen Who Stood Up to Putin." *Daily Beast*, March 10, 2014. www.thedailybeast.com/articles/2014/03/10/the-feminists-of-pussy-riot-and-femen-who-stood-up-to-putin.html.

Cui, Dan, and Jennifer Kelly. "'Too Asian?' or the Invisible Citizen on the Other Side of the Nation?" *Journal of International Migration and Integration* 14, no. 1 (2013): 157–74.

Currie, Dawn H., Deirdre M. Kelly, and Shauna Pomerantz. "'The Geeks Shall Inherit the Earth': Girls' Agency, Subjectivity and Empowerment." *Journal of Youth Studies* 9, no.4 (2006): 419–36.

———. *"Girl Power": Girls Reinventing Girlhoods*. New York: Peter Lang, 2009.

———. "The Power to Squash People: Understanding Girls' Relational Aggression." *British Journal of Sociology of Education* 28, no. 1 (2007), 23–37.

Daily Life. "Celebs Who've Spoken Out against Showbiz Sexism." Accessed July 29, 2015. www.dailylife.com.au/photogallery/news-and-views /dl-culture/celebs-whove-spoken-out-against-showbiz-sexism-20150521-gh6sgs.html.

Davies, Bronwyn. "Reading Anger in Early Childhood Intra-Actions: A Diffractive Analysis." *Qualitative Inquiry* 20, no. 6 (2014): 734–41.

———. "The Subject of Post-Structuralism: A Reply to Alison Jones." *Gender and Education* 9, no. 3 (1997): 271–84.

Davis-Kean, Pamela. "The Influence of Parent Education and Family Income on Child Achievement: The Indirect Role of Parental Expectations and the Home Environment." *Journal of Family Psychology* 19, no. 2 (2005): 294–304.

Day, Lori. "Why Boys Are Failing in an Educational System Stacked against Them." *Huffington Post Education,* August 27, 2011. www .huffingtonpost.com/lori-day/why-boys-are-failing-in-a_b_884262 .html.

Deleuze, Giles, and Félix Guattari. *A Thousand Plateaus: Capitalism and Schizophrenia.* Minneapolis: University of Minnesota Press, 1987.

Deliovsky, Karen. *White Femininity: Race, Gender, and Power.* Nova Scotia: Fernwood, 2010.

DiPrete, Thomas A., and Claudia Buchmann. *The Rise of Women: The Growing Gender Gap in Education and What It Means for American Schools.* New York: Russell Sage Foundation, 2013.

Douglas, Susan. *The Rise of Enlightened Sexism: How Pop Culture Took Us from Girl Power to Girls Gone Wild.* New York: St. Martin's, 2010.

Dyer, Richard. "The Matter of Whiteness." In *Theories of Race and Racism: A Reader,* edited by Les Back and John Solomos London, 539–48. London: Routledge, 2000.

Eckert, Penelope. *Jocks and Burnouts: Social Categories and Identity in High School.* New York: Teachers College Press, 1989.

Eliot, Lise. *Pink Brain, Blue Brain: How Small Differences Grow into Troublesome Gaps—And What We Can Do about It.* Boston: Mariner Books, 2010.

Ely, Robin J., Pamela Stone, and Colleen Ammerman. "Rethink What You 'Know' about High-Achieving Women." *Harvard Business Review* 92, no. 12 (December 2014): 101–9.

Epstein, Debbie, Janette Elwood, Valerie Hey, and Janet Maw. *Failing Boys? Issues in Gender and Achievement.* Maidenhead, UK: Open University Press, 1998.

Esters, Lorenzo, and Richard Whitmire. "Where the Boys Aren't: Obama Must Attack the Gender Gap in Schooling." *Daily News,* May 16, 2010. www.nydailynews.com/opinion/boys-aren-college-obama-attack-gender-gap-schooling-article-1.449738.

Everyday Sexism Project. Accessed August 31, 2015. www.everydaysexism .com.

Farrugia, David. "Young People and Structural Inequality: Beyond the Middle Ground." *Journal of Youth Studies* 16, no. 5 (2013): 670–93.

Ferguson, Ann Arnett. *Bad Boys: Public Schools and the Making of Black Masculinity.* Ann Arbor: University of Michigan Press, 2000.

Fine, Michelle. "Foreword." In *All about the Girl,* edited by Anita Harris, xi–xv. Routledge: New York, 2004.

Fisher, Celia B., Scyatta A. Wallace, and Rose E. Fenton. "Discrimination Distress during Adolescence." *Journal of Youth and Adolescence* 29, no. 6 (2000): 679–95.

Francis, Becky. *Boys, Girls, and Achievement: Addressing the Classroom Issues.* New York: RoutledgeFalmer, 2000.

Francis, Becky, Barbara Read, and Christine Skelton. *The Identities and Practices of High Achieving Pupils: Negotiating Achievement and Peer Cultures.* London: Bloomsbury, 2012.

Francis, Becky, Christine Skelton, and Barbara Read. "The Simultaneous Production of Educational Achievement and Popularity: How Do Some Pupils Accomplish It?" *British Educational Research Journal* 36, no. 2 (2010): 317–40.

Fredericks, Jennifer A. "Extracurricular Participation and Academic Outcomes: Testing the Over-Scheduling Hypothesis." *Journal of Youth and Adolescence* 41 (2012): 295–306.

Frosh, Stephen, Ann Phoenix, and Rob Pattman. *Young Masculinities: Understanding Boys in Contemporary Society.* Basingstoke, UK: Palgrave, 2001.

Funk, Liz. *Supergirls Speak Out.* New York: Touchstone, 2009.

Furlong, Andy, and Fred Cartmel. *Young People and Social Change: Individualization and Risk in Late Modernity.* Buckingham: Open University Press, 1997.

Gardener, Howard. *Frames of Mind: The Theory of Multiple Intelligences.* New York: Basic Books, 1983.

Garrison, Ednie D. "U.S. Feminism—Grrrl Style!: Youth (Sub)Cultures and the Technologics of the Third Wave." *Feminist Studies* 26, no. 1 (2000): 141–70.

Giddens, Anthony. *Modernity and Self Identity: Self and Society in the Late Modern Age.* Cambridge, UK: Polity Press, 1991.

Giffort, Danielle M. "Feminist Dilemmas and Implicit Feminism at Girls' Rock Camp." *Gender and Society* 25, no. 5 (2001): 569–88.

Gill, Rosalind. "Empowerment/Sexism: Figuring Female Sexual Agency in Contemporary Advertising." *Feminism and Psychology* 18, no. 1 (2008): 35–60.

———. "Postfeminist Media Culture: Elements of a Sensibility." *European Journal of Cultural Studies* 10, no. 2 (2007): 147–66.

———. "Sexism Reloaded, or, It's Time to Get Angry Again." *Feminist Media Studies* 11, no. 1 (2011): 62.

Gill, Rosalind, and Christina Scharff, eds. *New Femininities? Postfeminism, Neoliberalism and Identity.* Basingstoke, UK: Palgrave, 2011.

Gilligan, Carol, Nona Lyons, Trudy J. Hanmer, and Emma Willard School. *Making Connections: The Relational Worlds of Adolescent Girls at Emma Willard School.* Cambridge, MA: Harvard University Press, 1990.

Girl Effect. Accessed May 4, 2015. www.girleffect.org.

Gonick, Marnina. *Between Femininities: Ambivalence, Identity, and the Education of Girls.* New York: State University of New York Press, 2003.

———. "Between 'Girl Power' and 'Reviving Ophelia': Constituting the Neoliberal Girl Subject." *NWSA Journal* 18, no. 2 (2006): 1–23.

———. "Girl Power." In *Girl Culture: An Encyclopedia,* edited by Claudia A. Mitchel and Jacqueline Reid-Walsh, 310–14. Westport, CA: Greenwood Press, 2008.

Government of Canada. *Chief Public Health Officer's Report on the State of Public Health in Canada.* Public Health Agency of Canada, 2011. www.phac-aspc .gc.ca/cphorsphc-respcacsp/2011/cphorsphc-respcacsp-06-eng.php.

Graham, Sandra, April Z. Taylor, and Alice Y. Ho. "Race and Ethnicity in Peer Relations Research." In *Handbook of Peer Interactions, Relationships and Groups,* edited by Kenneth H. Rubin, William M. Bukowski, and Brett Laursen, 394–413. New York: Guilford, 2009.

Gurian, Michael, and Kathy Stevens. *Girls and Boys Learn Differently: A Guide For Teachers and Parents.* New York: Jossey-Bass, 2010.

———. *The Minds of Boys: Saving Our Sons from Falling behind in School and in Life.* New York: Jossey-Bass, 2007.

Hamad, Ruby. "Five Times the Women against Feminism Tumblr Proved Women Really Need Feminism." *Daily Life,* July 17, 2014. www.dailylife .com.au/news-and-views/dl-opinion/five-times-the-women-against-feminism-tumblr-proved-women-really-need-feminism-20140717–3c2s0.html.

Hammer, Kate. "Feminization of Education: One of Five Reasons Why Boys Are Failing." *Globe and Mail,* October 15, 2010. www.theglobeandmail.com /news/national/time-to-lead/feminization-of-education-one-of-five-reasons-why-boys-are-failing/article1215014.

Harris, Anita. *Future Girl: Young Women in the Twenty-First Century.* New York: Routledge, 2004.

Hatt, Beth. "Smartness as a Cultural Practice in Schools." *American Educational Research Journal* 49, no. 3 (2012): 438–60.

———. "Street Smarts vs. Book Smarts: The Figured World of Smartness in the Lives of Marginalized, Urban Youth." *Urban Review* 39, no. 2 (2007): 145–66.

Haughney, Christine. "Teenage Girls Lobby Teen Vogue Magazine over Depiction of Women." *New York Times,* July 11, 2012. http://mediadecoder .blogs.nytimes.com/2012/07/11/teenage-girls-lobby-teen-vogue-magazine-over-depiction-of-women.

Henry, Frances, and Carol Tator. *The Colour of Democracy: Racism in Canadian Society.* 3rd ed. Toronto: Nelson, 2006.

Henry, Frances, Carol Tator, Winston Mattis, and Tim Rees. "The Ideology of Racism." In *The Politics of Race in Canada: Readings in Historical Perspectives, Contemporary Realities, and Future Possibilities,* edited by Maria Wallis and Augie Fleras, 108–18. Don Mills, ON: Oxford University Press, 2009.

Hey, Valerie. *The Company She Keeps: An Ethnography of Girls' Friendships.* Buckingham, UK: Open University Press, 1997.

Hill, Catherine. *The Simple Truth about the Gender Pay Gap (Spring 2015).* Washington, DC: AAUW, 2015. www.aauw.org/research/the-simple-truth-about-the-gender-pay-gap.

hooks, bell. *Feminism Is for Everybody: Passionate Politics.* Boston: South End, 2010.

Horbury, Alison. "Post-Feminist Impasses in Popular Heroine Television." *Continuum: Journal of Media and Cultural Studies* 28, no. 2 (2014): 213–25.

Huhman, Heather R. "STEM Fields and the Gender Gap: Where Are the Women?" *Forbes,* June 20, 2012. www.forbes.com/sites/work-in-progress/2012/06/20/stem-fields-and-the-gender-gap-where-are-the-women.

Hymowitz, Kay. *Manning Up: How the Rise of Women Has Turned Men into Boys.* New York: Basic Books, 2012.

Inness, Sherrie A. *Geek Chic: Smart Women in Popular Culture.* New York: Palgrave Macmillan, 2007.

Ivinson, Gabrielle, and Emma Renold. "Valleys' Girls: Re-Theorising Bodies and Agency in a Semi-Rural Post-Industrial Locale." *Gender and Education* 25, no. 6 (2013): 704–21.

Jackson, Carolyn, Carrie Paechter, and Emma Renold. *Girls and Education 3–16: Continuing Concerns, New Agendas.* Buckingham: Open University Press, 2010.

Jackson, Sue, and Tiina M. Vares. "Media 'Sluts': 'Tween' Girls' Negotiations of Postfeminist Sexual Subjectivities in Popular Culture." In *New Femininities: Postfeminism, Neoliberalism and Subjectivity,* edited by Rosalind Gill and Christina Scharff, 134–46. Basingstoke, UK: Palgrave, 2011.

James, Carl. "Students 'at Risk': Stereotypes and the Schooling of Black Boys." *Urban Education* 47, no. 2 (2012): 464–94.

Jarvis, Alice-Azania. "The New Girl Power: Why We're Living in a Young Woman's World." *Independent,* September 9, 2010. www.independent.co .uk/voices/commentators/the-new-girl-power-why-were-living-in-a-young-womans-world-2074042.html.

"Jersey Shore Wiki." Wikia. Accessed December 8, 2015. www.jerseyshore .wikia.com/wiki/Nicole_Polizzi.

Jiwani, Yasmin, Candis Steenbergen, and Claudia Mitchell. *Girlhood: Redefining the Limits.* Montreal: Black Rose, 2006.

Joshi, Nalini. "The Future of Science: Women." Address to the National Press Club of Australia. Canberra, Australia, March 30, 2016.

Kearney, Mary Celeste. "The Missing Links: Riot Grrrl-Feminism-Lesbian Culture." In *Sexing the Groove: Popular Music and Gender,* edited by Sheila Whiteley, 67–99. London: Routledge, 1997.

Kehily, Mary Jane, and Anoop Nayak. "'Lads and Laughter': Humour and the Production of Heterosexual Hierarchies." *Gender and Education* 9, no. 1 (1997): 69–88.

Kelly, Deirdre M., and Shauna Pomerantz. "Mean, Wild, and Alienated: Girls and the State of Feminism in Popular Culture." *Girlhood Studies: An Interdisciplinary Journal* 2, no. 1 (2009): 1–17.

Kimmel, Michael. "'What about the Boys?': What Current Debates Tell Us—and Don't Tell Us—about Boys in School." In *Reconstructing Gender: A Multicultural Anthology,* edited by Estelle Disch, 369–81. New York: McGraw Hill, 2009.

Kindlon, Daniel J. *Alpha Girls: Understanding the New American Girl and How She is Changing the World.* Emmaus, PA: Rodale Books, 2006.

Kindlon, Daniel J., and Michael Thompson. *Raising Cain: Protecting the Emotional Life of Boys.* New York: Ballantine Books, 2000.

Knowles, Beyoncé. "Run the World (Girls)." Digital download. New York City: Columbia Records, 2011.

Kupchik, Aaron, and Nicholas Ellis. "School Discipline and Security: Fair for All Students?" *Youth and Society* 39, no. 4 (2008): 549–74.

Laksmi Chaundhry. "The Supergirl Syndrome." *Nation,* May 1, 2007. www .thenation.com/article/supergirl-syndrome.

Lareau, Annette. *Unequal Childhoods: Class, Race, and Family Life.* Berkeley: University of California Press, 2003.

Layton, Lyndsay. "National High School Graduation Rates at Historic High, but Disparities Still Exist." *Washington Post,* April 8, 2014. www .washingtonpost.com/local/education/high-school-graduation-rates-at-historic-high/2014/04/28/84eb0122-cee0-11e3-937f-d3026234b51c_story. html.

Leblanc, Lauraine. *Pretty in Punk: Girls' Gender Resistance in a Boys' Subculture.* New Brunswick, NJ: Rutgers University Press, 1999.

Lee, Nick. *Childhood and Society: Growing Up in an Age of Uncertainty.* Buckingham: Open University Press, 2005.

Lee, Stacey J. "Additional Complexities: Social Class, Ethnicity, Generation, and Gender in Asian American Student Experiences." *Race, Ethnicity and Education* 9, no. 1 (2006): 17–28.

———. *Unraveling the "Model Minority" Stereotype: Listening to Asian American Youth.* New York: Teachers College Press, 2009.

———. *Up against Whiteness: Race, School, and Immigrant Youth.* New York: Teachers College Press, 2005.

Legendary Entertainment. "Legendary Acquires Amy Poehler's Smart Girls at the Party Network." Legendary Entertainment press release. October 13, 2014. http://corporate.legendary.com/amy-poehlers-smart-girl.

Leonard, Diana. "Single-Sex Schooling." In The SAGE Handbook of Gender and Education, edited by Christine Skelton, Becky Francis, and Lisa Smulyan, 190–204. London: SAGE, 2006.

Leonard, Marion. "'Rebel Girl, You Are the Queen of My World': Feminism, 'Subculture' and Grrrl Power." In *Sexing The Groove: Popular Music and Gender,* edited by Sheila Whitely, 230–55. London: Routledge, 1997.

Levine-Rasky, Cynthia. "Whiteness: Normalization and the Everyday Practice of Power." In *Power and Everyday Practices,* edited by Deborah Brock, Rebecca Raby, and Mark P. Thomas, 86–109. Toronto: Nelson, 2012.

Levy, Ariel. *Female Chauvinist Pigs: Women and the Rise of Raunch Culture.* New York: Free Press, 2005.

Lewin, Tamar. "At Colleges, Women Are Leaving Men in the Dust." *New York Times,* July 9, 2006. www.nytimes.com/2006/07/09/education /09college.html.

———. "How Boys Lost Out to Girl Power." *New York Times,* December 13, 1998. www.nytimes.com/1998/12/13/weekinreview/ideas-trends-how-boys-lost-out-to-girl-power.html.

Lingard, Bob. "Contextualising and Utilising the 'What about the Boys?' Discourse in Education." *Change: Transformations in Education* 1 no. 2 (1998): 16–30.

Lingard, Bob, Wayne Martino, and Martin Mills. *Boys and Schooling: Beyond Structural Reform.* Hampshire, UK: Palgrave Macmillan. 2009.

Mac an Ghaill, Máirtín. *The Making of Men: Masculinities, Sexualities and Schooling.* Buckingham: Open University Press, 1994.

Mahoney, Joseph L., Angel L. Harris, and Jacqelynne S. Eccles. "Organized Activity Participation, Positive Youth Development, and the Over-Scheduling Hypothesis." *Social Policy Report* 20, no. 4 (2006): 1–32.

Martin, Courtenay. *Perfect Girls, Starving Daughters.* New York: Berkley Books, 2007.

Martino, Wayne. "Failing Boys!: Beyond Crisis, Moral Panic and Limiting Stereotypes." *Education Canada* 51, no. 4 (Fall 2011). www.cea-ace.ca /education-canada/article/failing-boys-beyond-crisis-moral-panic-and-limiting-stereotypes.

Martino, Wayne, and Bob Meyenn, eds. *What about the Boys? Issues of Masculinity and Schooling.* Buckingham: Open University Press, 2001.

Martino, Wayne, and Deborah Berrill. "Boys, Schooling, and Masculinities: Interrogating the 'Right' Way to Educate Boys." *Educational Review* 55, no. 2 (2003): 99–117.

Martino, Wayne, and Gol Rezai Rashti. "Neoliberal Accountability and the Politics of Boys' Underachievement: Steering Policy by Numbers in the Ontario Context." *International Journal of Inclusive Education* 16, no. 4 (2012): 423–40.

Martins, Chris. "Zayn Malik's Own Direction." *Billboard* 128, no. 1 (2016). www.billboard.com/articles/news/cover-story/6835305/zayn-malik-solo-career-one-direction-new-music.

Matthews, Julie. "Racialised Schooling, 'Ethnic Success' and Asian-Australian Students." *British Journal of Sociology and Education* 23, no. 2 (2002): 193–207.

McLaren, Peter. *Life in Schools: An Introduction to Critical Pedagogy and the Foundations of Education.* 6th ed. Boulder, CO: Paradigm Publishers, 2014.

McRobbie, Angela. *The Aftermath of Feminism: Gender, Culture and Social Change.* London: SAGE, 2009.

———. *Feminism and Youth Culture.* 2nd ed. Basingstoke, UK: Palgrave, 2000.

———. "Notes on Postfeminism and Popular Culture: Bridget Jones and the New Gender Regime." In *All about the Girl: Culture, Power, and Identity*, edited by Anita Harris, 3–14. New York: Routledge, 2004.

———. "Top Girls? Young Women and the Post-Feminist Sexual Contract." *Cultural Studies* 21, no. 4 (2007): 720.

———. "Young Women and Consumer Culture: An Intervention." *Cultural Studies* 22, no. 5 (2008): 531–50.

McRobbie, Angela, and Jenny Garber. "Girls and Subcultures." In *The Subcultures Reader,* 2nd ed., edited by Ken Gelder, 112–20. London: Routledge, 1997.

Meadows, Susannah, and Mary Carmichael. "Meet the GAMMA Girls." *Newsweek,* June 3, 2002, 44–51.

Mendrick, Heather, and Becky Francis. "Boffin and Geek Identities: Abject or Privileged?" *Gender and Education* 24, no. 1 (2012): 15–24.

Moeller, Kathryn K. "Proving 'the Girl Effect': Corporate Knowledge Production and Educational Intervention." *International Journal of Educational Development* 33, no. 6 (2013): 612–21.

Mohanty, Chandra. "Under Western Eyes: Feminist Scholarship and Colonial Discourses." *Feminist Review* 30, no. 10 (1988): 51–79.

Morris, Edward W. "'Tuck In That Shirt!' Race, Class, Gender and Discipline in an Urban School." *Sociological Perspectives* 48, no. 1 (2005): 25–48.

Nicholson, Linda, ed. *The Second Wave: A Reader in Feminist Theory.* New York: Routledge, 1999.

Noël, Lauren, and Christine H. Arscott. *Millennial Women: What Executives Need to Know about Millennial Women.* Lexington, MA: International Consortium for Executive Development Research, 2016. www.icedr.org /research/documents/15_millennial_women.pdf.

Nurka, Camille. "Postfeminist Autopsies." *Australian Feminist Studies* 17, no. 38 (2002): 185.

O'Donnell, Mike, and Sue Sharpe. *Uncertain Masculinities: Youth, Uncertainty and Class in Contemporary Britain.* London: Routledge, 2000.

Orenstein, Peggy, and American Association of University Women. *Schoolgirls: Young Women, Self-Esteem, and the Confidence Gap.* New York: Doubleday, 1994.

Paquette, Danielle. "Why Young Women Leave Their Jobs." *Washington Post,* March 28, 2016.

Parker, Andrew. "The Construction of Masculinity within Boys' Physical Education." *Gender and Education* 8, no. 2 (1996): 141–58.

Pascoe, C.J. *Dude, You're a Fag: Masculinity and Sexuality in High School.* Berkeley: University of California Press, 2006.

Pink. "Stupid Girls." Digital download. Atlanta: LaFace Records, 2006.

Pipher, Mary Bray. *Reviving Ophelia: Saving the Selves of Adolescent Girls.* New York: Putnam, 1994.

Pomerantz, Shauna. *Girls, Style, and School Identities: Dressing the Part.* New York: Palgrave, 2008.

————. "Spaces of Possibility: Mapping the Molecular in the Lives of Girls." *Girlhood Studies: An International Journal* 8, no. 2 (2015): 157–61.

Pomerantz, Shauna, and Rebecca Raby. "'Oh, She's So Smart': Girls' Complex Engagements with Post-Feminist Narratives of Academic Success." *Gender and Education* 23, no. 5 (2011): 549–64.

————. "Reading Smart Girls: Post-Nerds in Post-Feminist Popular Culture." In *Girls, Texts, Cultures,* edited by Clare Bradford and Mavis Reimer, 287–312. Waterloo, ON: Wilfred Laurier University Press, 2015.

————. "Taking on School Dress Codes: Teen Rebels with a Cause." *Globe andMail*June1,2015.www.theglobeandmail.com/globe-debate/taking-on-school-dress-codesteen-rebels-with-a-cause/article24704035.

Pomerantz, Shauna, Rebecca Raby, and Andrea Stefanik. "Girls Run the World? Caught between Sexism and Post-Feminism in the School." *Gender and Society* 27, no. 2 (2013): 185–207.

Proweller, Amira. *Constructing Female Identities: Meaning Making in an Upper Middle Class Youth Culture.* New York: State University of New York Press, 1998.

Pugh, Alison. *Longing and Belonging: Parents, Children, and Consumer Culture.* Berkeley: University of California Press, 2009.

Raby, Rebecca. *School Rules: Obedience, Discipline and Elusive Democracy.* Toronto: University of Toronto Press, 2012.

————. "Talking (behind Your) Back: Young Women and Resistance." In *Girlhood: Redefining the Limits,* edited by Yasmin Jiwani, Candis Steenbergen, and Claudia Mitchell, 138–54. Montreal: Black Rose, 2006.

————. "'Tank Tops Are OK but I Don't Want to See Her Thong': Girls' Engagements with Secondary School Dress Codes." *Youth and Society* 41, no. 3 (2010): 333–56.

————. "'There's No Racism at My School, It's Just Joking Around': Ramifications for Anti-Racist Education." *Race, Ethnicity and Education* 7 no. 4 (2004): 367–83.

————. "What Is Resistance?" *Journal of Youth Studies* 8 no. 2 (2005): 151–71.

Raby, Rebecca, and Shauna Pomerantz. "Landscapes of Academic Success: Girls, Location, and the Importance of School Culture." In *Girlhood Studies and the Politics of Place: Contemporary Paradigms for Research,* edited by Claudia A. Mitchell and Carrie Rentschler, 68–86. New York: Berghahn Books, 2016.

———. "Playing It Down or Playing It Up: The Pleasures and Hazards of Doing 'Smart Girl' in High School." *British Journal of Sociology of Education* 36, no. 4 (2015): 507–25.

Rajiva, Mythili. "Brown Girls, White Worlds: Adolescence and the Making of Racialized Selves." *Canadian Review and Anthropology* 43, no. 2 (2006): 165–83.

Ralina L. Joseph. "'Tyra Banks Is Fat': Reading (Post-)Racism and (Post-)Feminism in the New Millenium," *Critical Studies in Media Communication* 26, no. 3 (2009): 237–54.

Renold, Emma. *Girls, Boys, and Junior Sexualities: Exploring Children's Gender and Sexual Relations in the Primary School.* London: Routledge, 2005.

———. "Learning the 'Hard' Way: Boys, Hegemonic Masculinity and the Negotiation of Learner Identities in the Primary School." *British Journal of Sociology of Education* 22, no. 3 (2001): 369–85.

———. "'Other' Boys: Negotiating Non-Hegemonic Masculinities in the Primary School." *Gender and Education* 16 no. 2 (2004): 247–65.

———. "'Square-Girls': Femininity and the Negotiation of Academic Success in the Primary School." *British Educational Research Journal* 27, no. 5 (2001): 577–88

Renold, Emma, and Alexandra Allan. "Bright and Beautiful: High Achieving Girls, Ambivalent Femininities, and the Feminization of Success in the Primary School." *Discourse: Studies in the Cultural Politics of Education* 27, no. 4 (2006): 457–73.

Renold, Emma, and Jessica Ringrose. "Regulation and Rupture: Mapping Tween and Teenage Resistances to the Heterosexual Matrix." *Feminist Theory* 9, no. 3 (2008): 313–38.

———. "Schizoid Subjectivities? Re-Theorizing Teen Girls' Sexual Cultures in an Era of 'Sexualization.'" *Journal of Sociology* 47, no. 4 (2011): 389–409.

Ricks, Shawn Arango. "Falling through the Cracks: Black Girls and Education," *Interdisciplinary Journal of Teaching and Learning* 4, no. 1 (2014): 10–21.

Rimer, Sara. "For Girls, It's Be Yourself, and Be Perfect, Too." *New York Times,* April 1, 2007. www.nytimes.com/2007/04/01/education/01girls.html.

Ringrose, Jessica. *Postfeminist Education? Girls and the Sexual Politics of Schooling.* London: Routledge, 2013.

———. "Successful Girls? Complicating Post-Feminist, Neoliberal Discourses of Educational Achievement and Gender Equality." *Gender and Education* 19, no. 4 (2007): 471–89.

Ringrose, Jessica, and Valerie Walkerdine. "What Does It Mean to Be a Girl in the Twenty-First Century? Exploring Some Contemporary Dilemmas of Femininity and Girlhood in the West." In *Girl Culture: An Encyclopedia,* vol. 1, edited by Claudia A. Mitchell and Jacqueline Reid-Walsh, 6–16. Westport, CT: Greenwood Press, 2007.

Roberts, Steven. "Misrepresenting 'Choice Biographies'? A Reply to Woodman." *Journal of Youth Studies* 13, no. 1 (2010): 137–49.

Rose, Nikolas. *Inventing Our Selves: Psychology, Power and Personhood.* Cambridge: Cambridge University Press, 1996.

Rosenbloom, Susan, and Niobe Way. "Experiences of Discrimination among African American, Asian American, and Latino Adolescents in an Urban High School." *Youth and Society* 35, no. 4 (2004): 420–51.

Rosin, Hannah. *The End of Men: And the Rise of Women.* New York: Riverhead Books, 2012.

Rubin, Jeff. "The Future Looks Bleak for Ontario's Manufacturing Sector." *Globe and Mail,* December 30, 2013. www.theglobeandmail.com/report-on-business/economy/the-future-looks-bleak-for-ontarios-manufacturing-sector/article16132219.

Sadker, David Miller, and Karen R. Zittleman. *Still Failing at Fairness: How Gender Bias Cheats Girls and Boys in School and What We Can Do about It.* New York: Scribner, 2009.

Sadker, Myra, and David Miller Sadker. *Failing at Fairness: How America's Schools Cheat Girls.* New York: Scribner, 1994.

Sax, Leonard. *Boys Adrift: The Five Factors Driving the Growing Epidemic of Unmotivated Boys and Underachieving Young Men.* New York: Basic Books, 2009.

———. *Why Gender Matters: What Parents and Teachers Need to Know about the Emerging Science of Sex Difference.* New York: Harmony, 2006.

Scharff, Christina. *Repudiating Feminism: Young Women in a Neoliberal World.* Aldershot, UK: Ashgate, 2011.

Schippers, Mimi. "Recovering the Feminine Other: Masculinity, Femininity and Gender Hegemony." *Theoretical Sociology* 36 (2007): 85–102.

Sessions Stepp, Laura. "Alpha Girls in Middle School: Learning to Handle the ABCs of Power." *Washington Post,* February 23, 2002, C1.

Shields, Stephanie A. "Gender: An Intersectionality Perspective." *Sex Roles* 59, no. 5 (2008): 301–11.

Sinikka Aapola, Marnina Gonick, and Anita Harris. *Young Femininities: Girlhood, Power, and Social Change.* New York: Palgrave, 2005.

Skelton, Christine. "Gender and Achievement: Are Girls the 'Success Stories' of Restructured Education Systems?" *Educational Review* 62, no. 10 (2010): 131–42.

Skelton, Christine, and Becky Francis. "The 'Renaissance Child': High Achievement and Gender in Late Modernity." *International Journal of Inclusive Education* 16, no. 4 (2012): 441–59.

———. "Successful Boys and Literacy." *Curriculum Inquiry* 41, no. 4 (2011): 456–78.

Skelton, Christine, Becky Francis, and Barbara Read. "Brains before 'Beauty'? High Achieving Girls, School and Gender Identities." *Educational Studies* 36, no. 2 (2010): 185–94.

Skiba, Russell J., and M. Karega Rausch. "Zero Tolerance, Suspension, and Expulsion: Questions of Equity and Effectiveness." In *Handbook of Classroom Management: Research, Practice and Contemporary Issues,* edited by Carolyn M. Evertson and Carol S. Weinstein, 1063–92. Mahway, NJ: Lawrence Erlbaum Associates, 2006.

Smith, Emma. "Underachievement, Failing Youth and Moral Panics." *Evaluation and Research in Education* 23, no. 1 (2010): 37–49.

Smith, Linda Tuhiwai. *Decolonizing Methodologies: Research and Indigenous Peoples.* Dunedin, NZ: University of Otago Press, 1999.

Smith, Michelle. "Actually, Women, You Do Need Feminism." *The Conversation,* April 17, 2014. www.theconversation.com/actuCandace-women-you-do-need-feminism-30415.

Smoi, Robert. "Why Our Schools Are Failing Boys." *CBC News Canada,* January 8, 2010. www.cbc.ca/news/canada/why-our-schools-are-failing-boys-1.952880.

Sommers, Christina Hoff. "The Boys at the Back." *New York Times,* February 2, 2013. http://opinionator.blogs.nytimes.com/2013/02/02 /the-boys-at-the-back.

———. "How to Make School Better for Boys." *Atlantic,* September 13, 2013. www.theatlantic.com/education/archive/2013/09/how-to-make-school-better-for-boys/279635.

———. "The War against Boys." *Atlantic,* May 2000.www.theatlantic.com /magazine/archive/2000/05/the-war-against-boys/304659.

———. *The War against Boys: How Misguided Policies are Harming Our Young Men.* New York: Simon and Schuster, 2013.

Spice Girls. *Girl Power: The Official Book by the Spice Girls.* London: Andre Deutsch, 1997.

St. Pierre, Elizabeth Adams. "Poststructural Feminism in Education: An Overview." *International Journal of Qualitative Studies in Education* 13, no. 5 (2000): 477–515.

Swain, Jon. "The Role of Sport in the Construction of Masculinities in an English Independent Junior School." *Sport, Education and Society* 11, no. 4 (2006): 317–35.

Taft, Jessica. "Girl Power Politics: Pop-Culture Barriers and Organizational Resistance." In *All about the Girl: Culture, Power, and Identity,* edited by Anita Harris, 69–78. New York, London: Routledge, 2004.

Tasker, Yvonne, and Dianne Negra. *Interrogating Postfeminism: Gender and the Politics of Popular Culture.* Durham: Duke University Press, 2007.

Threadgold, Steven. "Should I Pitch My Tent in the Middle Ground? On 'Middling Tendency', Beck and Inequality in Youth Sociology." *Journal of Youth Studies* 14, no. 4 (2011): 381–93.

Tiessen, Kaylie. *Seismic Shift: Ontario's Changing Labour Market.* Toronto: Canadian Centre for Policy Alternatives, 2014. www.policyalternatives .ca/publications/reports/seismic-shift.

Twomey, Sarah Jane. Review of *The Rise of Women: The Growing Gender Gap in Education and What It Means for American Schools,* by Thomas A. DiPrete and Claudia Buchmann. *Teacher's College Record,* April 13, 2015. www.tcrecord.org/Content.asp?ContentID=17929.

Verdugo, Richard R. "Race-Ethnicity, Social Class, and Zero Tolerance Policies: The Cultural and Structural Wars." *Education and Urban Society* 35, no. 1 (2002): 50–75.

Vincent, Carol, and Stephen Ball. *Childcare, Choice and Class Practices.* London: Routledge, 2006.

Voyer, Daniel, and Susan D. Voyer. "Gender Differences in Scholastic Achievement: A Meta-Analysis." *Psychological Bulletin* 140, no. 4 (2014): 1174–204.

Wacquant, Loïc J. D. "Three Pernicious Premises in the Study of the American Ghetto." *Journal of Urban and Regional Research* 21, no. 2 (1997): 341–53.

Walk, R. Alan, and Larry S. Bourne. "Ghettos in Canada's Cities? Racial Segregation, Ethnic Enclaves and Poverty Concentration in Canadian Urban Areas." *Canadian Geographer* 50, no. 3 (2006): 273–97.

Walkerdine, Valerie. *Schoolgirl Fictions.* London: Verso, 1990.

Walkerdine, Valerie, Helen Lucey, and June Melody. *Growing Up Girl: Psychosocial Explorations of Gender and Class.* Basingstoke, UK: Palgrave, 2001.

Wallace, John M., Sara Goodkind, Cynthia M. Wallace, and Jerald G. Bachman. "Racial, Ethnic and Gender Differences in School Discipline among U.S. High School Students: 1991–2005." *Negro Educational Review* 59, nos. 1–2 (2008): 47–62.

Wallace, Rachel. "By the Numbers: A Look at the Gender Pay Gap." *AAUW Career and Workplace Blog,* September 18, 2014. www.aauw.org/2014/09/18/gender-pay-gap.

Warrington, Molly, and Michael Younger. "The Other Side of the Gender Gap." *Gender and Education* 12, no. 4 (2000): 493–508.

Weis, Lois. *Working Class without Work: High School Students in a De-Industrializing Economy.* New York: Routledge, 1990.

Whitmire, Richard. *Why Boys Fail: Saving Our Sons from an Educational System That's Leaving Them Behind.* New York: AMACOM, 2011.

Williams, Cara. *Economic Well-Being.* Statistics Canada, May 13, 2013. www.statcan.gc.ca/pub/89-503-x/2010001/article/11388-eng.htm.

Willis, Paul. *Learning to Labour: How Working Class Kids Get Working Class Jobs.* Farnborough, UK: Saxon House, 1977.

Wing, Jean Yonemura. "Beyond Black and White: The Model Minority Myth and the Invisibility of Asian American Students." *Urban Review* 39, no. 4 (2007): 455–87.

Women against Feminism. Accessed August 20, 2015. www.womenagainstfeminism.tumblr.com.

Woodman, Dan. "The Mysterious Case of the Pervasive Choice Biography: Ulrich Beck, Structure/Agency, and the Middling State of Theory in the Sociology of Youth." *Journal of Youth Studies* 12, no. 3 (2009): 243–56.

World Bank. "Proportion of Seats Held by Women in National Parliaments (%)." Accessed May 3, 2015. http://data.worldbank.org/indicator/SG.GEN.PARL.ZS.

Yon, Daniel A. *Elusive Cultures: Schooling, Race and Identity in Global Times.* New York: State University of New York Press, 2000.

———. "Urban Portraits of Identity: On the Problem of Knowing Culture and Identity in Intercultural Studies." *Journal of Intercultural Studies* 21, no. 2 (2000): 143–57.

Yousafzai, Malala, and Christina Lamb. *I Am Malala: The Girl Who Stood Up for Education and Was Shot by the Taliban.* New York: Little, Brown, 2013.

Zarzour, Kim. "Asian Students Are Feeling Stressed, Survey Shows." Yorkregion.com, July 12, 2013. www.yorkregion.com/news-story/3890884-asian-students-are-feeling-stressed-survey-shows.

Zhang, Qin. "Asian Americans beyond the Model Minority Stereotype: The Nerdy and the Leftout." *Journal of International and Intercultural Communication* 3, no. 1 (2010): 20–37.

Index